The MAN *who had been*
KING

The MAN *who had been* KING

The American Exile of Napoleon's Brother Joseph

PATRICIA TYSON STROUD

UNIVERSITY OF PENNSYLVANIA PRESS

PHILADELPHIA

10 9 8 7 6 5 4 3 2 1

PUBLISHED BY
UNIVERSITY OF PENNSYLVANIA PRESS
PHILADELPHIA, PENNSYLVANIA 19104-4011

LIBRARY OF CONGRESS CATALOGING-IN-PUBLICATION DATA

STROUD, PATRICIA TYSON.
   THE MAN WHO HAD BEEN KING : THE AMERICAN EXILE OF NAPOLEON'S BROTHER JOSEPH /
PATRICIA TYSON STROUD.
      P.   CM.
   INCLUDES BIBLIOGRAPHICAL REFERENCES AND INDEX.
   ISBN 0-8122-3872-9 (CLOTH : ALK. PAPER)
   1. JOSEPH BONAPARTE, KING OF SPAIN, 1768–1844 — EXILE — UNITED STATES.   2. SPAIN —
KINGS AND RULERS — BIOGRAPHY.   3. NAPOLEON I, EMPEROR OF THE FRENCH, 1769–1821 —
FAMILY.   I. TITLE.
DC216.5.S77   2005
944.05′092 — DC22
[B]   2004061162

FRONTISPIECE:
PORTRAIT OF JOSEPH BONAPARTE BY CHARLES WILLSON PEALE, 1824.
OIL ON CANVAS.
HISTORICAL SOCIETY OF PENNSYLVANIA.

For Lisa, Peter, and John
and in memory of Noel

Contents

ILLUSTRATIONS

PREFACE

Ever since its founding, the United States has been a refuge for millions of people, of all nationalities and classes. Following the Revolution of 1789, many members of the French aristocracy crossed the ocean to escape the guillotine. Less than twenty years later, a second wave of French émigrés would arrive—the generals, soldiers, sympathizers of Napoleon, who sought a safe haven following the final defeat at Waterloo. Among these was the emperor's oldest brother, Joseph (1768–1844), ex-King of Naples and Spain.

It comes as a surprise to most people that Joseph Bonaparte spent more than seventeen years in exile, living in splendor high above the banks of the Delaware River in New Jersey. Even before his escape from France in 1815 he had American connections. When negotiating the peace treaty of 1800 between Napoleon and the United States, he had met the leading diplomats of the day at his château of Mortefontaine, outside Paris. Before leaving Europe, he had acquired vast tracts of land in upstate New York. He arrived in America with a fortune in hand, and would shortly embark upon building and fitting out the magnificent estate he would call Point Breeze.

But as his friend Madame de Staël wrote when banished from France, "Exile acts on imagination and constantly presents itself as an obstacle to all desires, all plans, all hopes." Joseph would never cease to long for his homeland. An intelligent man who knew French, Italian, and Spanish, he would never manage to learn English adequately, even after living in his adopted country for over seventeen years. He never wished to become an American citizen, and even in the elegant setting of Point Breeze, surrounded by cultured, gifted new friends and neighbors, he continually dreamed of returning to France. Although he would repeatedly plead with his wife to join him, he had never been a faithful husband, and this amorous man would find other loves. But he felt the separation from his two daughters keenly.

Joseph claimed that he had never wanted the overpowering roles thrust upon him by his illustrious younger brother Napoleon. Left to his own devices, he would probably have been a lawyer in his native Corsica, a country gentleman with leisure to read the great literature he treasured and time to oversee the maintenance of his property. When Napoleon's downfall forced Joseph into exile, he was able to become that country gentleman at last, but far away from so much he held dear.

What follows is the story of a man who was nevertheless able to turn the memories of his and his family's glorious and tumultuous recent past to his advantage— and, as it happened, to the advantage of his adopted home as well. For the superb collection of European art that Joseph had shipped to America to embellish the estate at Point Breeze made of that house the finest gallery of its kind by far in the young country, one that served to educate and influence generations of aspiring artists. In that sense at least, his exile was indeed beneficial for Americans. Ever glancing back at his beloved France, the man who had been king and whose brother had been an emperor helped to shape the fabric of the new republic.

Fate will serve you well, but you will be good to fate.
—Madame de Staël to Joseph Bonaparte,
Coppet, 18 September 1804

You have proved, Sire, that you know how to be worthily the citizen of a republic.
—Victor Hugo to Joseph Bonaparte,
Paris, 27 February 1833

What dethroned monarch has been more fortunate than he to fall in such a way? Generally they have become beggars for aid, or pensioners, or prisoners. This is a change rather than a fall.
—Joseph Hopkinson to Louis Mailliard,
Philadelphia, 18 April 1837

Chapter 1

A NEW LIFE

We are disgusted to learn that an officer of the American Navy is in the company of this Corsican Adventurer.
— United States Gazette, *15 September 1815*

$\mathcal{I}$n the early morning of 25 July 1815, as the small American brigantine *Commerce* attempted to slip away on a favorable tide from the coast of France just over a month after Napoleon's defeat at Waterloo, the British warship *Bacchus* loomed out of the fog and blocked its passage. Officers of the English ship came aboard to examine the passports of a Spaniard, an American, and a Monsieur Surviglieri, who kept to his cabin. As the officers knew that the deposed emperor Napoleon was already aboard the *Bellerophon*, headed for England, they did not press their investigation of the mysterious Frenchman. Thus Joseph Bonaparte, ex-king of Naples and Spain and Napoleon's older brother (see plate 1), evaded detection on his way to self-imposed exile in the United States. Had Joseph remained in France, he would have been executed by the restored Bourbon, King Louis XVIII, or, if captured by the Allies, deported to a remote part of Russia.

Joseph's entourage included his Spanish ordinance officer, Unzaga, his American interpreter James Carret, his cook François Parrot, and his twenty-year-old secretary Louis Mailliard. Joseph left behind his wife and two daughters in Paris at the Luxembourg Palace where they had been living. He had chosen escape to a new though uncertain existence in America rather than share his brother's fate in surrendering to the English, as several of Napoleon's generals had done. He could go with a clear conscience since he had offered to pretend to be Napoleon, feigning illness and keeping to his bed in the inn at Rochefort, while the real Napoleon escaped to America on the ship Joseph had chartered. But Napoleon had refused his brother's offer, not wanting to put Joseph in danger of arrest and believing it beneath his dignity as emperor of France to leave his country in disguise. He preferred to place himself at the mercy of the English. Joseph would blame himself for encouraging this decision, which may have been the result of his own earlier friendship with Lord Cornwallis while negotiating the Treaty of Amiens, a short-lived agreement of peace between France and England in 1802. Cornwallis had refused to deal with the wily Marquis de Talleyrand, Napoleon's foreign minister, but he and Joseph had hit it off famously, no doubt giving the latter a warmer feeling about the English.

The Bonaparte family was originally from Corsica. The father, Carlo Buonaparte, when an eighteen-year-old law student at Pisa University, left his studies for an arranged marriage to the fourteen-year-old Marie-Letizia Ramolino on 2 June 1764. Both families had pretensions to nobility. The Buonapartes traced their lineage to Florence where they were members of the small ruling noble class. Carlo's ancestor, Guglielmo di Buonaparte, had, as a nobleman, been a member of the Ghibelline-controlled municipal council of the city in the thirteenth century. When the opposite party, the Guelphs, took over Florence, he and his family fled to Sarzana and eventual impoverishment. In the sixteenth century, Guglielmo's descendant, Francesco di Buonaparte, sailed to Corsica for a new life.[1] Joseph's mother's family, the Ramolinos, descended from noble Lombard antecedents and established in Corsica for 250 years, was decidedly more aristocratic, although as poor financially as the Buonapartes.

Joseph (Giuseppe Buonaparte—Napoleon would change the spelling to Bonaparte) was born on 7 January 1768 at Corte, Corsica, the eldest of eight children. Napoleon was his next younger brother, born on 15 August 1769. Next came Lucien (1775–1840) (fig. 1), by far the most politically radical of the brothers, but in many ways the most sincere in his beliefs. Lucien always felt that Napoleon turned his back on the principles of the French Revolution when he declared himself emperor of the French. After the death of Lucien's first wife, Christine Boyer, he had married, much to Napoleon's fury, Alexandrine de Bleschamps Jouberthou, a widow, yet from a noble family. Napoleon, at that point First Consul of France, had wanted his brothers and sisters to marry European royalty in order to cement the empire he planned. He repeatedly petitioned Lucien to divorce his wife, but to no avail. Lucien held fast to his devotion to Alexandrine and to their son, Charles-Lucien. Although Lucien and Alexandrine were married five months after the child's birth in 1803, Napoleon always considered him illegitimate and refused both father and son a place in the line of succession of his proposed empire. Charles-Lucien was Napoleon's oldest nephew and should have been his potential heir until Napoleon had a son of his own, eight

1. **Portrait of Lucien Bonaparte** *by François Xavier Fabre. Oil on canvas. Courtesy of the Museo Napoleonico, Rome.*

years later. Furious at his brother's attitude, Lucien fled to Italy. When Napoleon made life especially vexing for him there, he attempted to escape to America with his entire family—by then there were other children by Alexandrine, as well as his two daughters by Christine Boyer. But the family was captured by the British and taken to Malta, then to England, where they spent three years until Napoleon's exile to Elba made possible their return to Italy. Lucien returned to Paris to support his brother during the hundred days of the emperor's rule after his escape from Elba, but by July 1815 Lucien was imprisoned in Turin. In a few months he would be released.

Joseph's sister, Elisa (1777–1820), who had married Felix Bacciochi, member of a Corsican noble family, was made Grand Duchess of Tuscany by Napoleon, although her relations with him were often strained. After Napoleon's abdication, she moved to Trieste. Another brother, Louis (1778–1846), one-time king of Holland under Napoleon, had married Hortense de Beauharnais, daughter of Napoleon's wife Josephine, but the marriage had been a disaster from the start. They had been separated for some time, with Hortense living in Switzerland and Louis established in Florence. Pauline (1780–1825), the family beauty and inveterate flirt, first married General C. V. E. Leclerc and accompanied him to Saint Domingue (modern-day Haiti) where Leclerc died of yellow fever. After Pauline returned to Paris she married the Italian prince, Camillo Borghese, and lived in Rome. Joseph's youngest sister, Caroline (1782–1839), was the wife of Joachim Murat, Napoleon's daring and flamboyant marshal whom he had made king of Naples. Murat later betrayed the emperor to the Austrians and died on 13 October 1815 by a Neapolitan firing squad. Joseph's youngest brother, Jérôme (1784–1860), whose marriage to an American from Baltimore was annulled by Napoleon, later married Catherine of Württemberg. With his second wife, Jérôme now lived, a virtual prisoner, in Trieste.

The year Carlo and Marie-Letizia's first child, Joseph, was born, the Republic of Genoa, after tiring of the fight against the independence-seeking Corsicans led by Pasquale Paoli, sold the island to France. The following year, on 8 May 1769, Paoli was defeated by the French at the battle of Ponte Nuovo, and among his supporters Carlo with his wife and small child fled into the mountains toward Corte. When Paoli surrendered, the young couple returned to their home in Ajaccio by way of a rugged mountain route. To the end of her life Letizia remembered carrying Joseph in her arms while pregnant with Napoleon, staggering and slipping along precipitous paths.[2]

Throughout Joseph's childhood and youth the issue of the family's bona fide aristocracy was extremely important. In order to secure a free education for his children in France it was necessary for his father to prove the Buonapartes' noble lineage.

The French military governor of Corsica, Charles René, Count de Marbeuf and a favorite of Louis XV's, was instrumental in arranging Carlo's job as deputy for the nobility representing Corsica at Versailles in 1777. While he was away obtaining the necessary endorsements for his children, the beautiful young Letizia reputedly had an affair with the sixty-year-old governor, perhaps to further secure her children's educational plans. Marbeuf, a noted womanizer whose "virility belied his age," had conveniently left his wife behind in Paris.[3] Carlo, too, had a history of dalliances; with his charm and attractive looks he was apparently a ladies' man, a trait his oldest son would inherit.

Thus, by various means, the necessary noble credentials were presented, and Joseph and Napoleon were sent to school at Autun on the mainland to learn French. Afterward, Joseph was to study for the priesthood at Aix-en-Provence while Napoleon would be sent to military school. Before he left Autun, however, Joseph decided to abandon his religious studies to join the military. Napoleon was furious at this move, for by law the two brothers were not allowed to have the same career and Napoleon would need to change his plans. In a long letter to an uncle, the precocious fourteen-year-old Napoleon attempted to persuade his relative to squelch Joseph's new ambition. "He lacks the necessary boldness to face the perils of battle," Napoleon wrote of his older brother, adding a patent falsehood: "his feeble health could never sustain the rigours of a campaign." The catalogue of Joseph's shortcomings was extensive: ignorance of mathematics would keep him from the artillery and Joseph's frivolous character and extravagant habits would be his downfall. Joseph had to be persuaded to become an ecclesiastic, the younger brother concluded, for his education and talents would one day make him a bishop.[4] (Apparently a "frivolous character" and "extravagant habits" were no impediment to becoming a bishop.) Not only was an ecclesiastical career far from Joseph's inclinations but most Corsicans, although nominally Catholic, were uninterested in organized religion, believing more in luck, destiny, and fate than in the doctrines of original sin or damnation or a Christian God.[5] Although Joseph at times attended mass, he was essentially indifferent to the Church.

As it turned out, Joseph's plans for a military career were derailed by the death of his father. Joseph promised Carlo on his deathbed that he would return to Corsica to take care of his mother and six younger siblings. So after spending a few weeks at Aix with his uncle, Joseph Fesch, his mother's half-brother, who was studying for the priesthood and, as a cardinal under Napoleon, would acquire extravagant habits, he set sail for Corsica.

At home, Joseph assumed management of the family's olive groves, orange and mulberry trees, vineyards, and vegetable gardens. It was probably during this period that he developed a lifelong love of gardening and agriculture.[6] At the same time he worked out plans for a career in the law like that of his father. Always a serious student, Joseph took full advantage of his father's library and read deeply while preparing for his vocation. When Napoleon came home on leave, Joseph left to attend the university at Pisa. In May 1788, having passed his examinations, he received the degree of doctor in civil and canon law.

Back in Corsica, as a young man of twenty, he describes in his memoirs a particular day when he and Napoleon rode horseback from Ajaccio to Orezzo where Joseph had been chosen to represent the district of Ajaccio at a meeting. As they rode slowly along, Napoleon was preoccupied with the maneuvers and strategic positions of ancient warriors who for so many years had fought over the countryside, while Joseph reports that his own thoughts focused on "the singularity and beauty of the landscape."[7]

Joseph was making a name for himself in Corsica under the French, having been selected by the mayor of Ajaccio as his assistant. Within the year he was qualified to plead before the high court at Bastia and he soon became the protégé of the secretary general of the Corsican parliament. Napoleon had gone back to France but, unfortunately, he returned for a few months, only to unsettle Joseph's life through his passionate adherence to Corsican nationalism. The French Revolution in 1789 caused chaos in Corsica where Joseph, as a moderate, worked to establish order. Meanwhile, the French National Assembly invited General Paoli to return from exile in England to govern the island. Joseph was with the delegation that sailed to Marseilles to bring him back to Corsica.[8]

Several years later, the conflict that Napoleon had been stirring up with Paoli ever since the latter's return to Corsica erupted. In 1792 Napoleon campaigned for the job of commander of the volunteer battalions in Ajaccio, opposing Joseph's friend and Paoli's endorsed candidate, Pozzo di Borgo, whose family had rented the third floor of the Buonapartes' house in Ajaccio for years. A series of disastrous events—exacerbated by Joseph and Napoleon's brother Lucien, a radical Jacobin who accused Paoli of treason—led to the flight of the entire Buonaparte family to the mainland. They landed at Toulon on 13 June 1793. In France, it was the year of the Terror and it behooved Joseph and the others to renounce any pretensions to nobility and to be designated simply "citizen." On Corsica, the Buonapartes' house and properties were sacked. Considering the times, it was something of a saving grace that the whole family was impoverished.

Joseph soon set off for Paris to obtain money for them as patriot refugees. Corsican deputies of the Convention paved his way to the Administration where he solicited and was granted a relief fund for Corsican exiles. He also urged the government to send troops to drive the English from Corsica. For himself, he secured a job as *commissaire de guerre*, in charge of provisioning the army, with a salary of 6,000 francs a year, the usual black market deals, and more salary added when he was appointed commissioner to the Executive Committee of the Department of Corsica.[9] The bloodbath then taking place in Paris between the ultra-Jacobin party and the moderate Girondists goes unnoted in his memoirs, except for the assassination of Marat by Charlotte Corday. Several months later Joseph returned to his family in Toulon. Civil war by that time was raging in the south and he was fortunate to have secured a military post. At this point he seems to have assumed the role of an ardent republican, espousing the revolutionary government of Robespierre.

Aware that the Girondist faction (moderate republicans) was preparing to cede Toulon to the English, Joseph moved his family near Marseilles. While there, supporting his mother and younger siblings, Joseph met the charming sixteen-year-old Désirée Clary, daughter of a rich merchant. He had been influential in freeing a family member from prison, and soon became an intimate of the Clary household. The Clarys' wealth made them subject to confiscation of their property and incarceration, and they were deeply grateful for the handsome young officer's assistance. Before long Joseph proposed to Désirée. When he brought Napoleon to visit the Clarys, however, his brash younger brother almost immediately claimed her for himself, suggesting in all seriousness that Joseph court her older sister, Julie (fig. 2). Joseph seems to have acquiesced without much argument, perhaps thinking that it would be doubly advantageous for the brothers to both marry the well-dowried sisters. Julie was plainer, but more serious, and she was already in love with Joseph. They were married on 1 August 1794. Napoleon's affair with Désirée went on for a while, but he would gradually drift away and in time would marry Rose (Josephine) de Beauharnais. Désirée would marry General Jean-Baptiste-Jules Bernadotte and become his consort as Queen of Sweden.

Joseph performed a variety of diplomatic and political undertakings for Napoleon, proving himself quite useful to his younger brother. The following year Joseph went on a mission to Genoa in connection with plans for the French recovery of Corsica. Later, he accompanied Napoleon in the early part of the Italian campaign, by which time Napoleon had become a powerful general, and was personally involved in the French expedition to win back Corsica. There Joseph helped the commissioner of the French republic, Miot de Melito, in the island's political reorganization. In 1797, Joseph was elected to the Council of Five Hundred, but was soon involved in

2. **Julie Clary Bonaparte with Her Daughter Zénaïde** *by Robert Lefèvre. Oil on canvas. Musée National du Château de Versailles.*

a diplomatic career as French consul to the court of Parma. But Napoleon, now in a place of power, saw to it that his older brother was appointed minister to Rome. His assignment was to overthrow papal secular order, replacing it with French control under the guise of a "Roman Republic." In the Holy City where he was to encourage revolutionary movements, Joseph barely escaped assassination when a riot broke out before the embassy that resulted in the death of the French general Léonard Duphot, his sister Pauline's fiancé.

Back in Paris, his coffers swelled by handsome bribes and gifts, Joseph bought the estate of Mortefontaine, subsequently spending hundreds of thousands of francs on embellishing the château and buying additional land. By the coup d'état of 18 Brumaire (19 November 1799), Napoleon was consolidating the power that would eventually lead to his crowning himself Emperor of the French in December 1804.

Joseph's star had risen along with his brother's, but circumstances catapulted him to positions in life to which he never aspired. He was by far the best educated and the most highly cultured member of his family. His education and tastes had prepared him for the existence of a well-to-do lawyer and country squire, enjoying his family and friends, entertaining, reading great literature, collecting art, and building gardens.

Joseph's secretary, Louis Mailliard, wrote in his journal that Joseph's life had been a series of contradictions before he came to the United States. His natural preference had been for a tranquil life far from cities and politics.[10] He had married an heiress whose father died the following year leaving her a considerable inheritance. Mortefontaine, outside Paris, had been for him a paradise, surrounded by his small family, Zénaïde born in 1801 and Charlotte in 1803, and good friends. He enjoyed being in the country and he would have been content to spend the rest of his life in this secluded château. But not until Napoleon was permanently incarcerated was Joseph free to live according to his own dictates.

When Napoleon became First Consul, he made Joseph his representative to arrange a treaty ending hostilities between France and the United States caused by American trade agreements with the British that France found insulting. The treaty, signed at Mortefontaine in 1800, was celebrated with lavish festivities: illuminations, fireworks, a gala concert, and a play featuring prominent actors and actresses of the day. One of the provisions of this iniquitous agreement stipulated that United States citizens withdraw from the French-owned Caribbean island of Saint-Domingue, which had become a slave-free country under the rule of General Pierre Dominique Toussaint L'Ouverture, a black man originally installed as commander-in-chief by Napoleon several years earlier and a loyal subject of France.[11] The French were not

planning to leave Saint-Domingue alone. Napoleon, in a stunning about-face, reject-
ing the abolition of slavery that had been decreed by the Revolution, had decided
that a free black republic was a threat to West Indian trade. The Treaty of Amiens
that Joseph negotiated on 27 March 1802 with Lord Cornwallis between England and
France insured the safety of French ships, loaded with 20,000 troops and led by
Joseph's brother-in-law, Pauline's husband, General Leclerc, to reach Saint-Domingue and destroy the "first multiracial government in the New World."[12] The expedition was a disaster and thousands died, both French and citizens of Saint-Domingue.
Toussaint was sent to France in chains to die in prison.

　　Napoleon had sent Joseph to conclude the Treaty of Lunéville with the Austrian
plenipotentiary, Count Ludwig von Cobenzl, in February 1801, which effectively
brought an end to the second Coalition against France, securing peace for the first
time in ten years. And the following summer, at his magnificent mansion in Paris,
the Hôtel Marbeuf, Joseph signed the Concordat with Cardinals Consalvi, Spira, and
Caselli, representing Pope Pius VII, restoring the Catholic religion to France. (The
French Revolution had banned the Church.) Joseph's legal training had taught him
to be moderate and diplomatic, thus his brother used him for many private transactions as well. Despite Napoleon's early skepticism regarding his brother's aptitude, he
also made him study military art so he could command an army. When Napoleon
was planning the invasion of England, he named Joseph colonel of the fourth regiment at Boulogne.

　　The peace with Austria that Joseph had signed was not to last, for an Austro-
Russian coalition menaced France in 1805. In August, while away in Germany fighting the armies of this alliance, Napoleon appointed Joseph Regent of France. After
Napoleon's great victory at Austerlitz on 2 December, the emperor decided to take
possession of the Kingdom of Naples. In October the British had taken over Sicily
after the Battle of Trafalgar, and in order to prevent the British from dominating the
Mediterranean Napoleon needed to control Naples and Sicily.

　　He advised a no doubt astonished Joseph, in Paris, that he had named him
commander-in-chief of the Army of Naples: "I wish you to set off for Rome forty
hours after receipt of this letter," he said, "and let your first dispatch inform me that
you have entered Naples, driven out the treacherous court and subjected that part of
Italy to our authority."[13] He wrote again from Stuttgart three weeks later: "You will
make no truce, you will hear of no capitulation. My will is that the Bourbons shall
have ceased to reign at Naples. I intend to seat on that throne a Prince of my own
House—first of all you, if not, another."[14]

　　Joseph left at once, and traveling via Turin and Rome he at last reached Capua, where he learned that his advance guard already occupied Naples without firing a shot. The Bourbons had taken flight across the straits of Messina to Palermo. Joseph set about reestablishing peace in the kingdom of Naples, made many changes in the infrastructure of the country by suppressing feudalism, dissolving what he considered too-powerful convents, selling crown lands, founding universities and art centers, and establishing courts free from his own oversight. He tried to improve the Neapolitans' lot after the cruelty they had suffered under the repressive Bourbon Queen Caroline, sister of the beheaded Marie Antoinette of France.

But Napoleon constantly criticized Joseph's administration. "My Brother," he wrote in July 1806 from Paris. "Your government is not sufficiently vigorous; it is not sufficiently organized. You are too fearful of making enemies; you are too kind. You place too much confidence in the Neapolitans at this juncture."[15] Three weeks later he admonished Joseph again: "I have received your letter of the 17th. I see that all your military operations are wrong. I cannot understand how, surrounded as you are by men of military experience, there are so few who can give you good advice. . . . Your measures have no life or movement, no organization or method. Till now you have made nothing but mistakes: but I ought not to distress you. . . . Your policy with regard to Naples is just the reverse of what ought to be pursued towards a conquered nation. . . . What is the meaning of this Neapolitan National Guard? It is leaning on a reed, perhaps putting arms into the hands of your enemies. How little you know of men!"[16] And a few days later, "You should not make one retrograde step: perish, if necessary, upon the Neapolitan territory. Your dispositions have not all been good."[17]

General Jean Maximilien Lamarque, in contrast, would write to Joseph some years later: "You, there (in Naples), realized that which Plato wished so much for the good of humanity—a philosopher on a throne. I remember well, in your travels, how strongly you inspired the nobles with a love of the people; to the people—respect for the laws—toleration for the priests, and order and moderation in the army."[18]

But this potentially fortuitous match of king and country in Naples, notwithstanding Napoleon's criticism, was not to last. In the interests of imperial expansion and to drive the British out of Gibraltar, Napoleon moved Joseph, like a chess piece, to Spain, without considering Joseph's deep reluctance to the move. To a ladylove left behind in Naples, Joseph wrote that he would much prefer to lead the private life to which he was born than to be a king, and that if he behaved like an ambitious man, it was only due to the force of circumstances. "What will become of all this?" he had said. "How can I find happiness when my position is quite incompatible with my character; when I have to use all my courage and reason to reconcile the two. . . .

I am like a lost voyager, out of sight of land, carried away by irresistible currents on a distant sea." But he concludes, "I believe in what I have to do and in what I am doing."[19]

Joseph had reason to be apprehensive of his new assignment. The Spanish deeply resented the imposition of a foreigner, *el rey intruso*, on the throne in Madrid, and the new king's rule was thwarted at every turn. In addition, he had only nominal authority over the Spanish people. The personal tyranny of his brother continually forced him into the shadows, obliging him to renounce all his own initiatives. His generals constantly contradicted him because they took orders only from Napoleon. Joseph pleaded with his brother to withdraw his troops and leave him alone with the Spaniards, but Napoleon refused to listen. Joseph wrote to the emperor on three occasions renouncing the Spanish throne, but to no avail. "What an existence for a man of his tastes!" Louis Mailliard wrote in his journal.[20]

And yet, after the debacle in Spain, Joseph could tell his wife: "in spite of the disagreements [*brouilleries*] that have existed between the emperor and myself, it is true to say my dear, that he is still the man I love most in the world."[21]

But Joseph Bonaparte was leaving all that behind, sailing to America and potential freedom, while Napoleon was a British prisoner. At the time, Joseph thought that his brother would be treated with the same respect the English had shown Lucien during his house arrest there from late 1810 until 1814, and allow the fallen emperor to live quietly in retirement.

On the open sea, safe for the moment, Joseph relaxed for the first time in many months. The turmoil of the defeat at Waterloo, Napoleon's abdication, the leave-taking with his wife and children, the frantic ride to the coast to meet Napoleon at Rochefort, and the desperate attempt to find an American ship to charter all had taken their toll. Before Waterloo there had been Napoleon's first abdication in 1814, his exile to the island of Elba off the Italian coast, then the turbulent hundred days after his escape from Elba and his triumphant return to Paris.

Americans had watched in awe as this drama unfolded in France. Charles Jared Ingersoll, attorney, author, and future Democratic Congressman, who would become one of Joseph's most devoted friends, wrote to Alexander J. Dallas, Secretary of the Treasury, in the spring of 1815 about Napoleon's return from Elba: "Well, and what do you think of this? We have seen the scenes changed at a theatre, we have read the Arabian night's entertainment, and we have heard the wind blow at Washington— But they are all nothing to this. . . . To invade France at the head of a thousand vagabonds, and have 'em all to dine with him at the Tuileries three weeks afterwards—Happy he who has lived, a spectator, not an actor, for the last eighteen months at Paris—he will have had the historical experience of many ages—he may die when he likes."[22] Joseph Bonaparte, a principal actor in these events, no doubt welcomed the tranquillity of a monotonous ocean voyage, regardless of the weather.

Revived by the sea air and soothed by the gentle rolling of the ship as he sailed for America, Joseph was soon entertaining his companions and the captain, Philippe Misservey from Boulogne, with recitations from memory of dramatic passages from French and Italian poetry: Corneille, Racine, and his favorite author, Tasso. His old friend Laure d'Abrantes, the French wife of Marshal Junot, once said that Joseph spoke French with less of a foreign accent than any Corsican she ever knew. She described him as handsome, strong, and well read in French literature as well as Italian and English. According to her, Joseph loved poetry and belle-lettres and surrounded himself with learned and scientific men. She knew him to have "goodness of heart, gentleness, clemency, and accuracy of judgment." Some said he was weak, but she discounted that.[23] Perhaps it was inevitable he would always appear in such a way when placed beside his all-powerful brother. But Captain Misservey, not knowing the true identity of his passenger, was most impressed by the man he strongly suspected was the French statesman and general Lazare Carnot, who had been Napoleon's minister of the interior during the Hundred Days.

Several times during the crossing English ships gave chase, but the *Commerce* eluded them each time. At last, on 19 August, the lookout spotted New York. That night the ship lay safely off shore, but in the morning it had to run the gauntlet of two British frigates off Sandy Hook. Luckily, a harbor pilot who had come aboard sailed the *Commerce* so close to the shore to avoid "the damned English" that the warships, fearing to run aground, pulled away.

After disembarking his passengers, Captain Misservey apparently conveyed his suspicion as to the identity of Monsieur Surviglieri to a reporter from the *New York Evening Post*, for the paper promptly made it public that the man was Carnot. In order to remain anonymous, Joseph selected a modest boardinghouse instead of a grand hotel, but his precautions were to no avail since the mayor of New York, Jacob Radcliff, immediately came to pay his respects to the supposed Carnot. Joseph denied he was Carnot, and told Radcliff only that he was part of the imperial French household and wished to keep his identity secret, at least for a while.

By an odd coincidence, Commodore Jacob Lewis, who had been to Paris and had once been presented to Joseph, had come to the same boardinghouse to visit his son. On meeting and recognizing the former king of Spain, Lewis invited him to his country estate across the bay in Amboy, New Jersey. Joseph at first refused the invitation, as he was not quite prepared for a social visit, but to escape the mayor and any possible publicity, he accepted. The few days he spent in Amboy were actually a welcome respite from more than a month of fear of being apprehended on the high seas by the English. But being a robust and active man—he was forty-seven—he was eager to pursue his new life, and so on 5 September, accompanied by his secretary Mailliard, he returned to New York.

Joseph Bonaparte could not, however, long remain in obscurity in one of the largest cities in America. The next day, walking down Broadway, he was accosted by an elderly man who threw himself at Joseph's feet, grabbed his hand and covered it with kisses. With tears streaming down his face, the old soldier cried in French: "Your Majesty, here! Ah! How happy I am to see your Majesty again!" The embarrassed ex-king of Spain tried to force this former guardsman from his Spanish corps to his feet, but to no avail. A large crowd began to gather and it was no use hiding under a pseudonym. Joseph's only choice was to find the mayor and determine his course of action. He feared the American authorities might refuse him asylum and deport him to England.[24]

Mayor Radcliff recommended that Joseph go at once to Washington in order to place himself under the protection of President James Madison. He set off the next day, arriving at the Mansion House in Philadelphia on 11 September. The hotel was full, most of the rooms having been taken by Congressman Henry Clay, but Clay, learning of Joseph's predicament, offered him several rooms from his suite. At daybreak, Joseph resumed his journey, accompanied by Commodore Lewis.

He did not get far. Secretary of the Treasury Alexander J. Dallas had warned President Madison that Joseph Bonaparte was in Philadelphia en route to Washington. The president answered Dallas that he refused to meet with the brother of Napoleon, as it would be troubling to the restored Bourbon government, thus diplomatically unwise for Franco-American relations. Madison said he had written Richard Rush, his Attorney General, to dissuade Joseph from his journey and to assure him that he was perfectly free in this country and had no need of the president's protection. There was a precedent for Madison's action. President Washington, twenty years earlier, had refused to meet with Talleyrand, then an exile from the French Revolution.[25] Rush notified Madison that he had received his confidential letter and would take every precaution. "I am astonished at the gross indiscretion that could have dictated or permitted the measure, and you may confidently trust to its being defeated," he assured the president in cryptic language.[26]

Later that morning, Rush wrote Madison of his plan to waylay the travelers in

Baltimore. Edward Duvall of the Navy Office had been dispatched at 11 A.M. with a letter for Commodore Lewis. Duvall was expected to reach Baltimore by ten that night.[27] The Attorney General's letter to Lewis stated: "I have understood through an authentic channel, that one of the brothers of the late Emperor of France is at present travelling to this city under an assumed name, with a view probably of proceeding on as far as Montpelier, the residence of the President in Virginia; and that he has the good fortune to be in your company. It is evident that this conspicuous stranger comes to our shores as all others, upon the mere footing of the hospitality and protection which the laws hold out to all, without discrimination, whom choice or misfortune may bring to us, and that beyond this the executive authority of the country can interpose none." Rush continues that if the object is to pay respects, the president would "prefer declining at this time its personal offering." Rush cautions sternly, "I will take the farther liberty to subjoin that in no way, or at no time, would it be acceptable to the President to become a party to the concealment under which the stranger in question, may, for all other purposes, find it necessary or convenient to travel."[28] In an attempt at anonymity, Joseph had assumed the title of the Count of Survilliers (a small property he owned near his estate of Mortefontaine). Retracing his route, with a brief stopover in Lancaster, Pennsylvania, Joseph returned to Philadelphia where he had a good friend, Stephen Girard. Originally from Bordeaux, France, Girard was at the time president of the Second Bank of the United States and an immensely successful shipping magnate with an international trading empire that included Europe, the West Indies, and China. Joseph was indeed fortunate to have such a connection, for Girard served as his adviser and banker, and in the next few years would arrange to have furniture, rugs, paintings, tapestries, sculptures, and numerous household effects transported across the Atlantic on his own ships. Girard immediately rented a suitable house for Joseph in Philadelphia at (present number) 260 South Ninth Street, a building that still stands.[29] Installed in the dining room were panels on the theme of Cupid and Psyche designed by Jacques-Louis David that remained there well into the twentieth century.[30]

In early 1816, Joseph leased, in addition, a much grander place, Lansdowne (fig. 3), originally built by John Penn, son of the founder of Pennsylvania, on the outskirts of Philadelphia in what is now Fairmount Park. The estate had also been one of the homes of William Bingham, one of the wealthiest men in the country. His wife, Anne Willing, had been a great society hostess, entertaining distinguished foreign visitors such as the Duke of Orléans (later King Louis-Philippe) and the Duke de la Rochefoucauld-Liancourt, as well as such great English financiers as Alexander and Henry Baring, who married two of the Binghams' daughters.[31] The firm of Baring Brothers

3. **Lansdowne** *by William Russell Birch from* The Country Seats of the United States of America *(1809), plate 4. Historical Society of Pennsylvania.*

would handle some of Joseph's finances, and he would have more personal business dealings with Alexander Baring concerning his collection of art.

After Joseph moved into Lansdowne, Charles Ingersoll wrote to A. J. Dallas that "several gentlemen" had visited the ex-king and others, including Ingersoll himself, had entertained him.

We had at table yesterday [Joseph Bonaparte], Count Regnaud de St. Jean d'Angély, Generals Clauzel and Lefebvre des Nouettes [*sic*] and some of their attendants. . . . Joseph is a good looking middle aged man and talks, I am told (for tho I have had two or three little entretiens with him; I have not heard him) without any restraint of "quand j'etais roi de Naples and quand j'etais roi d'Espagne." He did so, I know, yesterday to Gen[eral] Isard who sat between him and me and mentioned it to me the moment afterwards—They were perfect strangers—As you are to be vis a vis sa majeste this summer on the banks of the Schuylkill you will have the means of taking his altitude yourself. He receives and returns the visits of such persons as think proper to call on him and professes, I understand, to prefer the society of Philadelphia to that of New York.[32]

Apparently, there were those who did not "think proper" to call on the brother of Napoleon. One of these might have been Congressman Joseph Hopkinson, author of "Hail Columbia" and future judge of the United States district court. In June 1814, after Napoleon's first abdication and his banishment to Elba by the combined forces of Austria, Prussia, Great Britain, and Russia, Hopkinson wrote to His Excellency Andrew Daschkoff, the Russian consul-general at Philadelphia, to offer him his "ecstatic, profound congratulations" on the "glorious news." "If a scourge or a pestilence had suddenly left the earth; if a fire which threatened to devour the world had been in a moment extinguished," he said, "it could not have excited in my heart more lively and deep emotions of gratitude and joy. And is it really so? Is the scourge of humanity gone? Is he sunk again into a harmless and despised reptile? I agree too that he has lost his character with his fortune; that he has slunk away like a detected thief, and has not dared to fall like an overthrown hero—This will have a good moral effect on the world—such a rascal ought not to leave behind the remembrance of a single act or quality calculated to command either praise or regret" (fig. 4).[33] Ironically, Hopkinson would become one of Joseph's most devoted friends.

Well-read Americans may have seen sentiments similar to Hopkinson's in Byron's "Ode to Napoleon," written after the emperor's 1814 banishment:

> *Thine evil deeds are writ in gore,*
> *Nor written thus in vain—*
> *Thy triumphs tell of fame no more,*
> *Or deepen every stain:*
> *If thou hadst died as honour dies,*
> *Some new Napoleon might arise,*
> *To shame the world again—*
> *But who would soar the solar height,*
> *To set in such a starless night?*[34]

More pertinent to the United States were the remarks of Richard Rush, who, in a letter to his friend Ingersoll, thought that "the late stupendous changes" might in the end be beneficial to America. "We should keep it in mind," Rush wrote, "that Bonaparte was, personally and peculiarly, a deadly enemy to us. He hated us, or rather despised us with a most hearty and durable contempt." Rush asserts that Jef-

4. **Triumph of the Year 1813** *by Johann Michael Voltz. Satiric engraving of Napoleon. German. Author's collection. Photo: Lisa Tyson Ennis.*

ferson, Madison, Gallatin, Monroe, and all the prominent men of the time agreed with him. "But," he continues about Napoleon, "he was a check to England, granted. But was he to the power of her marine? No! To her commerce? No! To her floods of money? Still, he kept Lord Wellington employed."[35]

These various writings were all in reaction to Napoleon's first abdication in 1814. After his defeat at Waterloo the following year, Rush confided to Ingersoll his loathing of the fallen emperor, and this time adds his feelings about the advantage taken by the English. "While Napoleon was the ascendant, all Europe, with England at the head, was held together by a community of hatred, with him as its constant and invigorating food. England, by a union of address and falsehood, had contrived to exhibit us as connected in interest or in sentiment with him. She made Europe believe it . . . thus Europe was shy of us."[36]

Only a few weeks after Joseph Bonaparte landed in America, a Philadelphia newspaper stated, "in these United States there was, in the minds of wise and good men, a fearful apprehension that the political freedom of the whole Christian world would be crushed by a military adventurer."[37] Although a secondary player in his brother's empire, Joseph did not escape criticism. The *United States Gazette* observed, "We are disgusted to learn that an officer of the American Navy [Commodore Lewis] is in the company of this Corsican adventurer."[38] Nathaniel Chapman (fig. 5), the Philadelphia-based physician whom in later years Joseph would claim as his closest friend in America, wrote in the *Port Folio*, in 1801: "Is not Buonaparte an atheist and a murderer, a robber, a hypocrite, an usurper, and a tyrant?"[39] These examples demonstrate the mountain of adverse feeling that Joseph would repeatedly come up against in various levels of American society and need to counteract in order to be accepted for himself alone in his adopted country.

At the same time, others accepted Joseph Bonaparte as they found him, and with a certain approbation. Deborah Norris Logan of Philadelphia noted in her diary for 1816 that large numbers of Frenchmen, fleeing from proscription, had lately arrived in America, Joseph Bonaparte amongst them, and that he had paid a visit to her husband. "I was not present," she says, "but the account given of Joseph, is that he might be easily taken for a jolly good natured Dutchman. . . . He is said to have brought with him great wealth. And spoke of preferring Pennsylvania as a residence because of the domestic manners, and sobriety of its inhabitants."[40]

But though Joseph may have appeared affable, his past had not left him without painful memories. Some years later, a Philadelphia gentleman, Samuel Breck, would record in his diary: "In the afternoon we visited Belmont, the seat of Judge [William] Peters. In walking through his fine grove of spruce hemlock, the Judge told me that Joseph Bonaparte, when he occupied the adjoining estate of Lansdowne, walked over one afternoon to see him, and whilst rambling about under the shade of these lofty hemlocks, the Ex-King asked by his interpreter what name the Judge had given to this umbrageous walk? I call it, said the Judge, the Grove of Oblivion. Ah! exclaimed Joseph, what would I not give to possess such a treasure."[41]

Joseph left Lansdowne in late spring 1817, after just more than a year. The property had not been in good shape. That summer Samuel Breck noted: "In the afternoon I accompanied the ladies to Lansdowne . . . This fine house is going to decay for want of a tenant and want of care." Breck reported that Joseph Bonaparte had offered an estate in Switzerland (Prangins) in exchange for the mansion in addition to the northwest square in Philadelphia at the intersection of Ninth and Walnut

5. **Portrait of Dr. Nathaniel Chapman** *by Samuel Bell Waugh, after Thomas Sully, 1859. Oil on canvas. American Philosophical Society.*

Streets, "on which he is desirous of building a palace, to include a private theatre."[42] Nothing came of the plan.

Lansdowne had been only a temporary home for the Count de Survilliers. While there he had begun to look for the large estate he envisioned, situated somewhere between Philadelphia and New York where news from Europe could reach him easily. Napoleon had thought of adopting such a plan for himself sometime before he decided at Rochefort to take his chances and surrender to the British. As the imprisoned emperor languished on the forbidding volcanic island of St. Helena, 1,500 miles off the West African coast, however, it was Joseph who lived out his brother's idea of freedom in America.

Chapter 2 A MAN OF PROPERTY

I take this opportunity of expressing to you, the sincere gratification I feel, at the partiality you have shown this State, by selecting it, as the place of your residence.
—Mahlon Dickerson, Governor of New Jersey,
to Joseph Bonaparte, 22 January 1817

Joseph's home for most of his time in the United States, the estate of Point Breeze, in central New Jersey, was actually his second land purchase in America. He already owned a large tract of land in northern New York State before he arrived in the New World. In 1814 when James Donatien Le Ray was visiting his legendary château de Chaumont in the Loire Valley (once the home of Diane de Poitiers and Marie de Medici), he learned that Joseph Bonaparte, a fugitive, was across the Loire River at the château de Blois. Joseph was in flight from the allied forces that were soon to force Napoleon to abdicate. Le Ray hastened to Blois to lend the emperor's brother his respects and sympathy. [1,2]

Joseph was in desperate straits the night Le Ray appeared at Blois. The allies were closing in and he would have to flee the country. He told Le Ray at dinner that his friend had arrived at a propitious time. In the courtyard were several wagons loaded with silver and fine furniture that could be confiscated at any moment and these he proposed exchanging for part of Le Ray's extensive landholdings in northern New York State. Le Ray protested that Joseph would be buying real estate sight unseen, but Joseph assured him of his complete trust and the sale was agreed on.

While at Blois, Le Ray introduced Joseph to Emmanuel Laurent Jacques (James) Carret, a young American in his employ who had grown up in northern New York State and whose father and brothers also worked for him at Chaumont. Joseph was impressed with the bilingual Carret and hired him as his interpreter. He would take him to America the following year after Napoleon's return from Elba, his defeat at Waterloo, and his second abdication, when the allies again forced Joseph to flee France for good.

On 2 July 1816, Joseph purchased another large property in the United States, from Stephen Sayre who, ironically, had once been High Sheriff of London. This was a two-hundred-and-eleven-acre farm called Point Breeze (see plate 7), just outside the small town of Bordentown, New Jersey, on the banks of the Delaware River. Mme. de Staël, Joseph's devoted friend (though Napoleon's erstwhile enemy), had recommended this area of New Jersey to him. Her reason had been that General Moreau, exiled by Napoleon out of jealousy, had once lived just across the river in Morrisville, Pennsylvania. Bordentown had also been home to Thomas Paine (1739– 1809), the author of *Common Sense* (1776) and *The Rights of Man* (1791–92), the latter defending measures taken in revolutionary France and appealing to the English to overthrow their monarchy and organize a republic.

In the following four months Joseph added nearly three hundred acres to his holding, and for the next nineteen years, until 1835, he constantly increased his estate by buying surrounding farms, orchards, fields, woods, and marshland from many owners. Through the marsh ran Crosswicks Creek and its tributary, Thornton Creek (possibly unnamed at the time), which he would dam with earth to create a large lake. The estate would eventually encompass approximately eighteen hundred acres.

Because he was not an American citizen, the Count de Survilliers was prohibited from purchasing land, so James Carret, as his agent, signed the Point Breeze transaction papers in Joseph's stead, as he would in New York State. But the count became the legal owner of Point Breeze just over six months later, on 22 January 1817, when the New Jersey legislature passed an act authorizing a non-naturalized foreigner whose country was not at war with the United States to hold real estate and to bequeath it to his heirs. "I take this opportunity of expressing to you, the sincere gratification I feel, at the partiality you have shown to this State, by selecting it, as the place of your residence," wrote the governor, Mahlon Dickerson. "That the members of the State Legislature participate with me, in sentiments of kindness towards you, the act they have passed, must afford the most satisfactory proof."[3]

In America, Joseph found some measure of the tranquility he had longed for all his life, and as soon as he bought Point Breeze he set to work with plans for improving his estate. He moved the Sayre house to Farnsworth Avenue in Bordentown and built a much larger edifice, spacious and airy and set out on a high triangular promontory overlooking the Delaware River. His so-called architect (to the extent that he allowed anyone beside himself to design the building) and master mason was a

Frenchman, Theodore Mauroy, whom he had employed at Mortefontaine.[4] But his most invaluable assistance, from building the house to filling its larders, came from the merchant Stephen Girard.

In early December 1816, Girard, an entrepreneur with multiple business interests, wrote that he was sending two thousand feet of yellow Carolina pine flooring boards, noting that "this quality of pine is the best that we have in America and exceeds that of Europe." He advises that the door and window frames be made with this wood and says he awaits new instructions from the count on the subject.[5] The following August, Girard notified Joseph that two hundred pieces of Nanking china and six cases of marble had arrived on his ship *Le Linet*, and that they were on the wharf in Philadelphia and would be expedited as soon as possible.[6]

Girard's services went beyond building materials. "I wish to send you four barrels of red Bordeaux wine of 1815," Girard had written in the fall of 1816, "and one barrel of old Médoc wine; I will add to this shipment a barrel of white wine of St. Croix du Mont, if you desire; kindly let me know your intention on this subject. If you need a cooper to bottle your wine, I might be able to send you the one who works for me."[7] It sounds as though Joseph Bonaparte was quite a tippler, but Charles Ingersoll observed that Joseph drank only a small amount of wine at each of his two meals. Amazingly for a Frenchman, he diluted his champagne with water. Ingersoll described him as a "heavy feeder, and so extremely abstemious of drink that it seemed to me his health would have been better for eating less and drinking more."[8] The impressive cellar was mostly for guests. In Spain Joseph had been nicknamed Pepe Botellas, "Joe Bottles," because of the scale of his entertaining.

Even though Joseph had spent several years as pampered royalty, he soon entered into the American spirit of self-reliance. According to a report in the *Baltimore American* of September 1816, just a year after his arrival: "[The count] seems determined to conform to the manners and customs of our country. I saw old Mr. Sayre, of whom he purchased the farm. He said when Mr. Buonaparte came to take possession of that place he [Sayre] was called out from dinner, and found him [the new owner] busily engaged, with his own hands, unloading the furniture he had bought. Something was said about sending for other hands, but he said no—everybody worked in this country."[9] Recent aristocratic arrivals from Europe were looked on with suspicion if they did not appear somehow gainfully employed: In 1822, *Niles Weekly Register*, in announcing that Achille and Lucien Murat had been granted permission to depart for the United States, had commented: "If they are willing to *work* to get an honest living, we shall be glad of their arrival—but we have consumers enough already."[10]

One incident in the Bonaparte legend (whether it actually took place is uncertain) showed Joseph as an appreciative resident of the republic. In early summer 1817, when he had only recently moved into the completed Point Breeze, a servant announced to him in his study that a group of strangers waited in the hall. Joseph was surprised to see a delegation of Spanish and Mexican revolutionaries headed by General Francisco Xavier Mina, then only twenty-eight. Mina was the nephew of the most famous of all the Spanish guerrilla leaders who had fought against Joseph in Spain, and he himself had caused Joseph countless headaches by harassing his line of communications with France. The young general entered the study quickly and sank to his knees, declaiming dramatically that he and his compatriots had come to place the crown of Mexico on Joseph Bonaparte's head and to declare his majesty king of the Indies.[11]

Joseph responded kindly, though probably with barely concealed amusement: "I know of nothing more rewarding in my public life, than to see men who did not recognize my authority in Madrid come to me now that I am in exile, but every day in this hospitable country proves to me the excellence of the republican form of government for America. Preserve it in Mexico as a precious gift of Providence. Calm your internal quarrels and look in the midst of your fellow-citizens for a man more capable than myself to fill the role of Washington."[12] General Mina did not press his case, and, after being handsomely entertained at dinner, the delegation withdrew. Mina apparently ignored Joseph's sound advice, for several months later he died before a Spanish firing squad in Mexico.

Others tried to persuade Joseph Bonaparte to accept the throne of Mexico. Joseph Lakanal, a professor of philosophy and rhetoric in France, planned to "restore" Joseph as King of the Indies (part of his Spanish title), as the Spanish possessions in Latin America were called. Lakanal was an intellectual, known for having laid the cornerstone of the modern French educational system centered upon the eminent École Polytechnique.[13] In America, where he had fled after the Restoration in 1815 (as a delegate to the National Convention he had voted for the death of Louis XVI), he put his prodigious powers of mind to a plan for rescuing Napoleon from St. Helena. This he hoped to achieve by invading Mexico with experienced French officers and American soldiers recruited from the frontier and financing the venture by seizing Mexico's rich silver mines.

A Philadelphia periodical reported in March 1817 on the impossibility of rescuing Napoleon from St. Helena. "The garrison consists of 2500 men, with upwards of

500 pieces of artillery and about 20 mortars. The only plain on the island is that where Bonaparte resides, on which a regiment is also encamped. This plain is surrounded by tremendous precipices, on which are stationed sentinels and telegraphs. An hourly report is made with these to the governor of what the prisoner is doing; and in two minutes he can be apprised of any particular occurrence, as well at night as in the daytime. In addition to these, two frigates and two brigs are constantly sailing round the island, and at night the whole coast is patrolled by armed boats." The writer concludes, "such are the preparations to guard against the influence and power of one man—ever represented to us as a monster, to be hated rather than loved."[14]

In mid-1817, Lakanal sent an emissary to Joseph with a packet that included letters and documents concerning the imminent invasion of Mexico. He included with his plans, a report on conditions in Mexico and the Louisiana Territory, a list of Indian tribes, as well as an Indian vocabulary. Forewarned, Joseph refused to accept this compromising collection of documents. Somehow it came into the hands of Hyde de Neuville, the nervous French ambassador to the United States appointed by Louis XVIII to monitor the activities of suspected ex-patriots, especially any Bona-partists. Neuville at once turned the papers over to Secretary of State John Quincy Adams, alerting him that the exiled French military, mobilizing for this invasion and meeting at Point Breeze, was a dangerous threat to the peace of the United States. The American government was not particularly concerned, as newspapers and jour-nals often reported that many French officers frequently visited Joseph Bonaparte at Point Breeze, including Marshal Grouchy, Generals Clauzel, Lefebvre-Desnouettes, Vandamme, and the brothers Charles and Henri Lallemand. In contrast, when the Spanish ambassador, Louis de Onis, learned of the damaging information he has-tened to demand an investigation. Fortunately for Joseph, Henry Clay, a friend of Lakanal, deemed the whole affair comical and convinced President James Monroe that Joseph Bonaparte was innocent and should not be questioned.

The Bonaparte family was still dogged by a news report casting suspicion on their potential for insurrection. Joseph's younger brother, Lucien, tried to come to the United States at this time since his situation in Europe as Napoleon's brother was increasingly tenuous. *Niles Weekly Register* reported at the end of April on a docu-ment containing the determination of the allied powers to prevent the "escape" of Lucien to the United States. The paper mentioned the "ulterior plans" that discon-tented refugees proposed for the purpose of making America "a theater of revolution-ary ideas, and a new field for ambition and intrigue." Lucien should not be allowed into the country since "North America having received a great number of malcon-tents and French refugees, the presence of Lucien Bonaparte in the United States would be still more dangerous than it is in Europe, where he can be better watched. Therefore, his passports must be refused." The statement's signers in Paris were the Duke of Richelieu, Prime Minister of France from 1815 to 1818, Wellington, and Charles André Pozzo di Borgo, the Bonapartes' implacable enemy, then Russian ambassador.[15] These men could not have known that the hot-headed youth—who, as a professed Jacobin (a radical branch of revolutionaries), had earlier called himself "Brutus"—had mellowed into a middle-aged art aficionado who spent lavish sums on his collections and would soon be more interested in excavating and cataloguing the Etruscan artifacts he was finding on his vast lands outside Rome than in stirring up revolution anywhere.

Joseph's troubles with the American establishment were not over. In 1816, Congress had granted land on the Tombigbee River in Alabama, bought from the Indians, to a group of French émigrés who called their agricultural project for developing this land the Society for the Cultivation of the Vine and the Olive. The Count de Survilliers, always willing to help his countrymen, had contributed generously to this means of livelihood for exiled French soldiers. But Joseph was again implicated as a conspirator when, after the Lakanal affair came to light, the authorities began to suspect that the Tombigbee organization was a front for a planned invasion of Mexico and was perhaps coupled with Lakanal. General Charles Lallemand, president of the Tombigbee group, insisted that he did not know Lakanal and that his own project was genuine.

Since Lallemand and his society did not find the soil in Alabama suitable for growing grapes and olives, they decided instead to set up a colony called the Champ d'Asile (field of refuge) on the Trinity River in Texas. Unfortunately, the land they selected was disputed by the United States and Mexico. The four hundred men in this organization were all former French soldiers quite unaccustomed to an agricultural existence on the frontier, they faced challenges for which they were totally unprepared. They had known only military life as battle-hardened veterans of Cairo, Jaffa, Marengo, Jena, Austerlitz, Moscow, Spain, and Waterloo.

Charles Lallemand had been part of the expedition to Egypt with Napoleon and with only a handful of others had returned to France with the future emperor. He had fought in Spain, been wounded at Waterloo, and after Napoleon's abdication and flight to the coast, had been charged by Napoleon to go aboard the *Bellerophon* and request England's hospitality for the fallen emperor. At Plymouth he had been arrested and sent to prison on Malta. In Paris he was charged with treason and sentenced to death, but the Maltese freed him in 1816 and he eventually succeeded in reaching America and Point Breeze where Joseph helped to establish him in a foreign country. It was in 1817 that he founded the Champ d'Asile for French soldier refugees.[16]

His brother, Henri Dominique Lallemand, three years younger, had also had a military career. He had served in Spain, and with his brother had marched on Paris after Napoleon's escape from Elba. He, too, was wounded at Waterloo, condemned to death by the restored monarchy, and escaped to America. Through his friendship with Joseph, who aided him in many ways, he met Stephen Girard and fell in love with Girard's niece and ward, Henriette. They were married in Philadelphia on 28 October 1817, with the Count de Survilliers, Charles Lallemand, Marshal Grouchy, and other former officers of the empire present.[17]

The principal concern of the United States government was actually not its disruption by former French soldiers. President Monroe in Washington and Andrew Jackson on the frontier were more apprehensive that the Spanish colonies could serve as a base for a Negro insurrection, a Negro-Indian alliance, or an effort to abolish slavery in the South.[18] Hyde de Neuville informed John Quincy Adams that the Lallemands' scheme was similar to that of Aaron Burr, some thirteen years earlier, for seizing the Mexican mines of San Luis Potosi and Vera Cruz, as well as Mexican land, and creating a new republic in the Southwest. Neuville was further able to assure Adams that his suspicions were correct when a New Orleans newspaper reported that Stephen Girard had given fifty thousand dollars "to finance a filibustering [insurrectionary] expedition against Mexico, supplemented with very considerable sums from Joseph Bonaparte and 'other distinguished Frenchmen.' "[19]

An indignant Henri wrote Girard (his uncle-in-law) from New Orleans, sending him two newspapers with incriminating reports that mentioned the settlements established by his brother and himself on the Trinity River in "the province of Texas." "Although a man is not called upon to answer an unsigned article," he said, "I thought it better not to maintain silence in this case because of the incorrect reference to you as well as to the Count of Survilliers and Marshal Grouchy, as my silence might have been misinterpreted. You will see that my answers are short and concise, as they ought to be. When one's intentions are pure, one has nothing to fear and one does not need to indulge in fine phrases in replying to calumnies." He added that the people in New Orleans had "shown their contempt for this attack of the journalists."[20]

Henri said he had just heard from his brother, recently arrived at the Trinity River after many hardships caused by the weather and bad roads. Charles had bought oxen and horses to be used until some could be caught from the "wild herds in the country," and was getting the colonists settled on the banks of the river. Henri himself was sending out plows and seed from New Orleans. He confided to Girard that since it was unnecessary for both brothers to be in the settlement, he planned to take advantage of this fact for returning to Philadelphia to see his wife, whom he missed dreadfully. "Perhaps you will say it is a weakness to be too fond of one's wife," he told Girard. "Possibly it is; but for all that I shall not apologize for loving her a great deal and finding it a hardship to be separated from her. Anyhow, though I may be madly in love with her, my love will never make a fool of me; for you see that I can leave her when my business renders it necessary."[21]

As far as plans went for the Lallemand brothers to invade Mexico, the rumor appears to have been unfounded. The brothers sincerely wished to establish a refuge for their fellow expatriates. But the experiment turned out a fiasco, lasting only a year before succumbing to the climate, disease, lack of supplies, and hostility from the Spanish and Mexican authorities. Contemporary accounts even told of several colonists being burned at the stake by warring Indians.

All the panicky suspicions of Hyde de Neuville about Joseph's involvement in nefarious schemes were for nothing. Henri told Girard, "What we had most to fear, what we were bound carefully to avoid was displeasing the American government, and putting it in the position of being forced to declare itself against us. . . . We were also bound to put ourselves in a safe position with the Spanish government, to allow it no excuse for complaining to the Americans that we had made armed invasion of its territory from American soil."[22]

As for the Mexican monarchy, not only Joseph thought it a bad idea. Barry O'Meara, Napoleon's physician on St. Helena, noted in his journal on 30 January 1817 that Napoleon did not attach much importance to the information that Joseph had been offered the crown of Mexico. "Joseph has brains and talent," the emperor observed, "but he is too taken up with pleasures and literature to be a king."[23] Napoleon had told Joseph when he was king of Naples, "You live too much with letters and savants. These are coquettes with which one must maintain *un commerce de galanterie*, but which one must never dream of making his wife or his minister."[24]

Chapter 3 ALONE

> *I hope that some day I will have the pleasure to be here with you.*
> *Today I am all alone.*
>
> —Joseph Bonaparte to his daughter Zénaïde,
> Point Breeze, 14 September 1817

*I*n the winter of 1818, Joseph received a letter from Count Emmanuel Augustin Dieudonné de Las Cases, who had just been hospitably received by Joseph's wife, Julie, in Frankfurt. Las Cases, a French historian to whom Napoleon had dictated part of his memoirs and the emperor's favorite of all the devotees who accompanied him to St. Helena, had been abruptly sent away by the British authorities for smuggling correspondence off the island. He had been deported to the Cape of Good Hope, he told Joseph, and would have written "Votre Majesté" sooner had it not been for the strict surveillance of his captivity. "You will no doubt see in the English papers that this same letter, as well as others, were seized on my arrival in the Thames." Austria had granted Las Cases asylum, but by then the precarious state of his health kept him in Frankfurt, where he was living quietly. His devotion to Napoleon remained. "Near or far, I have no other occupation, no other thoughts than to alleviate his horrible situation, if it is possible. . . . If your majesty vouchsafes to allow me, by way of the queen, to send that which she believes necessary, I will take care of this with pleasure."[1]

Joseph told Julie in June that he had written to Las Cases and to let him know he was doing everything he could for him. He instructed his banker in London to send Las Cases money and also wrote to his mother on the same subject: "Las Cases must be reimbursed for all he has advanced to the emperor."[2]

By mid-July 1817, Joseph was able to write Julie in Frankfurt: "I have finished the house and all the expenses of a first establishment which have been considerable because we will be many and everything is very expensive in this country. I have invested all the money I have here"—presumably with Girard—"and with the interest from the funds and of that from Holland I will be able to manage, but with much economy. It is necessary to renounce all acts of charity—I must think only of you and the children. We have no means of acquiring money. Others can get it by work or by the generosity [*bienfaisance*] of their relations, today richer than we are who are isolated and besieged with difficulties [*battus par l'orage*]. I repeat that this country is excellent, but the worst thing is not to have enough income to live moderately for there is no hope of making money."[3]

Joseph proposed to Baring, his London banker, that he remit to him the value of all his lands sold in France and in return give him an annual revenue, with the capital staying in Baring's hands for five or ten years. But he thinks the Baring firm will not accept his proposition. (He was correct.) He sends embraces and kisses to her and their two daughters, Lolotte (Charlotte) and Zénaïde, and says he fervently desires the arrival of all three the following spring, which did not take place.[4] Julie's finances are not mentioned; no question as to whether or not she has enough to live on in comfort in Frankfurt. Perhaps he assumed that he had been sufficiently generous.

In some ways it had been useful for Joseph to have his wife still in Europe so she could send him all he needed for the house he was furnishing. In January 1818, he told her he had received three hundred books from Prangins (his château in Switzerland), four paintings, and eighty bottles of wine. He asks her to send the rest of his library, the rugs, curtains, beds, and Gobelin tapestries, all presumably from Prangins and Mortefontaine. From their house in Paris she is to send "the two Venus de Medicis and the gladiator from the burgher of Bruges—it cost me 15,000 livres, if one could get eight it would be necessary to sell it." He says, "jewels have no value here—if the diamonds are worth what they were when I left—sell all that you have of my jewels. I have received the little pictures of Zénaïde and Lolotte and the large portrait by Robert Le Fefèvre that was at Prangins, but I have not received your portrait. I ask you to have an original or a copy made of the one by Gérard."[5] Joseph discounts the fact that Gérard had been appointed "First Painter of the King" to the despised Bourbon Louis XVIII.

A month later Julie still had not satisfied him about the Gérard. "I have asked many times to send me the painting by Gérard of you and the children—it was at Madrid and then at Mortefontaine. If it has been damaged it must be repaired by Gérard and if it is lost he must make another," he wrote. The portrait (see plate 2) had been damaged by Prussian troops who slashed it, notably Julie's face, with their sabers. But it was not lost and Gérard would supervise a copy for Julie to be sent to Frankfurt. Joseph ends his letter with a detail intended to show his wife that he had been thinking about her while embellishing Point Breeze: "I have planted trees of all kinds hoping that their fruits, their flowers and their shade will please you."[6]

Joseph also made America sound appealing to his daughter. While on a visit to New York he told the fifteen-year-old Zénaïde: "The city where I am is very large. There are plays, concerts, excursions [*promenades*], and all that you could desire—one finds only friends in this country—you can live as you want without finding any bad people. I hope you will have the courage to put up with the inconveniences of travel that you would find on a voyage to this large and beautiful country and your little Papa who loves you so tenderly and who hopes to embrace you soon."[7] Sometime later he informed her that he had put two of her drawings of landscapes in his *salon de ville* (his Philadelphia sitting room), where he thought they looked very well.

From (the newly completed) Point Breeze, he wrote, "One could call this time of year an Indian summer [*l'été des sauvages*]. . . . I am writing from a room which is the most appealing in the house and perhaps of all the left bank of the Delaware. It has seven windows of which five are on the river. Four times a day the steamboats stop below the windows—I hope that someday I will have the pleasure to be here with you. Today I am all alone."[8] At that time, steamboats came part way up the Crosswicks Creek to a landing below the bluff where Joseph's house stood.

King Louis XVIII had permitted Joseph's wife to remain in France with their two daughters, in spite of the fact that Julie would not separate her fortunes from her husband's. But Julie soon found it unpleasant in Paris and moved her family to Frankfurt and eventually to Brussels. While Joseph had occupied Lansdowne, the grand and beautiful mansion outside Philadelphia, spending untold sums building and furbishing Point Breeze, and enjoying a busy social life, Julie inhabited a cold, damp villa in Frankfurt where it rained so much the water at times reached the first floor. She told her brother, Nicholas Clary, in the fall of 1816 that she had no company and did not expect that anyone would hasten to come see her. But she was occupied with her children and liked to be alone.[9]

As her health was fragile she had been reluctant to cross the Atlantic—not an unfounded fear in those days—and once she had suffered appalling seasickness sailing from Marseilles to Genoa. There may have been still another reason holding Julie back. Joseph would tell the company assembled at Nicholas Biddle's house for dinner in 1818 that there were those who sought "to frighten my wife and children by stories of Serpents and all sorts of things to prevent their coming over here. I have written them that never have I seen fewer serpents than since my arrival in America, that during a residence of almost two years I have seen but one."[10] Even with all her misgivings, Julie's unpleasant surroundings and loneliness must for a short time have overcome her reluctance to face an ocean voyage and she had at last decided on coming to America. In the summer of 1817 Girard wrote Joseph that he (Girard) had been informed that "Madame J. Bonaparte" had applied for passage in one of his ships, the *Montesquieu*. Girard was unable to comply with this request, however. "From the moment the English commenced to annoy our *Pavillon*, under the pretext there were enemy passengers on board, I gave orders to my captains to take on board only American sailors and merchandise to be charged to my account. I regret that this precaution on my part prevents your family from using my ships."[11]

By November, Girard was more confident the English would not harass his vessels. He wrote Joseph that he had three ships in the Indian Ocean returning to Amsterdam where one of them would be the following March, April, or May. "Let me know if you would like to use this occasion for your family."[12] Presumably by then Julie had again changed her mind about the hazardous crossing because she did not avail herself of Girard's offer.

It was always difficult for Joseph to get letters to his wife, even by regular mail routes, for they could be intercepted and confiscated. Girard told him in mid-December that he intended sending his ship *Le Voltaire* to the north of Europe in two days with orders to put in at Amsterdam if the ice in the port permitted. "If you desire to send letters by this occasion I will give them under cover to Mr. Edward George."[13] At the time Joseph was not certain where his wife and children were. Girard, in writing to his agents in Amsterdam, enclosed a letter "from the count to the countess in Frankfurt where he believes she has her two daughters with her."[14]

In spite of the fact that Julie had been allowed to stay in France, the Allies' Amnesty Act proscribed all other Bonapartes from entering the country. Ingersoll had written Rush the previous May 1817, that Lucien Bonaparte, then living in Rome, had asked permission of Pope Pius VII "to transplant himself and wife and ten children" to the United States." Lucien intended first to come alone "in order to reconnoitre and make arrangements." Ingersoll added that Lucien was a great favorite with the pope, and that his motive for emigrating was probably that his holiness was very old and might soon die, "in which event Lucien would be exposed, without a powerful protector, to the Bourbon influence."[15] Lucien's move would have pleased Joseph in more than one respect, since in order to have his progeny bear the name Bonaparte, he had his eye on Lucien's oldest son, Charles-Lucien, as a possible future husband for Zénaïde. The boy was just a year younger than she (fig. 6).

In April 1819, Joseph complained to Julie, "You do not speak to me about the

6. **Charles-Lucien Bonaparte as a Young Man** *by Charles de Châtillon. Pencil drawing. Courtesy of the Museo Napoleonico, Rome.*

son of Lucien—I don't know how to interpret your silence on the subject. Lucien always has the same idea in mind—immigrating to the United States. Lucien's son has no money, but the health, the name, an education conforming to our actual state makes me think he is right for the happiness of our child. Adieu, ma chère Julie. I embrace you with all my heart and hope that I won't have too much longer to wait to embrace you in reality."[16] Julie's silence on the subject of Charles-Lucien as a husband for Zénaïde may have been due to her resentment at the dowry of 700,000 francs that Lucien demanded. Joseph fails to comment on the enormous sum in his letter. To entice Zénaïde to come to America with her future husband, Joseph wrote to her, "If you come here at the end of summer, I will have nine months to build a house for you on the lake's edge—cool and airy in summer—I can definitely buy the land that surrounds the lake." As an added attraction, he comments, "We are three days from New York and half the journey one makes by steamboat."[17]

The following August he tells her that he approves her marriage to Charles-Lucien if her mother agrees to it, but he greatly regrets that he cannot attend the wedding. When they are married they can live at Prangins if they would prefer that to Florence, or Rome (where Charles's family have residences). He thinks Charles should live with her because Lucien has so many children still at home.[18] For the time being, however, Joseph remained focused on establishing a grand and suitable place in America for her and the rest of his family. His daughters would join him in New Jersey within a few years; he did not see Julie for another twenty years.

The house that Joseph built at Point Breeze was much admired. An Englishman, writing of his visit in the summer of 1819, observed that only the White House in Washington surpassed it. He described the first floor as consisting of nine rooms, magnificently decorated and furnished, the walls covered with numerous works of renowned artists.[19] Another English guest, the radical activist, reformer, and writer Frances Wright, who came to Point Breeze that same summer, described the house's marvelous panorama overlooking Crosswicks Creek with the Delaware River beyond. Entering the estate, she wrote, one perceives across the lawn magnolias and rhodo-dendron harmoniously planted under the great American forest trees that serve as a border, the green rug of the lawn setting off the large white house. She described Joseph as "leaving his workmen to meet her in an old coat from which he had barely shaken off the mortar, and—a sign of the true gentleman—made no apologies. His air, figure, and address, have the character of the English country gentleman—open, unaffected, and independent, but perhaps combining more mildness and suavity."

She said his face was "fine" and it was difficult to decide which of the busts in the house were of Napoleon and which of Joseph.

While walking in the park, she said, "he gathered a wild flower, and in presenting it to me, carelessly drew a comparison between its minute beauties and the pleasures of private life; contrasting those of ambition and power with the more gaudy flowers of the parterre, which look better at a distance than upon nearer approach. He said this so naturally, with a manner so simple, and an accent so mild, that it was impossible to see in it an attempt at display of any kind." She added that after she had departed, she mused that the Count de Survilliers had given her the feeling that, rather than otherwise, fortune "had spited him in making him the brother of the ambitious Napoleon."[20]

In the late summer of 1817, when Julia Rush, the beautiful young daughter of the celebrated Dr. Benjamin Rush of Philadelphia, had dined with Joseph at Point Breeze, she said that his conversation—presumably she spoke French, for others said Joseph had little command of spoken English—was very communicative and that he was often "severe" on his brother Napoleon. It may have been politic to criticize Napoleon in America, where so much bad feeling about him existed. Joseph told her that when he was king of Spain he would direct his marshals and generals to do one thing, but they would immediately do something else, on orders from the emperor. He said that Napoleon's intention was to annex the greater part of Spain to France and to leave him (Joseph) only a small kingdom in the south. She added that the Count de Survilliers's manners were "urbane and polished," and that he was a "very good looking man."[21] Most women, no matter what age, agreed on that.

Joseph had been so occupied with establishing himself in the New World and developing his estate at Point Breeze that he did not visit his lands in New York for several years. Twenty-five years earlier this part of the country had been the destination of certain French aristocrats escaping the horrors of their country's bloody revolution. They had been told that Castorland, the colony they planned, was overrun with profitable beaver. The promoters of the enterprise envisioned planting untold acres of vineyards for a bounteous harvest in addition to the beaver trade, as well as the production of maple syrup that in time would outstrip the sugar cane industry of the West Indies. A great port would be established on Lake Ontario for shipping goods up the St. Lawrence River to the Atlantic Ocean. Many of the early settlers were men of wealth and refinement who dreamed of vast estates carved out of this woodland country traversed by the Black River and abounding with fish and game.

But the attempt of the Castorland colonists, pitifully unprepared to cope with the wilderness, was a failure and most of them left in disgust. They had at least charted and mapped a substantial portion of the area, and their surveys and the road they built were of great value to the English-speaking pioneers who followed them a few years later.[22]

Napoleon himself had dreamed of establishing a great colony in this part of the world. The Count de Las Cases, writing on St. Helena in May 1816, says that he and the emperor had learned from the press that Joseph had bought a great quantity of land in northern New York State on the St. Lawrence River, that it was surrounded by a large number of Frenchmen, and that he would soon found a community. The emperor was reportedly pleased at the prospect of this endeavor because of the proximity of Canada where much of the population was French. He thought this French presence would strengthen their resistance to the English who were in control of Canada.[23]

According to Las Cases, Napoleon said that if he had reached America he would have called together all those who were close to him and these people would have formed the nucleus of a new country. Before a year was out, the events of Europe would drive thousands more to him. He yearned to realize this dream, as America to him was a true refuge, an immense continent with a particular quality of liberty.[24]

Joseph, in acquiring his vast lands in northern New York, may have had his brother's future in mind. At the crucial time when Napoleon had been forced by the allied armies to escape from France and Joseph had offered to change places with him, he may have thought when he bought his Black River holdings that the land would be the perfect place for Napoleon to establish a new domain. But since this was not to be, he would enjoy the hunting and fishing himself while entertaining numerous friends. In addition he would help penniless émigrés to establish themselves with gifts of small land parcels.

Joseph first visited his northern lands in the late summer of 1817. A Philadelphia newspaper reported that he had been in Buffalo on 16 September: "on Wednesday last, Joseph Bonaparte, Ex-King of Spain, arrived in this village. The next day he passed down the Niagara River and viewed the Falls; after which he returned to this place and on Saturday proceeded on his route to Philadelphia via Erie, Pennsylvania. He was accompanied by several French gentlemen."[25]

Joseph again traveled north in the summer of 1818. The same Philadelphia newspaper reported from Watertown, New York, that, "On Monday last, Joseph Bonaparte, ex-king of Spain, arrived at the seat of M. Le Ray de Chaumont; and on Tuesday, he with his attendants, accompanied by M. Le Ray de Chaumont, passed through the village. He spent two hours in visiting the cotton factory, pulling-mill, trip hammer, paper mill, the park etc. and appeared highly gratified with the many public improvements witnessed in this vicinity—and which have generally been completed in the short space of four years."[26] Ironically, on the same page with this notice was a report from France that the Duke of Wellington had just dined with the Austrian ambassador and was expected to leave Paris at the end of the week. This adversary who, in his war against France, had driven Joseph ignominiously from Spain on the battlefield in northern Spain only five years earlier, was now in Paris as an honored guest of the restored Bourbon king, Louis XVIII, while Joseph, secure in the United States, quietly surveyed the immense land holdings that he planned to use for hunting deer and rabbits. Fate had allowed both men to survive a horrible massacre to pursue their lives in security and affluence.

For seven years, Joseph's land was held in the name of his agent, James Carret, as Point Breeze had been. On 1 March 1825, Joseph petitioned the State of New York to allow him to own property in the state:

> Joseph Bonaparte begs the Legislature of New York to author-
> ise him to hold land in this State. Although a foreigner, he is not
> one of those who daily solicit in order to quit this hospitable coun-
> try, where the true rights of man are the most respected; but never-
> theless being more than ever attached to his own country, and
> bound to it by duties rendered still more sacred by misfortune, he
> is not in a position to profit by the law which offers him the hon-
> ourable and precious title of American Citizen, and thereby confer
> upon him the right of holding land. He must continue to be a
> Frenchman; hoping, however, to find in the Legislature of the State
> of New York the same kindness and good will which he has experi-
> enced in the other States of the Union, he begs the Legislature will
> grant him the right of holding land in this State of New York.[27]

His request was granted a few months later.

One wonders how successful Napoleon would have been in establishing himself in this part of the world, for feelings toward him were decidedly negative as far as the general populace was concerned. A week earlier, the same newspaper that mentioned Joseph's visit to Buffalo quoted a certain captain, just out of Gibraltar, whose ship had been boarded by some one from a British man-of-war bound for England from St. Helena. The boarding officer had reported that "Bonaparte" was in good health, that he took very little exercise, and was in the habit of taking warm baths in which he stayed four or five hours at a time. "As he has kept the world for so long in *warm water*," stated the writer, "it is proper enough that he should try an experiment of its effects on *himself.*"[28]

The land Joseph bought with silver and furniture worth 600,000 francs (about $120,000), some 25,000 acres, essentially comprised the virgin forests between the Black River and the Adirondack Mountains. Heavily wooded, it contained a 1,200-acre lake surrounded by bold rocky shores, alternating with tree-filled swamps, encompassing several islands, and adorned in summer with masses of yellow water lilies. He called it Lake Diana after the goddess of the hunt, but it would eventually be known as Lake Bonaparte. Perhaps a painting of Peter Paul Rubens he had at Point Breeze, *The Hunt of Diana,* suggested the name, which may also have recalled the sumptuous royal palace gardens of Caserta, Italy, when he had been king of Naples. Below a grand cascade in this famous garden of the Bourbon rulers, statues tell the story of Diana and her nymphs interrupted while bathing by the huntsman Actaeon. In the myth, Diana turns Actaeon into a stag, and his own dogs tear him to pieces.

Joseph made extensive improvements to his Black River lands. He had a road cut from the old turnpike through to his lake, a boat taken through the woods and launched on its waters, and a log house built as a hunting lodge on an elevated part of the shore commanding a fine view. At the outlet of the lake, at the present-day village of Alpina, he would have a clearing made of some thirty acres and a framed building erected with icehouse, cellars for storing food and wine, outhouses, and other necessaries. This dwelling was intended as his summer residence.[29] It had a large dining room, sitting room, and kitchen on the first floor, and on the second floor, beside the count's "sleeping apartment," the first lavatory and toilet, made of hammered lead, set up in that part of the country.[30]

Elaborate tales would be told of Joseph's visits to his northern lands in future years. It was said that because he feared British or Bourbon spies were tracking him, he had a bodyguard of four giant grenadiers, veterans of the Napoleonic wars, and that he had built a bulletproof house furnished with works of art, cut glass, and silver. He was supposed to have arrived in a gilded coach drawn by six horses and accompanied by numerous guests and servants in other carriages. On Lake Diana it was said that he and his party floated in a large six-oared gondola, such as he had known in Venice, fashioned from a giant tree trunk. He was described as riding into the woods dressed in green velvet hunting attire and picnicking in the forest on gold plates.[31] However apocryphal these tales, Joseph maintained his regal lifestyle wherever he was. Deborah Logan reported in her diary for the summer of 1821 that "[Napoleon's] brother Joseph passed through Trenton a day or two ago on his visit to some of the watering places; he always takes a great train along with him on these excurtions. His cook and the Paraphernalia of Luxurious eating, always makes a part of this train."[32]

Chapter 4 FRIENDS, FAMILY, AND ANNA

> *You understand at least that Madame Julie tolerates things on your*
> *part that a great number of women I know would not allow. I do not*
> *except my own sweet Josephine.*
>
> > —Napoleon to Joseph Bonaparte, quoted in
> > Lucien Bonaparte's *Memoirs*

Joseph Bonaparte's male friends and acquaintances in America represented amazing crosscurrents of contemporary political, social, and military history. For the most part they were particularly erudite men. One American who spoke French and became a close friend, William Short (fig. 7), had been Thomas Jefferson's secretary when Jefferson was minister to France from 1794 to 1798. Short also fell in love with a Frenchwoman, Rosalie de la Rochefoucauld, and their intense affair lasted seven years, although they never married.[1] He would no doubt have been sympathetic concerning Joseph Bonaparte's *affaires de coeur*. Another French-speaking American was Nicholas Biddle, an important figure in early American banking and editor of the *Port Folio*, America's foremost literary magazine at the time. Charles Ingersoll, a lawyer, and like Biddle, some fourteen years younger than Joseph, also was literary. He wrote poetry, plays, pamphlets, and a two-volume history of the War of 1812. This *History of the Second War Between the United States of America and Great Britain,* which contained an account of the French Revolution and the Empire, incorporated the essence of many conversations with the Count de Survilliers and his fellow expatriates.[2] Ingersoll's pamphlets, in particular, which defended American culture as superior to that of England in several instances, were widely read and have been credited with helping to create an American cultural nationalism in the early

7. **Portrait of William Short** *by Rembrandt Peale, 1803. Oil on canvas. Muscarelle Museum of Art, College of William and Mary.*

republic.[3] Like Short, Ingersoll had been attached to the American legation in France, spoke French, and probably had met Joseph in Paris. Ingersoll was one of the first to entertain the ex-king in 1816, not long after he had settled in Philadelphia.

That fall Ingersoll would give his friend, Richard Rush, Secretary of State under Monroe, his opinion of Joseph Bonaparte. "Your reflections upon King Joseph are striking enough," answered Rush from Washington. "They reminded me of the Prince's upon the crown in Henry 4," referring to the speech in Shakespeare that ends, "Uneasy lies the head that wears a crown." Rush continued, "The occasions, to be sure, are different. After all, Joseph was but half a King. First, he was not born one, which, with a King, is every thing. Secondly, during the short time that the wires moved him, he seems to have wanted [lacked] all the wishes and the passions that belong to the throne. Richard Cromwell matches him, as well as any other parallel I recollect."[4] Richard Cromwell was Oliver Cromwell's son and decidedly passive successor who refused any attempt to keep his power when the Long Parliament and heads of the army agreed on his dismissal, much as Napoleon had dismissed Joseph from Spain.

Another friend with literary tastes was Dr. Nathaniel Chapman (see fig. 5), a founder of the College of Physicians in Philadelphia. Chapman, the Count de Survilliers's personal physician, was an editor of medical textbooks and in 1820 founded what would become the *American Journal of Medical Sciences*, as it is known today. His wit and courtly manners delighted Joseph, who would in time claim Chapman as his closest friend in the New World. Also a prominent medical man in Philadelphia was Philip Syng Physick, "the father of American surgery," whose teenaged daughter Susan described a visit to Point Breeze. While being shown through the house, Susan admired an engraving of Napoleon's son, the King of Rome. "You like it? You like it?" the count had said, "I give it you! I give it you!" Although Susan Physick protested, the picture was placed in the carriage beside her when she left.[5]

Among the count's neighbors in Bordentown was the jurist Joseph Hopkinson (fig. 8), who would become his intimate and valued confidant, as well as his lawyer. There was also the naval officer Admiral Charles Stewart, commander of the USS *Constitution* in the War of 1812, whose house (called Ironsides, like his vessel) could be seen from Joseph's belvedere. Joseph's close social ties with Biddle, Chapman, Ingersoll, Hopkinson, and Physick gained him introductions to other Philadelphians.

In 1823, the Count de Survilliers would be elected a member of the prestigious American Philosophical Society of which Thomas Jefferson had been president while he was U.S. president. At the society's meetings Joseph met statesmen like Daniel Webster, sixth U.S. president John Quincy Adams, Adams's secretary of state Henry

8. **Portrait of Joseph Hopkinson,** *lithograph after portrait by James Reid Lambdin, 1843.*
Athenaeum of Philadelphia.

Clay, and General Thomas Cadwalader. Others he knew from the society were French-born Peter Stephen Du Ponceau, a leading authority on international law and a philologist who made important contributions to the study of various North American Indian languages, and Joel Roberts Poinsett, the first U.S. ambassador to Mexico in 1825 and for whom the poinsettia was named. It is difficult to tell how well received Joseph was at this point in his exile. Some regarded him still with a certain amount of skepticism, but the Count de Survilliers charmed friends and acquaintances with his ties to recent European history, regardless of opinions concerning Napoleon, as well as with his erudition and interesting conversation.

At a dinner he hosted in the winter of 1818 in Philadelphia, Biddle recorded in his private journal many of these conversations with Joseph, probably held in French. Joseph spoke of Joseph Fouché, Duke of Otrante (1763–1820), Napoleon's brutal Minister of Police, whom he described as behaving worse than anyone else in political matters. Fouché betrayed the emperor after his abdication by drawing up a list for Louis XVIII of men who could not enter France, including most of the generals who visited Joseph at Point Breeze at one time or another.

As for Talleyrand (Charles Maurice de Talleyrand-Périgord, 1754–1838), the French statesman who took holy orders but was eventually excommunicated by the pope for proposing confiscation of church property to support the government, and who switched allegiance from Napoleon to the Bourbons when power shifted, Joseph was slightly less harsh. He said that Talleyrand might "be excused on the ground that in his coming out for the Bourbons, he fell back on the place he occupied before the Revolution. But Fouché soiled with all sorts of crimes, steeped in blood, what interest could he be in the eyes of the Bourbons? He is a mixture of mud, steeped in blood!" At another dinner at Biddle's house a month later, Joseph pronounced Talleyrand "an ignoramous." At Biddle's astonishment, the count replied: "Yes, but Talleyrand is an ignoramous. He is very lazy and all lazy people are ignorant. I distinguish between men who are something in themselves, who are familiar with science or proficient in Art, and those who have a mere smattering of everything." William Short, also present, agreed. "I saw a good deal of Talleyrand," he said. "I have had occasion to come in contact with many individuals, but in all my experience I never met one more despicable."[6]

The talk about Talleyrand naturally led to Germaine de Staël, who had been his lover. Because de Staël had strongly opposed the empire, Napoleon accused her of intriguing against him and banned her from France when he became emperor. Joseph told the assembled company at Biddle's that once he had spent an entire day trying to convince Napoleon to leave Germaine in peace and to pay back the two million francs advanced to France by her father, the French financier and statesman Jacques Necker. "What!" Napoleon had exclaimed, "you speak in favor of that hussy, you have only known her for a certain number of days—while Talleyrand who has known her a very long time is opposed to it." Joseph told the gathering that Madame de Staël said of Talleyrand: "he is an individual who always comes to the rescue of the victor."[7] This statement proved only too true, for he betrayed Napoleon to the allies before and after the disaster at Waterloo.

Joseph had many stories about de Staël and Talleyrand. When Talleyrand grew cold to her and commenced his liaison with another, she asked him one day, to test his affections, if she and Madame Grant were shipwrecked, which one would he save? He answered, "But, Madame, you have a charming house at Coppet on the lake of Geneva. Your father was a farseeing man who took precautions. Assuredly he had you taught to swim!"[8]

At Point Breeze, where Joseph frequently entertained these friends, among many others, there was constant but unostentatious hospitality. While staying there, one would be awakened by a servant bringing a cup of coffee or tea, then at ten or eleven a "meat breakfast" would be served. This was described as a center table spread with quantities of delicious fruits surrounded by smaller tables where tea, chocolate, coffee, eggs cooked in various ways, different meats, and a number of French delicacies were set out.[9] At one's disposal during the day would be an excellent library, horses and carriages for excursions, shooting, fishing, or whatever pastime one desired until dinner between six and seven. Afterward, one could choose a drive around the grounds or a game of billiards. Bedtime was usually ten o'clock. The domestic household consisted of Joseph's secretary Louis Mailliard, four or five men servants, a coachman, and the cook, François Parrot, who came with him from France.[10]

Mailliard, born at Mortefontaine in 1795, several years before Joseph acquired his property there, was fast becoming the count's closest confidant, young as he was. He married a Frenchwoman, Marguerite Angelique Redet (fig. 9), also a native of Mortefontaine, who was probably in the count's employ in Bordentown. Mailliard's son Adolphe was born at Point Breeze on 5 August 1819. But ten days later joy turned to grief when Marguerite died of complications from childbirth. Adolphe would be raised in France by his Redet grandparents, and Mailliard would mourn Marguerite all his life.[11]

Point Breeze was, especially in the early years, a place of refuge open to unfortunate Europeans driven by political upheavals to America. Joseph's friends among his

9. **Louis Mailliard and His Wife Marguerite Redet,** *miniature portraits, artist unknown, 1810–1820. Bancroft Library, University of California at Berkeley.*

fellow Frenchmen were principally exiled marshals and generals of Napoleon's army, such as Emmanuel, Marquis de Grouchy;[12] Count Charles Lefebvre-Desnouettes; Bertrand Clauzel; Count Dominique René Vandamme; and Michel, Count Regnaud de Saint-Jean d'Angély, who had been a crucial ally of Napoleon and served as his secretary of state in 1807, as well as being a witness for Napoleon's divorce from Josephine. When Count Regnaud came to the United States he lived in New York but was a frequent guest at Point Breeze. Reputed to be mentally unbalanced, he passed a number of worthless checks, and Joseph settled his debts while paying his passage back to Antwerp.[13]

For the most part, Joseph greatly enjoyed the company of the French exiles he had known so well in former times. At a wedding in New York he attended, along with St. Jean d'Angély, Grouchy, Vandamme, Lefebvre-Desnouettes, Charles Lalle-mand, and other expatriated followers of Napoleon, the friends had much to remi-nisce about and much to drink. All night the various marshals "enjoyed themselves as no other men on the face of the earth but Frenchmen could have under similar circumstances," according to Fitz-Greene Halleck, an American who was present. Halleck recorded how the ex-king blew vigorously on a newspaper trumpet, the cav-alry leader Lallemand crawled around on all fours with a small boy on his back, while another Waterloo general mimicked a stuttering French soldier.[14] They all sang songs and regaled each other with stories. One involved Marshal Andoche Junot when he was governor of Portugal. It seems that on a certain morning, Junot surprised the population of Lisbon by appearing in the great square before his palace on an empty pedestal, mounted on his horse personifying an equestrian statue—and completely naked. When the police came to arrest him they were astonished to find that the "statue" was their general-in-chief.[15]

All these men visited Joseph at Point Breeze, but the most prominent of his French visitors was the Marquis de Lafayette, hero of the American Revolution, who came to see Joseph twice on his triumphal return to the United States in 1824 and in 1825. In spite of the great cordiality with which the Count de Survilliers received Lafayette, his relationship with this hero of nearly mythical proportions was often at odds because of their different political views. Lafayette had been in favor of the Bourbon restoration after Napoleon's downfall at Waterloo. According to Ingersoll, Lafayette had "received considerable sums as indemnity for confiscated property, voted to his family by the French Chambers under the Bourbon government."[16]

Different levels of society—which involved his employees with whom he spent considerable time, as well as his peers—and their conflicting philosophies, were part of Joseph Bonaparte's world at Point Breeze. Francis Lieber, a German-born writer who came to the United States in June 1827 and two years later secured an introduc-tion to Joseph through his Philadelphia publisher, had dined with Joseph in company with an elderly man. The guest was formerly a hotheaded member of the Convention (the French regime several years after the Revolution of 1789 that decreed the aboli-tion of the monarchy and sentenced Louis XVI to death) who, recently arrived from South America, had gone directly to Bordentown to see the Count de Survilliers. This man had been a rabid supporter of Danton and Robespierre, and after the fall of the latter had fled to Colombia under the protection of the government of Simon Bolívar. Now as an old man seated at table with Joseph in the United States, using the French familiar "tu" popular under the Convention, he, a regicide, was addressing, some thirty years after the French Revolution, a man who had been king of Naples and of Spain. "You recall, Bonaparte," Lieber quoted him as saying, "when Robespierre did this or that."[17] Lieber, a much younger man once in the ranks of the Prussian army that had defeated and dethroned Napoleon, marveled to himself at the count's easy acceptance of such a familiar attitude and of the memories that were resurrected. There they were, three representatives of recent momentous periods and events in the history of Europe, two who had once been bitter enemies, seated at the same table quietly having dinner.[18]

This incident was not an exception. Even in the United States, where many regarded his brother with contempt, Joseph Bonaparte soon made friends with the leading men of the day and was accepted on his own terms. Nicholas Biddle (fig. 10), who summered at his wife's estate Andalusia across the Delaware River and spoke fluent French, was a boon to Joseph, who spoke almost no English when he first arrived in the United States. In 1804, Biddle had been to Paris as secretary to John Armstrong, the newly appointed minister to France. He had been present at Napoleon's coronation in 1804 and may have met Joseph at the time.[19] Biddle seems to have taken to the Count de Survilliers almost at once. He wrote to a friend in February 1818 that he regretted not being in Philadelphia at the time of his friend's visit because he wanted to introduce him to Joseph Bonaparte. "I have lately seen a good deal of him, and really he is by far the most interesting stranger that I have ever known in this country. He is free and communicative and talks of all the great events and the great persons of his day with a frankness, which assures you of his good nature as well as his veracity. I am going to dine with him as soon as I finish this letter."[20]

More than likely, since it was February, this dinner would have taken place at Joseph's winter home, a townhouse in Philadelphia that he rented from Stephen Girard for some years. Joseph usually spent the spring and early summer at Point Breeze, then July in northern New York State on his Black River property, and August at either Saratoga or Ballston Spa. By September, he was back at Point Breeze where he stayed until December. Then he moved to Philadelphia until March or April. But he was often back and forth between Point Breeze and Philadelphia, depending on events.

Called the Dunlop House (see plate 5), the Philadelphia mansion with its grounds occupied an entire city block between Market and Chestnut Streets and Twelfth and Thirteenth Streets. At a dinner party, Joseph had once offered to buy the house from Girard. The latter asked how much he was willing to pay for it, and Joseph answered that he would surround the entire city block with silver half dollars.

10. **Portrait of Nicholas Biddle** *by Rembrandt Peale. Engraving, partly colored. Engraved by James Barton Longacre and Thomas B. Welsh. American Philosophical Society.*

Girard smiled and replied that he accepted if the coins were stood on end; nothing came of the proposed sale. (The John Dunlop House has been gone for well over a century, but the entire block where it stood is still owned by the Stephen Girard Trust.) Entertaining frequently, at Point Breeze as well as in Philadelphia, was one of the ways Joseph came to know the intelligentsia of the city.

One evening in 1827, at the theater in Philadelphia where Francis Lieber had gone to see a French company from New Orleans, he spied the ex-king with his nephew Jérôme Patterson (son of his brother Jérôme Bonaparte and Elizabeth Patterson from Baltimore) and Joseph's friend Joseph Hopkinson. Lieber at the time had yet to meet the ex-king and was fascinated to see him. "Count Survilliers resembles his brother strongly," he noticed, "he has the short neck, round chin, full lips; the smooth hair, high shoulders and nose of the Emperor; the likeness to the portraits and engravings I had seen of the great General is very striking."[21]

The next morning Lieber called on Joseph at his hotel (he had given up renting houses in Philadelphia after his daughters had both returned to Europe). The young German had been corresponding with the count for a while about an article on Napoleon he was writing for the *Encyclopedia Americana* and Lieber was eager to meet him. When the count entered the room he greeted Lieber kindly, invited him to sit down beside him on the sofa, and requested they speak in French. "[He] spoke rapidly and fluently," Leiber said, corroborating Nicholas Biddle's statement about the count's conversation, "with a dignity of manner that charmed me, of a hundred remarkable things relating to his family, his ancestors, Robespierre, Napoleon as a young General in Italy, as Consul and Emperor—his own reign in Spain and Naples, the present Ministry in France, the Bourbons, Alexander (the czar of Russia), Josephine, the English and Fox, and a world of events."[22]

When he at last stood up to leave, Lieber said that Joseph's short stature and bearing again reminded him of Napoleon, whom young Franz had once seen surrounded by his proud bodyguard before the castle in Berlin, where the little boy had been lifted up on the shoulders of a family servant to get a better look. "It always seemed to me," Lieber recorded, "that the simple fact of my being brought into communication with this man so lately the King of Spain, and connected with the most mighty monarch of his day and his aiding me in a work [the article for the *Encyclopedia*] written by a former Pomeranian rifleman [himself], who was wounded in the battle waged against his imperial brother, condensed in a nut-shell the whole history of that agitated time."[23]

Although Joseph's brother had been a "mighty monarch" and he himself had twice been a king, Joseph always professed that his politics were republican. "I received my ideas in the Revolution," he once said at a dinner given by Ingersoll. "I am a Republican more even than you Americans are. I did not wish the formation of the French Empire."[24] Joseph may have found it only politic in America to profess his republicanism when he was living in unencumbered peace. And yet, his position may have been in some respects sincere. In France the majority of his friends were liberals, such as Stanislas de Girardin who acted as his equerry, the Bishop of Casal, as his chaplain,[25] and some so opposed to the empire like Madame de Staël that Napoleon banished her from the country. But, at her father's country house, Coppet, in Switzerland, she entertained many of those who shared her ideas, among them

Bernadotte, always at odds with Napoleon but who himself became a king, the writer Benjamin Constant, and frequently Joseph Bonaparte.

In 1814, when the great French actor François Joseph Talma visited Joseph at Prangins, Switzerland, Talma quoted him as saying: "My republican ideas are so fixed and so positive, that even though I was King of Naples and king of Spain, I never for an instant ceased to be republican."[26] Whatever contradictions in political philosophy this entailed, once in the United States Joseph succeeded in persuading his new friends that he did not share his brother's outlook. In the spring of 1817, Ingersoll, writing to Rush, said, "Joseph has repeatedly, and with all the apparent earnestness and animation of sincerity, assured me that the Emperor's cardinal error was preferring his Marshals and Dukes to the people—The people were his bulwark, he says and upon them alone he should have placed his whole reliance." Joseph had told Ingersoll, "after the battle of Waterloo Napoleon was betrayed by nearly all the most elevated of his former creatures, who forced him to abdicate, when Carnot and Sieyès and the republicans who had never flattered him were decidedly of opinion that at such a crisis resignation was not the watchword, but energy and decision."[27]

And it was this philosophy, or his profession of it, that soon overcame Americans' resistance to the brother of Napoleon; a man most Americans regarded as a monster.

Life was lonely without his family, however, and Joseph was not one to remain long without an intimate relationship. His record of fidelity to his wife, Julie, was far from unblemished. In a discussion with Napoleon in 1803 about his hereditary succession, while Joseph described his "petite Julie" as the best in the world, Napoleon observed that "we know that besides her known goodness, she also has the greatest indulgence for your little conjugal pranks [*vos petites fredaines conjugales*]. God knows on that point . . ." Joseph interrupted him, "Ah! On that point . . . I believe that it's the same with all husbands, and sometimes with wives; but not with mine." "All the better for you," dryly replied the First Consul. "You understand at least that Madame Julie tolerates things on your part that a great number of women I know would not allow. I do not except my own sweet Josephine."[28] Joseph insisted on this occasion that he loved and esteemed his wife, but this dedication did not prevent him from having affairs.

In 1804, a year after this discussion, Napoleon named Joseph Colonel Commandant of the 4th Regiment of the Line and sent him to Boulogne on the French coast to prepare for the invasion of England that never took place. Before long the dashing colonel enjoyed the favors of a Madame F, aggravating his commander-in-chief, Marshal Soult, whom Joseph had replaced in the lady's affections. Soult would bear a grudge and many years later enact it in Spain when Joseph was king by ignoring his orders. Joseph was also involved with Madame Regnaud de Saint-Jean-d'Angély, the wife of his friend, as well as Mademoiselle Le Gros of the Theatre Français and a certain "Adèle."[29]

After Napoleon named Joseph King of the Two Sicilies (March 1806), and shortly after he had taken up his post in Naples, he began a more serious affair with the beautiful twenty-one-year-old Maria-Guilia Colonna, Duchess d'Atri. The duchess fell passionately in love with the new king, wrote him a *billet-doux* once if not twice every day, and in 1807, bore him a son, Guilio. (The boy would not live to adulthood.) When Julie finally arrived in Naples with her two children to take up her duties as queen, the duchess wrote Joseph: "I love you. If I told you that I wished to abandon you, it was only for the sake of your family. You saw my tears, so you saw how much this cost me. But then, are you not the father of Guilio? Ah! This is enough for me to adore you forever!"[30]

After three years, Napoleon insisted that Joseph leave Naples and in 1808 assume instead the role of King of Spain and the Indies. This he did with reluctance, but only a few months away from the Duchess d'Atri, Joseph once again engaged in a romance. Stanislas de Girardin, one of Joseph's intimate friends, describes in his memoirs, published in 1829 much to Joseph's annoyance, how this came about.[31]

At Vitoria, on his way to Madrid to take on his royal responsibilities, Joseph was lodged in a *palacio* given over to him by the Marques and Marquesa del Montehermoso, who were themselves installed across the road in one of their other dwellings. On looking from the window one morning, Joseph spied a lovely dark-haired Spanish girl, and summoning his servant Christophe, he sent him to ask the young woman to spend the night with his master, offering her the extravagant sum of 13,000 francs. Christophe dutifully presented himself across the road and was introduced into the nursery, for the girl was the Montehermoso children's nanny. The nursemaid was not so much embarrassed by the proposition as by the presence of her mistress. The latter, however, gave her a smiling nod of permission.

The next day Girardin informed Joseph that the marquesa had spoken of the episode in society the previous evening. She had expressed her surprise that a man of the new king's standing should not have addressed himself to persons of higher rank, as she was sure there were many in Vitoria who would be flattered by his attentions. The day afterward, Girardin records that Joseph invited him to dine with the marques and the marquesa. "It was easy to see," Girdardin says, "that the Marquesa was already something more than just the mistress of the house in which we were."

The Marquesa del Montehermoso was elegant and charming, spoke both French and Italian fluently, sang accompanied by a guitar, and painted miniatures. Best of all, her husband seems not to have objected to Joseph's relations with his wife. The new king showed his gratitude by appointing the marques his chamberlain, naming him a grandee of Spain, and buying his house for three times its value.[32]

As for Julie, she had gone to Naples only toward the end of Joseph's reign, since Napoleon, ever solicitous of her welfare (perhaps because he had once been engaged to her sister Désirée), advised that she was better off staying in Paris due to the unsettled political situation. When Napoleon sent Joseph to Spain, the emperor was even more adamant that Julie not be involved in the volatile events taking place there. She therefore returned to Paris from Italy with her two daughters and never went to Spain. Whether or not she knew of her husband's romantic escapades is unknown, for she continued to write him loving letters without recriminations of any kind. But thinking back on Napoleon's remarks in 1803 of her enormous tolerance with her husband's affairs, she must have suspected the truth. She was a reserved, private person who had no desire for the pomp and splendor of the court, preferring a secluded, quiet existence alone with her children, and often with Désirée and their half-sister Honorine de Villeneuve. She was devoted to Joseph in her way, but much of their married life had been lived apart, so after he went into exile in America it is not surprising that, given her fragile health and terror of crossing the ocean, she preferred to stay in Europe.

By June 1818, Joseph wrote his wife repeatedly to tell her he missed his family and also that he suspected the life she was leading no longer pleased her or their children. "Zénaïde above all must suffer at her age"—she was seventeen—"from the monastic life that you have made for her, and her letters tell me enough that she is not happy. The children especially would have distractions here that they do not have at Frankfurt."[33]

The following month he learned that Julie would not be leaving Europe when it would be the best season for crossing the ocean. He had suggested the first of August as a good time to embark in order to enjoy the autumn in America.

> I think my dear that if you are still not in a state to leave this
> fall, we must take another course. I have been alone here for three
> years, if I could honorably be a prisoner in Europe I would come

to join the rest of my family, but in the position where I am, this choice would be dishonorable, and you would not advise me to do it. I am alone in liberty, but I must stay here. I do not look for events that could happen [*evenements*], but I do not avoid them, and I will be always ready to do my duty [of heading up a Bonpartist revival in France] that which others would do by passion. Therefore, I must stay where I am because it is my duty to stay here, but I am unhappy because I am isolated. The hope of your arrival, the establishing of a house, the preparations to receive you have supported my existence, but today this hope is extinguished, I blame all that I have done, I am disgusted [*dégoûté*] with my establishment, even though it is beautiful, because I have not made it for myself alone.

Joseph's secretary Mailliard, who had seen her in Frankfurt, "has not hidden from me that you do not plan to come this autumn, or the following spring. . . . I realize it is your health which prevents you from coming . . . but, if I must sympathize with your situation, you must sympathize with mine, and if you cannot come yourself, send me one of our children and keep the other. . . . Zénaïde is the largest and strongest to undertake the voyage and I will take as good care of her as you would." He knows this proposition is very painful for Julie, but Zénaïde is seventeen and old enough to be married. "Well! She will leave you for a father, or for a husband."[34]

It was inevitable given Joseph's loneliness, his gradual realization that his wife would never join him in America, and his past reputation with the fair sex, that he would have found in America a replacement for the Duchess d'Atri in Naples and the Marquesa del Montehermoso in Spain. Her name was Ann (or Anna) Savage (1800–1865), born in Philadelphia the eldest daughter of John Savage and his wife Margaret Larkey. Although not a duchess or a marquesa, she was descended from an old and distinguished Virginia family, albeit one fallen on hard times. The Savages are believed to be the oldest family of continuous English descent in America. Anna's ancestor, Thomas Savage left England on the first supply ship of the Virginia Company in 1607, and was an early settler on the Eastern Shore of Virginia. In 1608, he was taken hostage by Powhatan (the origin of the false claim that Anna was a descendant of Pocahontas). In 1619, Thomas Savage became a significant property owner when he was given a tract of 9,000 acres known as Savage's Neck in Northampton County. Anna's grandfather Nathaniel Lyttleton Savage was a member of the Virginia House of Delegates in 1776, had served as a lieutenant with the Virginia Light Dragoons throughout the war, and was a founding member of the Society of the Cincinnati.[35] The family had lost its prominence by the time his grandson, Anna's father, moved to Philadelphia, where he became a carpenter and then a maker of suspenders. Contrary to some accounts, Anna was not a Quaker, for, according to records at Christ Church in Philadelphia, she and her siblings were baptized in that Episcopal church in which her parents had been married.[36]

Joseph apparently met Anna one day in 1818 when he went to her family's shop to buy a pair of suspenders. At eighteen, she was a dark-eyed flirtatious beauty who may have spoken a little French, and Joseph, with his eye for beautiful women, was immediately interested. Anna, a simple shop girl, was no doubt thrilled by the attentions paid her by the former king and brother of Napoleon. Even at thirty-two years her senior and somewhat corpulent, he still had a great deal of charisma. By this time Anna's father was dead and her mother, reduced to keeping a shop, could not object to such good fortune for her penniless daughter.

Joseph had first set up Anna in a small house in Philadelphia, but she was so ostracized by Philadelphia society that it was necessary to find his mistress different accommodations. His liaison was also not helpful to his own reputation in a city that was decidedly not Paris, Naples, or Madrid. The French consul in Philadelphia, M. de la Forest, wrote to a friend in Paris that Joseph Bonaparte "had many mistresses" and that he "entertained them publicly at Bordentown."[37] The house he found was a handsome secluded brick mansion at the head of a long lane, lined with beautiful shade trees set back above the Delaware River outside Trenton, New Jersey, some five miles above Point Breeze. It was called Bow Hill, being located on a bow of the river, and belonged to his friend Barnt De Klyn, a rich merchant descended from French Huguenot nobility. Joseph hoped that Anna would be more acceptable to the people of Trenton, but in this he was mistaken, for they too refused to call on her.[38] The wits of the day called the house "Beau Hill," and their May–December situation was the subject of ridicule. But Joseph's romance was more than just a passing fancy, for the couple would have two children, Pauline Josephe Anne, born in 1819, and Caroline Charlotte, in 1822. As Joseph never mentions these children in his lettters or his memoirs, it is not possible to know how he felt about them. But it is clear that he was devoted to his legitimate daughters and thought of them as his heirs.

Chapter 5 POINT BREEZE

If you were here I don't think you would regret Mortefontaine, the
place where I am is more beautiful, and every day it becomes more so.
—Joseph Bonaparte to Julie Bonaparte, Point
Breeze, 17 April 1818

*T*he ex-king's elegant New Jersey estate, Point Breeze, would in time evolve
into a showplace to which groups of people would travel by steamboat from
Philadelphia on Sundays and certain holidays in order to see the collection of great
European paintings and statues that Joseph Bonaparte had shipped from abroad. The
entire New Jersey legislature even came upon occasion (fig. 11). Joseph's wife and
agents overseas had arranged to send these magnificent works of art, usually by way
of Stephen Girard's ships. A memorandum of 1818 in Joseph's handwriting lists nineteen cases of paintings and engravings, furniture, rugs, candelabra, *girandoles*
(sconces), mirrors, clocks, maps, wine, and a trunk containing table linen and kitch-
enware to be shipped from Le Havre to Philadelphia on the *James M.* In order not to
pay taxes on these items, Joseph wrote on the bottom of the inventory that, except
for the wine, all these effects had been in his various houses for twenty years. "This I
affirm on my honor and if it is necessary I swear on the Bible."[1] We do not know
whether these belongings included paintings from the royal Spanish collections Joseph acquired as king of Spain, in whose possession they would have been for considerably less than twenty years.

Joseph was not able to bring a great deal of money with him, but a certain
amount had been sewn into Louis Mailliard's clothes before leaving and this would
suffice for the time being. Joseph could also obtain credit on his large European
properties, Mortefontaine, with its surrounding four farms in France, and the château
of Prangins in Switzerland. Because of the proscription on the Bonapartes owning

11. **View on the Delaware Near Bordentown** *by Karl Bodmer, 1834, engraved by Ch. Vogel, Ackermann & Company, London. Author's collection. Photo: Lisa Tyson Ennis.*

land, both these estates had been placed in the name of Julie's half-sister, the Countess Honorine de Villeneuve. Joseph's money was with Baring Brothers in London—odd considering that his brother was a prisoner of the British—and in Stephen Girard's private bank.

Shortly after moving into Point Breeze in August 1817, Joseph sent Louis Mailliard to Europe to retrieve a large cache of diamonds, important papers, and money he had buried with Mailliard's help in a foxhole at Prangins two years earlier when he had had to leave the château forever. En route, Mailliard's ship was wrecked in a violent storm off the coast of Ireland, but he was rescued along with the other passengers. He eventually reached England, then crossed over to Frankfurt for an interview with Julie. She confided in him then that on the advice of her physicians she would probably never be able to join her husband in America.

Stephen Girard wrote from Philadelphia to his agent at Daniel Crommelin & Sons in Amsterdam on 16 July, informing him of the shipwreck: "Unforeseen circumstances having detained Mr. L. Mailliard, he is now about to depart for your City, where he will deliver you my Letter of the 1st of May last. . . . It is probable, that a short time after said Mr. Mailliard's arrival in the interior of your Country, that Gentleman will have occasion to forward you a Small Package containing important objects to be kept by you Subject to my order." Girard continued that it is "highly necessary" for a person of "good Character and repute well known to you" to accompany Mailliard and take charge of the package alluded to and deliver it to this agent.[2] The anticipated package contained Joseph's diamonds buried at Prangins.

Maillaird did not arrive at Nyon, the small town near Prangins, until Christmas Eve. There he presented himself to a Monsieur Veret, Joseph's financial administrator in Switzerland who was known to Mailliard. Joseph's faithful secretary had disguised himself as an Englishman with a red wig and a fake accent, both of which were sufficient to deceive Veret, who laughed heartily when Mailliard revealed his true identity. He aimed to pass himself off as an English speculator looking for deposits of metal and coal. Veret assured him he would not be recognized.

Mailliard hired two workmen, and to carry off the deception, had them dig at a distance from where he knew Joseph's treasure chest was buried. The next day, he took the workers to the exact spot and had them dig only to a certain depth after which he dismissed them. That night he returned with Veret to remove the final layer of dirt and at last, after some fear that he had mistaken the place, uncovered the casket. Back at Veret's house, the two men opened the lid and inventoried the contents against a list that Mailliard had brought with him. After drying out the humid parcels of important papers, among which, in small boxes, were sixteen large diamonds worth millions of francs, they ascertained that nothing was missing. Mailliard soon left to begin his arduous voyage back to Point Breeze.[3] On his return in April 1818, Joseph was able to write Girard that Mailliard had "fulfilled his errand well."[4]

Now the Count de Survilliers had enough money to develop his estate as he envisioned it. He rose early and spent a good part of every day outside with a hatchet in his side pocket and thirty to fifty workmen trimming and planting trees, making roads through the woods and along Crosswicks Creek, which, below his house, ran parallel to the Delaware. His workmen respectfully called him "Mr. Bonaparte,"[5] but to everyone else he was the Count de Survilliers. His republicanism seems to have stopped with his laborers.

He commissioned the Philadelphia artist Thomas Birch to paint the idyllic scene from the terrace of Point Breeze (see plate 8). In the foreground, Birch shows dogs cavorting to lend a playful touch and to give a sense of informality to the scene, characteristic of the ex-king's pleasant way of life. The gardens and potted plants shown on either side of the painting tell of Joseph's interest in horticulture. In the middle ground, before an elegant white railing, a group of guests are gathered, suggesting the hospitality the count offered to numerous friends and acquaintances. A statue of Apollo, carefully placed so that it gazes out to the horizon, is indicative of Joseph's love of the fine arts. In the distance, sailboats and a steamboat ply the Delaware.

It was lonely without his family, however, and at this point he had not yet met Anna Savage. In the spring of 1818 he wrote Julie that he was delighted to learn her health was better and he looked for her arrival within the year. He says he has stopped all expenses for furniture since she will bring such things with her. The house is comparatively larger than others in the neighborhood, although too small to lodge thirty or forty people, but there will be fewer at her arrival and if necessary it could be made larger. "It is certain that I have spent a lot to establish myself here in a manner that you would not regret compared to the other dwellings you have lived in," Joseph says in justification. "But I hope we will all be reunited and live within our means, in a way commensurate to the simplicity of our tastes. I have given much to unfortunate European refugees although not enough for their needs and desires, but one must give preference to one's own children." He says he has received some vague intimation about living in Austria, but circumstances there would not be as good or as tranquil as Point Breeze. "If you were here I don't think you would regret Mortefontaine, the place where I am is more beautiful, and every day it becomes more so."[6] Joseph's statement about "the simplicity of our tastes" is a relative phrase when discussing a house not quite large enough for thirty or forty people. A month later he told her, "I am always waiting for you to come. Everything I do now and have done is in this hope. You know how many things have to be accomplished in order to set up a household as large as ours."[7]

In July, on his way to Ballston Spa, New York, he lamented in a letter to Zénaïde that he was growing old, that three years had already passed, and that he could no longer bear to live alone in a country that is very fine, but where everyone else has their own family and enjoys the happiness that he hopes to find on her arrival. "I am occupied with buying, construction, of work today that the health of your mother will never allow her to see what I have done," he says. Although this letter to his daughter is only a few months after the one to his wife, he confides to Zénaïde that he does not believe her mother will ever join him. By this time Anna had entered his life and he may not have cared any more whether Julie came or not. "I am alone in this strange country—one of you [Zénaïde or Lolotte] could stay with your mother, but the other should come here—it is only fair—I need one of you [*j'ai besoin d'une de vous*]—I think it should be you because you are older and stronger than Lolotte— you could undertake the voyage and I hope you would be happy here. Your governess, another woman, Mr. Presle [his agent in France], your *valet de chambre*, and a cook could come with you."[8] In August, back at Point Breeze, he informs Zénaïde that he has two portraits of her by Robert Lefèvre that came on his birthday, but he has no portrait of her mother. "I look forward to seeing all three of you," he says although there was little likelihood of Julie making the voyage and he knew it.[9]

The following March, when his younger brother Lucien told Joseph that he seriously wanted to immigrate to America from Italy with his family because of the harassment he was enduring as Napoleon's sibling, Joseph wrote him a long letter describing the conditions Lucien would find in the New World, as he saw them. He says that the necessities of life, as well as luxury items, are much more expensive in the United States than in Italy. The day laborers' salaries are more, but the laborers are happy and do not "trouble the tranquillity of the richer classes." (Joseph is no doubt referring to the possibility of revolution by the lower classes that is moderated in the United States by paying adequate salaries.) In that part of the country where slavery is tolerated (the South), families who have a lot of land and live on it most of the year enjoy an abundance of produce, while in the part where he, Joseph, resides, slavery is not allowed and one must depend on the pleasures of fishing and hunting and pay dearly for the cultivation of one's own land. But he thinks the farmers in America are incomparably better off than in Europe.

However, he cautions, one must bring a lot of money because the chances for commerce are so uncertain and fortunes so unstable that it is not prudent to make investments. The end result is that one must live moderately, or have a great deal of money to satisfy one's tastes. As for the fine arts, they have not yet been born. Here, he asserts, one could not buy a Raphael for a hundred dollars or a Titian for ten thousand. There are no such paintings here. It would be necessary to bring all that kind of culture with him. There are plays in the large cities, but not one Italian singer.

He cautions Lucien, "I would not want you to reproach me one day if you came to this country, but you know my tastes and my character, and I can assure you that the government, the country, the climate, and the inhabitants please me equally—I am not exacting and they are not. Tranquillity, justice, calm, one finds all that. People are often crowded in the cities, at the balls, in traveling, on the steamboats, but they are never rude or offended [*blessés*]. Each respects his neighbor and is respected in return." He ends his letter: "I kiss you with heartfelt affection and also your family."[10]

Joseph had every reason to denigrate the performing arts in Philadelphia. Although the first opera given in the city had been Mozart's *Don Giovanni* on 26 December 1818, at the Chestnut Street Theater, the performance and those that followed for sometime were a curious mixture of other compositions. It frequently happened that the singers' abilities were not suited to the piece, so it was necessary to omit much of the composer's music and substitute popular airs that were sure to be applauded. The stated opera would be only part of the performance, each work sharing honors with a comedy, a tragedy, or a farce—possibly Shakespeare or Walter Scott—but often works by total unknowns. Performances began at six o'clock and lasted until midnight with no reservations, so the well-to-do sent their servants to hold seats until they arrived. Bars in the theaters unfortunately encouraged drunkenness and brawling.[11]

In 1825, Manuel Garcia's Italian opera company, the first in the United States, would come to New York. Garcia's greatest attraction was his beautiful daughter Maria, to be known famously in Europe as Madame Malibran. The Count de Survilliers must have taken his family to hear her, as his son-in-law would later comment: "America as you see *marche à grande* toward refinement of civilization, since she has taste in Italian opera."[12] But he would have spoken too soon. A newspaper writer in Philadelphia, noting that attendance in New York had fallen off, stated: "The fact is that excepting as a matter of curiosity, a nine-days wonder, an opera company cannot be supported in America."[13]

No matter how highly Joseph thought of the customs and manners of Americans and no matter how much he was willing to forgive what he saw as their lack of culture, Joseph still missed his relatives, especially those who shared his tastes as his brother Lucien did. However, by 1819 he had a nineteen-year-old mistress who would bear him a child that year. If his family would not come to him, at least he was creating a blood relation in America. The baby, Pauline, was probably delivered at Bow Hill where Joseph had Anna safely ensconced and where he could visit her frequently.

Less than a year after Joseph's letter to Lucien, he would have dramatic firsthand experience of neighborly assistance in the United States. On 4 January 1820, between eleven and twelve o'clock in the morning, his house at Point Breeze caught fire and in a short time burned to the ground. The count was on his way home from New York, but the local citizens rallied around and, in spite of the swiftness of the fire and the difficulty of opening such heavy doors and windows, were able to remove the majority of paintings, statues, furniture, silver, jewels, books, and linens. It was impossible to extinguish the fire; water froze in the hoses and the bucket brigade, attempting the nearly impossible task of bringing water from Crosswicks Creek up an embankment of some sixty feet, was inadequate for such a blaze.

Joseph entered his gates just as the roof fell in. The entire neighborhood was there, men and women risking their lives to save his property from the flames, no doubt whipped up by the northwest wind so often blowing hard on that point of land. He had to call some of them back and force them from the walls. According to a Philadelphia newspaper, the count appeared calm and stoical and more impressed by the efforts of his neighbors than by the loss of his house.[14] He later recounted that in the night of the fire and during the next day, drawers were brought to him containing the proper quantity of money, gold medals, and valuable jewels that might have been taken with impunity.[15] The night of the fire, some young people from Bordentown even formed a guard to protect the count's belongings until morning.[16]

Several days later, Joseph wrote a letter to one of the Bordentown magistrates expressing his gratitude to the citizens of the town for their help in saving his possessions. He said that what they did proved to him that men are generally good when they have not been perverted in their youth by bad examples, when they preserve their dignity on becoming men, and understand that true grandeur is in the heart and depends on oneself. He added that he thought Americans were the happiest people he had known. This letter was published in many American newspapers.[17] To Joseph's chagrin, a few local people felt insulted that he would even imagine they might steal his treasures.

The cause of the blaze was never confirmed. Some said a guest left a fire burning in his room, perhaps improperly screened, and locked the door when he departed for Philadelphia. Others wondered if it was arson. It was thought that Joseph had at Point Breeze copies of Napoleon's correspondence with foreign sovereigns and that certain governments wished to see this correspondence destroyed. A female member of a Russian consulate in the United States, who often stayed in Bordentown, was suspected of employing one of Joseph's servants to set the fire, but this was never proved.[18]

Now with no house outside Philadelphia, Joseph probably spent more time at Bow Hill with Anna and his infant daughter Pauline. As it turned out, this would probably be the happiest time for Anna with her charming, robust, though middle-aged lover.

Before starting to rebuild, it seems likely that Joseph looked into the possible purchase of another property with an elegant house on the west bank of the Schuylkill River just across from Philadelphia. The Woodlands had been built and the garden developed by the late William Hamilton, and it was apparently available. Stephen Girard wrote the Count de Survilliers on 22 February 1820: "Here is the letter that Mr. J. Lyle [James Lyle, Hamilton's son-in-law] has written me with a copy of the valuation of the Woodlands, made by experts who are known to me. I will send him the original and promise to communicate with you about it."[19] The mansion's splendid portico on its south front, twenty-four feet high and supported by six stately Tuscan columns with Doric capitals, would have appealed to Joseph's taste. As at Point Breeze, the river was below and beyond. The domed vestibule with its four statuary niches would have beautifully accommodated his finest Canovas, as would the grand saloon with its apsidal ends, also designed for statues. The ten acres of cultivated grounds contained a variety of indigenous and exotic trees and shrubs chosen for their foliage, or fragrance. The French botanist André Michaux, who visited Philadelphia in 1802, observed of Hamilton's "magnificent" garden: "His collection of exotics is immense, and remarkable for plants from New Holland [Australia], all the trees and shrubs of the United States, at least those that could stand the winter at Philadelphia . . . in short, it would be impossible to find a more agreeable situation than the residence of Mr. W. Hamilton."[20]

Joseph had been familiar with the Woodlands for many years. It was one of the first places he visited when he originally came to Philadelphia in 1815. Samuel Breck recorded this visit in his diary: "[The ex-king] expressed himself much pleased with the botanick garden, walks, shrubbery, house, paintings and prospect. He has ridden a good deal around this neighborhood."[21] However grand the house and gardens had been, William Hamilton's heirs had not maintained them after his death in 1813, and Joseph must have preferred his own garden and extensive hunting grounds. If he had thought to use the Woodlands as his winter home, its location outside the city would not have recommended it to one whose social life required that he be in the center of things. In any event, he turned instead to rebuilding at Point Breeze.

The site he chose was considerably further back from the promontory where the first house had been, without the devastating exposure to wind that had helped to demolish his previous dwelling. He decided to convert the unharmed brick stables into his second mansion, perhaps in order to save money. The location was near the road, called the New York Turnpike in those days, but presently Park Street, without a spectacular view, as the other house had, but a vista stretching for a distance over flat fields and woods. The new situation was decidedly more comfortable, however, being at all times warmer. In winter, particularly, the northwest wind howling down the Delaware was bitterly cold.

All that was left of the old house was the belvedere, built right on the Point, with an underground passageway that opened out halfway to the steep bank below where steps built into the embankment continued down to Crosswicks Creek. With the

12. **Manor House of Joseph Bonaparte near Bordentown** *by Karl Bodmer, 1832. Watercolor. Joslyn Art Museum, Omaha, Nebraska, gift of Enron Art Foundation.*

belvedere's winding stairs inside and balconies at various levels from where Joseph could view the sunsets he compared to those of Venice, the little structure was often the scene of open-air concerts and suppers. Above the entrance he had inscribed in Latin the motto from Virgil of his favorite author, Bernardin de St. Pierre: "Non ignara mali, miseris succurrere" (Not unaware of misfortune, I know to help the unfortunate).[22] He was known to have been generous with other French refugees, as well as his workmen and to have gone out of his way to find employment for anyone seeking it.

He wrote Julie that he had been reading about the turmoil in Europe, particularly in Spain, while in America all was perfect tranquility; he said this in spite of the ashes of his once beautiful mansion at his feet. "I expect to be in my own house in a month," he says, "and it will be as magnificent as the one we have lost, but more comfortable." He adds, with an eye to economics, "I have already written that you must sell Prangins."[23] The new house, built of brick and covered with white plaster, was patterned somewhat on the layout of his château at Prangins, with a central block and two perpendicular wings (fig. 12), but perhaps even more specifically on the château at Malmaison, Napoleon and Josephine's mansion just outside Paris with its horizontal plan of seven rooms opening onto each other. In a short time, the Count de Survilliers would embellish his abode as splendidly as his previous dwellings with all the furnishings the people of Bordentown had so bravely rescued. Yet again keeping up the illusion that Julie was still coming, the following August he told her, after returning from "a voyage of six weeks in the woods," that if she came to Point Breeze she would find a completed establishment that she would enjoy more than any in Europe.[24]

Joseph was fortunate in being able to employ a skilled cabinetmaker, or *ébéniste*, named Michel Bouvier, an ex-soldier who had fought under Napoleon at Waterloo. After Bouvier immigrated to the United States, he is believed to have honed his skills with the master cabinetmaker Charles-Honoré Lannuier in New York. By 1817, Bouvier had set up his own shop in Philadelphia making handsome furniture in the Empire style, many pieces being for his two French patrons, Stephen Girard and Joseph Bonaparte. He had worked on the first Point Breeze, and after the fire he had supervised the second mansion's construction and refurbishing. In addition, Bouvier executed more menial tasks for the Count de Survilliers, "moving furniture, assembling and dismantling beds, polishing wood pieces, sewing silk for tables, and even dispensing firewood and coal."[25]

On entering the spacious hall of the new mansion, through finely carved folding mahogany doors with an opening at the far end onto the terrace overlooking the Delaware at a distance, one was surrounded by paintings of the great Italian masters and impressive marble sculptures from antiquity. To the left was the billiard room (it is on the right at Malmaison) where the most striking object, set into the woodwork, was the great painting by Jacques Louis David, *Bonaparte Crossing the Alps at the Great St. Bernard* (see fig. 23). On the other walls of the room hung Franz Snyders's *Two Young Lions and a Fawn* (fig. 13) and Charles Natoire's *Toilette of Psyche* (fig. 14),[26] a painting surprising to most Americans unused to pictures of nude women, whether or not they were figures from mythology. A large table with Italian marble top, two sofas and eight chairs with horsehair seats, and a large billiard table completed the furnishings. At the windows hung curtains of white muslin bordered in green, a large red and white rug covered the floor, and from the ceiling hung four gilded copper chandeliers.

The grand salon was preceded by a small anteroom and a library on the left side of the entrance hall containing a portion of the count's 8,000 volumes. This was the largest collection in the country; at the time the Library of Congress contained 6,500 books.[27] The same handsome blue merino material on the chairs and sofas was also used for the draperies. Several large tables topped with black and gray marble and

13. **Two Lions and a Fawn** *by Franz Snyders. Oil on canvas. Bayerische Staatsgemaidesammlungen, Munich.*

ornamented with bronze stood against the walls. On them stood two magnificent candelabras from the Luxembourg Palace of five lights each with bronze figures of Baccanalian nymphs on solid stands of porphyry. The intricately carved marble fireplace mantle had been sent from Italy as a gift from Joseph's uncle, Cardinal Joseph Fesch. An unusual clock, a gift from Napoleon, graced the mantle. It featured an image of Urania (the muse of astronomy) and was inspired by an antique statue. A royal Gobelin medallion-figured carpet, also from the Luxembourg Palace, covered the floor.

The paintings in this elegant reception room were mostly of the imperial family by Baron François Pascal Simon Gérard: Napoleon in his grand court robes, Joseph as king of Spain wearing a mantle of green velvet edged with ermine (see plate 1), and Julie as Queen of Naples with her two young daughters (see plate 2) commissioned by Napoleon in 1808 for the emperors' *salon de famille* in the palace of St. Cloud. Seascapes by Joseph Vernet and views of Naples by Simon Denis completed this elegant space where the ex-king received many distinguished visitors. It was also in this room where the family would later often gather after dinner for recitations of tragic drama with everyone taking part in reading the classics, a common form of entertainment in nineteenth-century French aristocratic circles.[28]

14. **Toilette of
Psyche** *by Charles
Joseph Natoire, 1745. Oil
on canvas. New Orleans
Museum of Art, Museum
purchase through the
bequest of Judge Charles F.
Claiborne, 40.2.*

Across the hall was a room devoted entirely to statues of Joseph's family. The
ex-king would often spend time here in meditation, alone with the bust of Napoleon
by Antonio Canova (fig. 15); of his father, Carlo Buonaparte, and of his brothers
Louis and Jérôme, all by Lorenzo Bartolini; also by the same artist, his sisters-in-law,
Marie-Louise of Austria (Napoleon's second wife) and Catherine of Württemberg
(Jérôme's second wife). There were busts of his mother Letizia, designated Madame
Mère by Napoleon, and of his sisters Elisa Bacciochi and Pauline Borghese by Canova,
who also sculpted Napoleon's infant son, called the King of Rome by his father,
sleeping on a cushion. Regarding Canova, Frances Wright remarked that these were
"the first works of the Italian Phidias" that she had seen and she studied them "with
much curiosity."[29]

Wright was not alone in being fascinated by the great works of art at Point
Breeze, but not everyone saw them as masterpieces. Once Joseph was showing two
Quaker ladies the reduced-scale copy of Canova's statue of his voluptuous sister Pau-
line as Venus Victrix lying half-naked on a couch (fig. 16). He provoked their

15. **Bust of Napoleon** *by Antonio Canova. Marble. Presented to Stephen Girard by Joseph Bonaparte in 1817. Girard College Collection.*

shocked, though silent response by standing "some time perfectly enraptured before [the statue], pointing out to us what a beautiful head Pauline had; what hair; what eyes, nose, mouth, chin; what a throat; what a neck; what arms; what a beautiful bust; what a foot—enumerating all her charms one after another, and demanding our opinion of them. Necessity made us philosophers, and we were obliged to show as much *sang froid* on the subject as himself; for it was impossible to turn away without our prudery's exciting more attention than would have been pleasant."[30]

A visitor to the mansion's first floor reported that, "when all the doors were opened, the nine rooms, giving onto each other in a double line, produced a suite of

16. **Pauline Borghese as Venus Victrix** *by Antonio Canova. Reduced scale statue in marble.*
Athenaeum of Philadelphia.

great effect, above all at night when the apartments were brilliantly illuminated."[31]
The dining room, attended on gala evenings by liveried waiters with mustaches and
long beards—a striking anomaly among servants in America[32]—contained an impos-
ing table of seven leaves able to seat twenty-four, often set with the finest Sèvres
porcelain. Against the walls were two stunning pier tables ornamented with the heads
of sphinx and other Egyptian motifs inspired by Napoleon's expedition to North
Africa (fig. 17). These exceptional examples of high-style Egyptian taste may have
influenced patrons in Philadelphia and New York when they ordered furniture from
such cabinetmakers as Charles-Honoré Lannuier, Michel Bouvier, and Anthony G.
Quervelle.[33] Between the windows stood a pair of magnificent porphyry vases given
to the count by Jean Bernadotte (King Carl XIV Gustav of Sweden), Joseph's brother-
in-law married to Julie's sister Désirée, and a former general of Napoleon's. Four
enormous gilded candelabra, each with seven arms, graced the buffet, while on the
walls were exquisite works of Flemish artists as well as engravings of Napoleon's great
battles in Italy. Draperies of blue damask with gilt poles and ornaments as well as an

17. **Empire table from Point Breeze, c. 1800–1810.** *Mahogany, mahogany veneer, marble, mirror, ormolu. Gift of Edward Hopkinson. Philadelphia Museum of Art.*

immense Brussels carpet completed the room's decoration.[34] Henry James, in his novel *The Ambassadors*, evokes the sensation one might have felt after passing through these rooms at Point Breeze: "The whole thing made a vista, which he found high melancholy and sweet—full, once more, of dim historic shades, of the faint far-away cannon-roar of the great Empire."[35]

The Count de Survilliers's private apartment on the second floor consisted of bedroom, dressing room, study with an immense mahogany bookcase extending across one wall, and "bathing room." Its windows and balcony overlooked the garden. The same two Quaker women who visited Point Breeze in 1836 described his "chamber" as having curtains, chair upholstery, and bed canopy of light blue satin trimmed with silver. "Every room [of the suite] contained a mirror that reached from the ceiling to the ground," as one described it. "Over the bed hung a very splendid mirror, and another over the bath. The walls were covered with oil paintings, principally of young females, with less clothing about them than their originals would have found agreeable in our cold climate, and much less than we found agreeable when the count without ceremony, led us in front of them, and enumerated the beauties of the painting with the air of an accomplished amateur."[36] One of the paintings Joseph showed his straight-laced guests may have been Titian's *Tarquin and Lucretia* (plate 9), which depicted a mythological rape, a work so shocking to nineteenth-century sensibilities that it appeared six times at auction in London between 1845 and 1911—the entire Victorian age—before entering the Fitzwilliam Museum in Cambridge, England.[37]

The count appears to have been fond of provocative works of art for many years. When he was king of Spain he personally ordered the hanging of certain paintings of nudes such as the *Danaë* of Titian and *Atalanta and Hippomenes* of Guido Reni, both now in the Prado Museum, in the royal palace. Charles IV had relegated these pictures to an annex of the royal palace for "lack of decency." The king had even thought to have them burned, but he relented when assured they had then been shut up in the Academy of San Fernando. To add insult to Bourbon injury, Joseph had had Titian's *Venus and Adonis* hung in the very room where the previous king, Charles III, ate his lunch.[38]

Perhaps ahead of his time in relaxing his censorship of such pictures, Joseph Bonaparte, though indeed a sensual amorous person, was also a generous one; attributes that may go hand in hand. He loaned many of his paintings to the Pennsylvania Academy of the Fine Arts in Philadelphia for annual exhibitions. At first he had been reluctant to lend the David of *Bonaparte Crossing the Alps at the Great St. Bernard* because of its size and the difficulty of removing the painting from its frame in order to transport it, but his friend Joseph Hopkinson, president of the Academy, finally persuaded him and the picture was displayed every year from 1822 to 1829. There is no record, however, that the *Tarquin and Lucretia* was ever shown. No doubt the ex-king, or more likely the exhibits committee, hesitated to offend the ladies of Philadelphia, in spite of the painting being by Titian. In the early years of the Pennsylvania Academy, separate visiting days were allocated for ladies in the interest of modesty.

Joseph Bonaparte had every reason to be an accomplished connoisseur of art, having been surrounded with the magnificent collection of his Bourbon predecessors in the royal palace in Madrid for the five years he had been king of Spain. Not only were the great masters of Spain and Italy represented, but also those of the Netherlands, as Spain had occupied the Low Countries for much of the sixteenth century. Joseph's adviser about these works of art was Vivant Denon, who became the first director of the Louvre.

The count may also have bought European paintings in the United States. The artist John Trumbull wrote to his colleague Thomas Sully in March 1819 about a

Monsieur Alexandre de Longchamps of New York who wished to sell a collection of pictures. Trumbull suggests they be offered to Joseph Bonaparte, but cautions Sully, for political reasons, not to mention that they belong to a French gentleman.[39] Perhaps Trumbull thought Joseph would be uneasy about the provenance of the paintings after the turmoil he had so recently left behind in Europe.

Chapter 6 BONAPARTE'S PARK

If I was in [Joseph's] place I would found a great empire of all Spanish America, but you will see that he will be a bourgeois American and spend his fortune in making gardens.
—Napoleon to Montholon on St. Helena

*H*owever much he enjoyed his wilderness domain in New York State for hunting and summer recreation, the property Joseph cared most about was Point Breeze and its development into a picturesque landscape garden and park (fig. 18). When the ex-king came to America, he already had a background in garden art at his two European estates, Mortefontaine in France and Prangins in Switzerland. Although he lived at Prangins only from 1814 to 1815, he had accomplished much in the way of landscape improvement. But since he had lived off and on at Mortefontaine from 1798 until his flight from France in 1815, he was able to do a great deal more. When Joseph bought Mortefontaine, situated forty-five kilometers northeast of Paris in the *département* of Val d'Oise, the gardens were in a state of neglect. During the Revolution, two former owners had been tried as aristocrats and guillotined and the gardens had lain untouched for four years. The natural environment of the countryside consisted of rolling hills, river valleys, lakes, and woods. With such features the first owner was able to model a considerable landscape garden after that of his friend the Marquis René-Louis de Girardin at his neighboring estate of Ermenonville (fig. 19).[1]

Girardin had visited England and was familiar with the romantic landscape gardens that had become so popular there in the eighteenth century. The inspiration for these naturalistic landscapes had come, in many cases, from the paintings of Claude Lorain, whose lovely renderings of the Roman *campagna* with idealized terrain and classical ruins recalled the scenes traveling aristocrats had seen on their Grand Tour.

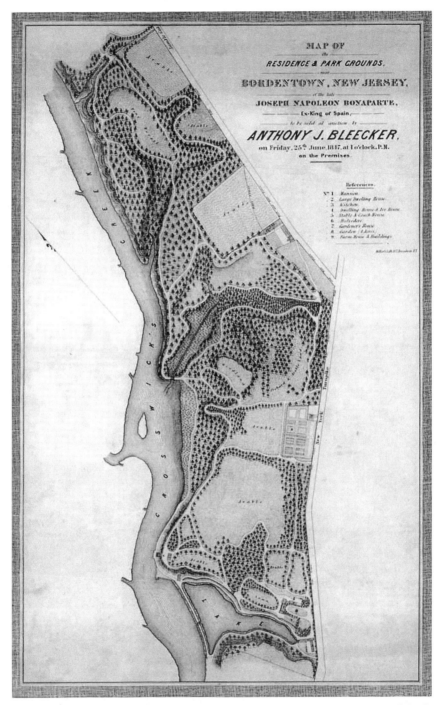

18. "Map of the Residence and Park Grounds, Bordentown, New Jersey, of the late Joseph Napoleon Bonaparte, Ex-King of Spain, to be sold at auction, by Anthony J. Bleecker on Friday, 25th June, 1847, at 1 o'clock P.M. on the premises." *Collection of the Library of Congress.*

19. "Le Petit Lac" and "Vue du Coté du Nord" from *Promenade ou Itinéraire des Jardins d'Ermenonville* by Louis-Stanislas-Xavier de Girardin, Paris, 1788. Photo: Lisa Tyson Ennis.

It was thought that nature should be combined with art, that is, gardens with trees and shrubs of various greens and different shapes and carefully placed, as they were depicted in the paintings of Claude.[2] "Where genius commands, nature obeys," Girardin, the consummate gardener, wrote in his *Promenade ou itinéraire des jardins d'Ermenonville* of 1788.[3] At Ermenonville, Girardin created picturesque vistas based on various paintings. This concept would have appealed to Joseph Bonaparte with his love of the fine arts and it no doubt inspired him when restoring the garden and park at Mortefontaine, designing the gardens at Prangins, and ultimately shaping the park at Point Breeze.

In keeping with the idea of re-creating a classical landscape, the English dotted their gardens with small temples, a practice the French, for the most part, found artificial and ridiculous. Once the formal French garden—culminating at Versailles—was no longer in fashion, usefulness and practicality became more in the French line of thought. The philosopher Jean-Jacques Rousseau inspired Girardin and subsequently, Joseph Bonaparte, with his philosophy of the natural man and a return to nature. In his *Julie: ou la nouvelle Héloïse* (1761) Rousseau criticized the unnaturalness of formal gardens, proposing that symmetry was antithetical to nature and variety. Rousseau visited England in 1766–67 and was quoted as saying that he wished the numerous temples of the English gardens "were changed into cottages, and other dwellings which (under the tenure of keeping up the picturesque circumstances required by the owner) might be made the reward of industry, and the consolation of distress."[4] This thought, too, could be said to have influenced the Count de Survilliers at Point Breeze, where he eschewed building temples, except for the belvedere, and erected several small houses for various members of his family and staff. There were stables, servants' lodges, farmers' and gardeners' cottages, and many outbuildings. Joseph even accommodated an old veteran from the Napoleonic wars who sought his help and was granted it until his death.

Napoleon at St. Helena had said to General Montholon: "Joseph will build a great establishment in America. It will be the refuge of all my relatives. If I was in his place, I would found a great empire of all Spanish America, but you will see that he will be a bourgeois American and spend his fortune in making gardens."[5] In the new French taste for natural landscapes, a political component associated the gardens' openness and informality with a certain sense of freedom that the emperor would not have understood; he preferred the structured gardens of the Tuileries, Versailles, and Fontainebleau.

In 1806, Joseph had commissioned the celebrated landscape painter Jean-Joseph-Xavier Bidauld (1758–1846) to paint the park at Mortefontaine, a picture he brought with him to the United States (see plate 6). There are many features in this work that Joseph would employ at Point Breeze: pleasure boats, swans, the vista, and the paths for strolling. The object was harmony between civilized man and sympathetic nature in a long-standing European tradition.

Having once been king of Spain, Joseph sought to pattern the park at Point Breeze somewhat on that of the Escorial, Philip II's enormous sixteenth-century palace northeast of Madrid. He planted formal gardens around the main house and created twelve miles of carriage roads winding through the woods and over small stone bridges as the road passed and repassed over Thornton Creek. Joseph had formed a half-mile-long lake by damming the creek, a tidal tributary of Crosswicks Creek, itself a tributary of the Delaware River, which ran through his property.[6] Several islands, covered with velvet grass, rare bushes, and trees, added interest to the peaceful scene, while anchored along the shore were the small swan-shaped pleasure boats he had had constructed for leisurely excursions. A carriage drive ran along one side of the lagoon down to the wharf below Point Breeze. In the winter months when the lake was frozen, skaters were welcomed and Joseph had his servants bring large baskets of oranges and tangerines, rare treats from Florida and Spain that the count delighted in rolling onto the ice where the skaters chased after them with great confusion and excitement.

Stephen Girard, who had a nursery in South Philadelphia, in addition to his other commercial affairs, was as much help with obtaining plants for Joseph's gardens as he was with materials for the house. "If you wish some raspberry bushes, let me know and I will reserve some for you," he had written in the spring of 1818. "I also have some plants of hazelnut trees which will blend with the trees you have received from France. As for the artichoke plants, I still haven't found them. I will tell you if they merit to be planted in your kitchen garden [*jardin potager*]."[7] Joseph often returned the favor. The same spring he told Girard he was sending him two dozen apricot (*abricotiers*) and peach trees, part of his French shipment.[8] By the end of May, Girard reported that the artichoke plants "have been transplanted and are ready to send to you, as their number is voluminous you should send a gardener, or some other reliable person."[9]

Aside from the plants Joseph received from Girard and those he ordered from France, he also bought a great deal from the Landreth Nursery in Philadelphia which specialized in roses, camellias, rhododendrons, azaleas, and magnolias, as well as the Osage orange that had been started from seed brought back by Lewis and Clark. At the time it was being planted in great quantities for hedges in every part of the East.[10] An impressive number of Landreth shrubs and trees were shipped to the count by steamboat and "sundry trees by wagon" for seventy-four dollars on an unspecified date in 1821. Various ornamental trees and four grapevines followed together with more trees. On 22 March 1821, a bill of lading noted that "20 White Lindens, 40 Athenia Poplars, 40 Lombardy Poplars, 20 Weeping Willows, 10 Button-Flowering Locusts for a total of $80" had been delivered to Point Breeze.[11]

From Europe the count imported swans, pheasants, quail, hares, and rabbits with the idea of expanding these species in the New World. He ordered all possible precautions taken to keep these animals from escaping before they could reproduce sufficiently and offered rewards for any found outside his property and returned. Joseph employed a local twelve-year-old named Alexander Carman to go out with him every morning in the fall before breakfast to hunt for rabbit traps set in the park by the town boys. To retrieve them, Carman would crawl under the shrubbery and bring the traps to the count, who smashed them with a hatchet.[12] One addition to the fauna at Point Breeze came about by chance. Joseph received a note from Girard saying that a friend of his, a Mr. Rodney, had brought back a curious animal from South America procured on the River Plate. As he is not able to care for this *précieux animal*, he has asked Girard to give it to the count in his name. Rodney had called the animal a Patagonian hare.[13]

At all times, Joseph allowed local children to climb on the garden's statuary deer and lions as hobby horses and to play hide and seek among the marble gods and goddesses on the grounds of the estate.[14] These statues, incongruously, also included two life-size figures in Carrara marble on brownstone bases of Richard the Lion-Hearted and Ivanhoe, both in full chain mail, and a bust of Caesar Augustus.[15] As for the first two, Joseph's love of history and literature must have overcome his antipathy to the British.

For the future accommodation of Zénaïde, who Joseph so earnestly desired to come to America, with her husband-to-be and cousin, Charles-Lucien Bonaparte, Joseph built the promised Lake House, probably in the spring of 1820. The architecture of the three-story house beside the lake (with an underground passage connected to the mansion for convenience during inclement weather) somewhat resembled the simple lines of the Bonaparte family house in Ajaccio, Corsica, where Joseph grew up. But the young couple would not arrive until September 1823, more than a year after their marriage in Brussels, where Zénaïde had been living with her mother.

In damming Thornton Creek to form a lake, in creating islands planted with velvet grass and rare shrubs, and in building a carriage road encircling the lake from which to view it from many points, Joseph mostly used ideas from Ermenonville in France for his picturesque landscape. But in the New World he had a fresh palette to work with, as so many of the trees and wildflowers were different from those in Europe. The twelve miles of carriage roads and bridle paths that wound through the park passed numerous sassafras and tulip trees, beech, chestnut, ash, white birch, sweet gum, dogwood, honey locust, and clusters of pines and oaks—twenty-five species of oaks, many of which were always green—persimmon trees, and eight species of walnuts. Joseph's son-in-law, Charles, an enthusiastic naturalist and already a budding ornithologist, would describe this New World vegetation in a letter to his mother in Rome.[16]

In the same letter, Charles would describe the azalea, mock orange, viburnum, and many species of rhododendron that his father-in-law had planted around the manor house, and a paradise of native spring wildflowers growing in the woods: creeping sorrel, mayapple, bluets, Solomon's seal, spiderwort, and bird's-foot violets. He said that forget-me-nots and veronica were in great quantities around the boathouse where the small swan-shaped pleasure craft were stored. And all about the aviary, housing rare pheasants from Europe, there was columbine, wood anemone, ranunculus, and cranesbill. Stargrass surrounded the "fountain Hopkinson," a spring circled by rustic seats, the name honoring Joseph's close friend and neighbor, Joseph Hopkinson. Andromeda was planted around another fountain, obscurely named "Claudine," and there was also a "fountain of tulips" elegantly edged with tulip trees. Many other spots had names as well, such as the "bridge of savages," where a number of Native American relics had been found when digging the bridge's foundation.[17] This naming of various locations on the property lent a uniquely personal aspect to Point Breeze that must have been endearing to Joseph's numerous friends and acquaintances.

Many of the ideas he employed at Point Breeze, such as the names of places, had their origin in his favorite book, Bernardin de St. Pierre's *Paul et Virginie*. The story takes place on the island of Mauritius in the Indian Ocean where Paul and Virginie, with their respective mothers, create a Garden of Eden out of the jungle. Various locations in the garden are given names with personal associations, such as Virginie's Resting Place, the Burial Place of Tears, and the Fountain of Cocoa Trees. A quotation from Virgil is placed over their cottage door, no doubt the source of Joseph's idea to place such an inscription over the entrance to his belvedere. Paul and Virginie plant seeds of violets and scabiosa from France to remind them of their native land in the same way that Joseph ordered apricot, peach, and other fruit trees from France; a bit of home for the exile at Point Breeze.

The Count de Survilliers, in his beautiful park and garden, must have found a kindred spirit in St. Pierre, a disciple of Rousseau and the unidentified narrator of the story in Mauritius: "In my present tranquillity, I pass in review the agitating pursuits of my past life, to which I formerly attached so much value,—patronage, fortune, reputation, pleasure, and the opinions which are ever at strife over all the earth. I compare the men whom I have seen disputing furiously over these vanities, and who are no more, to the tiny waves of my rivulet, which break in foam against its rocky bed, and disappear, never to return. As for me, I suffer myself to float calmly down the stream of time to the shoreless ocean of futurity."[18]

From the lake to the main house, Joseph constructed a forty-foot subterranean passage, near the Lake House, walled with brick and closed with heavy doors. The passage had two branches, one into the cellar for the transportation of wine, the other into the house for the butcher, the baker, and others bringing supplies. A third door opened into the icehouses, where ice cut from the Delaware in winter could easily be stored. An earlier tunnel, which opened halfway up the embankment with steps leading up from broad Crosswicks Creek, had served the count's first house in the same way. The precedent had been such a tunnel at Mortefontaine. For the new house, there was also a lattice-covered arcade somewhat in the shape of a long shed that connected the manor to Zénaïde's Lake House. Its purpose would be shelter from inclement weather for her and her servants, as well as for guests who had been enjoying the lake.[19] Joseph may have been inspired for this edifice in the lattice-covered passage built by Napoleon for Marie-Louise at Compiègne.[20] The local lore, at the time and later, was that the count had constructed the underground tunnels as escape routes should he be apprehended by the French or the British, and that the belvedere was a lookout tower to watch for the enemy approaching by water. In later years Louis Mailliard would refer to all these suspicions as nonsense.

In 1826 John Fanning Watson would write of Joseph's garden: "Nothing can be more romantic than the whole Scenery—the Shades, where so required, are so very deep & impressive—In the midst of the premises is a beautiful Lake, surrounded by high Banks covered with innumerable Shrubs & Trees—In the middle an Island (artificial) beautifully covered with weeping Willows—Swans & Exotic Geese, sported upon the bosom of the Lake. . . . The novelty of such costliness & elegance was like enchantment to my feelings & when I had traversed the various sections of the woods & lawns, through all their charming & meandering avenues & mazes, I could not forbear to think it was the best terrestrial paradise I had ever enjoyed."[21] Watson was a keen observer of places, people, manners, and customs, collecting his studies in his *Annals of Philadelphia and Pennsylvania*, published in 1845.

The beauty of the original Point Breeze's site, high on a bluff above the Delaware, the hospitality, and perhaps in certain respects the erudition of Joseph Bonaparte, puts one somewhat in mind of an1816 description of Monticello. Richard Rush wrote to Charles Ingersoll about Jefferson: "I need not tell you with what open doors he lives, as you well know that his mountain is made a sort of Mecca."[22] Point Breeze, too, served as a Mecca for the many French refugees who found their way there, and certainly it was for Joseph himself.

Plate 1. **Joseph Bonaparte as King of Spain** *by François Gérard, c. 1810. Oil on canvas. Musée National du Château de Fontainbleau. Photo: Réunion des Musées Nationaux/ Art Resource, NY.*

Plate 2. **Julie Bonaparte, Queen of Spain, with Her Daughters Zénaïde and Charlotte** *by François Gérard, 1808–1809. Oil on canvas. National Gallery of Ireland, Dublin.*

Plate 3. **Anna Savage and Her Daughters Pauline Josephe Ann and Caroline Charlotte by Joseph Bonaparte,** *by Bass Otis, 1823. Oil on canvas. Philadelphia Museum of Art, purchased with the Edgar V. Seeler Fund.*

Plate 4. **Emilie Lacoste** *by Charlotte Bonaparte, 1823. Watercolor. Athenaeum of Philadelphia.*

Plate 5. **Dunlop House** *by John James Barralet, 1807. Watercolor. Stephen Girard Collection, Girard College, Philadelphia.*

Plate 6. **Parc de la Mortefontaine** *by Jean Bidauld, 1806. Oil on canvas. Indianapolis Museum of Art, Alicia Ballard Fine Arts Purchase Fund, and the Allen Whitehill Clowes Fund 1985.189.*

Plate 7. **View of Point Breeze** *by Charles B. Lawrence, 1819. Oil on canvas. New Jersey State Museum.*

Plate 8. **Point Breeze on the Delaware** *by Thomas Birch, 1818. Oil on canvas. Private collection.*

Plate 9. **Tarquin and Lucretia**
by Titian, c. 1568–76. Oil on canvas.
Fitzwilliam Museum, Cambridge,
England.

Plate 10. **Adoration of the Shepherds** *by Anton-Raphael Mengs, 1764–1765. Oil on canvas. Corcoran Gallery of Art, Washington, D.C., gift of William Wilson Corcoran.*

Plate 11. **Joseph Bonaparte,** *Innocent-Joachim-Louis Goubaud, 1832. Maison Bonaparte, Ajaccio, Corsica, France. Réunion des Musées Nationaux/ Art Resource, NY. Photo: Gérard Blot.*

Chapter 7 THE LAST OF
NAPOLEON

Sire, I heard after I had been torn away from your august brother,
that he was extremely ill, according to all reports.
      —Count de Las Cases to Joseph Bonaparte,
       Frankfurt, 21 February 1818

O ne of Joseph's principal concerns at this time was the suffering of his
brother Napoleon. In the winter of 1818, Joseph had received a letter from
the Count de Las Cases: "Sire, I heard after I had been torn away from your august
brother that he was extremely ill, according to all reports. But although in bad health,
his spirits were unmoved [*impassible*] and he has raised himself above his adversities
and harmful treatment."[1] General Bertrand, who would stay with Napoleon until his
death, had written that the emperor suffered from a liver ailment, "a mortal illness
in this unhealthy climate." He added that if the emperor were forced to stay at St.
Helena he would be knowingly killed (*sciemment tué*).[2] These reports had been frustrating and painful for Joseph since he was helpless in freeing his brother from this
inaccessible island.

The previous spring Joseph himself had been ill with nephritis, a painful in-
flammation of the kidney. He felt sure that he was suffering from the same cancer
that killed his father and sought advice from several physicians, but they were unable
to find evidence of the dread disease. From Philadelphia, he wrote Nicholas Biddle
that he was convalescing from an illness that had kept him in bed for twenty days
and that he hoped soon "to take the waters."[3] He was able to do this at the spa in
Saratoga, New York, where news reached him of Napoleon's death.[4] He had died on
5 May 1821 from what many believe to have been hepatitis; others stomach cancer

like his father; still others that he had been poisoned.[5] Transatlantic communication being what it was in those days, Joseph only learned of it in August.

The news depressed Joseph deeply, for although he had disagreed with Napoleon's policies, he remained devoted to him and served him loyally in many capacities. As children they had been inseparable, galloping across the fields and hills of Corsica, Joseph enjoying the scenery and Napoleon playing soldier. It was a disappointment when they were sent to separate schools in France, but later, as young men back in Corsica, they had fled to France after falling out with the Corsican independence leader Pasquale Paoli. During Napoleon's early years in Paris when he was poor and struggling to be recognized, he and Joseph had been particularly close. In June 1795, when Napoleon was twenty-six, he wrote from Paris to Joseph in Genoa where, newly married, Joseph was in partnership with his wife's brother Nicholas Clary: "In whatever circumstances you may be placed by fortune, you know well, my friend, that you cannot have a better or a dearer friend than myself, or one who wishes more sincerely for your happiness. Life is a flimsy dream, soon to be over. If you are going away, and you think that it may be for some time, send me your portrait."[6] It is even possible that Napoleon's attachment to Joseph underlay his changing his wife's name from Rose to Josephine. Josephe was one of her names, but that would have been too close to his brother's; until Napoleon married her she had always been known as Rose.

Napoleon's sentiments would harden as he ascended to power, but Joseph believed that beneath his brother's cold exterior he still cared for him. Joseph once wrote to Napoleon from Naples on the occasion of his birthday: "The glorious Emperor will never replace for me the Napoleone [his childhood name] whom I so much loved, and whom I hope to find again, as I knew him twenty years ago, if we are to meet in the Elysian Fields."[7] Napoleon himself gave a somewhat humorous explanation for his coldness: "I had to create an external facade, an etiquette; otherwise people would have been slapping me on the back whenever they saw me."[8]

Joseph told Nicholas Biddle that everyone had gotten into the habit of cringing before Napoleon and that only he and Lucien could tell him the truth when circumstances demanded it. "In Councils of State, none dared give an opposite opinion. In discussions, the question was not what was right or wrong, but what the emperor thought or said about it. Talleyrand would reply to any remark, 'That may be, but the Emperor has said so and so.'" Napoleon would then turn to Joseph and say, "See now, you are the only person who thinks in such a way."[9]

Lucien in his memoirs recalled a conversation he had once had with Joseph about Napoleon as the two brothers walked in the park at Malmaison. Joseph had said he recognized Napoleon's talents and found him amiable three-quarters of the time, but although he loved, esteemed, and admired the emperor, he did not like the tone Napoleon often took with him. Joseph acknowledged that Napoleon's historic political life surpassed him, but in their personal relations, he, Joseph, was, and always would be, the elder brother. Lucien said that explained to him the uncharacteristically hostile attitude Joseph frequently adopted toward Napoleon; he was continually defending his rights of primogeniture.[10]

Joseph would have remembered only too vividly the confrontation with Napoleon over the sale of the Louisiana Territory, a scene that Lucien would record in his memoirs. Joseph had been intensely angry on learning from Lucien that Napoleon intended to bypass the Chamber of Deputies and sell the vast territory west of the Mississippi River directly to the Americans. Lucien was furious at the sale because he had negotiated the Treaty of San Ildefonso with Spain in 1800, transferring Louisiana to France. Joseph could hardly believe that the First Consul—some months later he would declare himself emperor—would so abandon his own republican principles as to bypass the chamber.

Lucien was already at the Tuileries Palace when Joseph, seeking Napoleon, found him in his bath. They both confronted him with their disapproval. "Messieurs," Napoleon answered them, "think whatever you want, but you will have to grieve over this affair; you, Lucien, for the sale itself; you, Joseph, because I pass by the assent you think I should have, you understand?" Lucien observed that a tempest was brewing, not in a "glass of water" (or a teapot), but in the bathtub of one who was beginning to make all the sovereigns of Europe tremble.

In approaching the bathtub, Joseph said to him, "And so, my dear brother, you do not intend to expose your plan to parliamentary discussion? Then, I tell you, since it is necessary, that I place myself at the head of the opposition to your doing this." At these words the First Consul merely smiled, but Joseph flushed red and nearly stammering with anger, shouted: "Laugh, laugh, laugh! I will do no less than I say although I do not like to go up before the tribune, but this time I will be there."

The First Consul raised his body from its reclining position and stated slowly but firmly: "You have no need to be an orator for the opposition because I repeat to you that this discussion doesn't mean anything, since the proposition that does not have the happiness to have your approbation is conceived by me, negotiated by me, and will be ratified and executed by me in mockery of your opposition." So saying, Napoleon, according to Lucien, "slipped down tranquilly into the white waves of eau de cologne." Joseph, angrier than before, "his handsome face still more inflamed," responded sarcastically: "Well, I tell you, general, that you, me, both of us, if you do what you say, must prepare to go join the poor innocent devils who you, so legally, with humanitarianism, above all so justly, deported to Sinnamari," referring to a small port in French Guyana.[11]

What followed was "an aquatic explosion," as Lucien described it, when Napoleon shot up out of the bathtub and then threw himself back in the water, drenching Joseph and shouting: "You are insolent! I must . . ." Lucien thought Napoleon had not finished his sentence, but he did notice that the pallor of the First Consul contrasted with Joseph's extreme redness. There was silence and Lucien dared not mediate between his two older brothers. To relieve the tension he started to recite a passage from Virgil where an angry Neptune rebukes the unchained waves, a comparison that had struck him as comical. Joseph replied to Lucien: "In any case, your god is definitely crazy [*bien fou*]." But Neptune/Napoleon, disarmed, or wishing to appear so, said jovially to Lucien, "Always a poem for the occasion!"

The scene changed abruptly. Joseph's face and clothes were soaked, but the "perfumed wave" had calmed his anger, which with him, as Lucien said, was always superficial and ephemeral. Joseph attempted to dry himself, aided by Napoleon's *valet de chambre*, but the poor valet, no doubt overcome by the drama he had witnessed, collapsed in a dead faint. Joseph caught the falling man while Lucien rang for Roustan, Napoleon's Turkish servant. The discussion was over.[12]

Napoleon's determination over the issue of Louisiana may have signaled his downfall. It had proved impossible to stop the sale by putting the debate before the chamber, though both Joseph and Lucien agreed that the deputies would definitely have vetoed it, convinced that the fifteen million dollars realized would have gone to finance more wars. In fact it did finance them; the disasters against Russia and Spain indirectly brought down the empire.

In a strange twist of fate, the son of Chancellor Robert Livingston, one of the American negotiators of the Louisiana Purchase, was now a friend of Joseph, who would visit Livingson's handsome house, Clermont, overlooking the Hudson River at Rhinebeck, on his way to northern New York state. And it was not Joseph who had been sent to Sinnamari, the equivalent of St. Helena, but Napoleon, as Joseph had warned.

General Bertrand wrote from London in early September 1821 that it was the first opportunity he had to contact Joseph and not knowing his address, he had deposited his letter with Joseph's London bankers, Baring Brothers, anticipating they would forward it. After describing Napoleon's suffering in detail and how he felt his end approaching, Bertrand said that, even so, "the hope of leaving this dreadful country often presented itself to his imagination; some newspaper articles and false reports excited our expectations. We sometimes fancied that we were on the eve of starting for America; we read travels, we made plans, we arrived at your house, we wandered over that immense country, where alone we might hope to enjoy liberty. Vain hopes! Vain projects! Which only made us doubly feel our misfortunes." Bertrand told Joseph that if the conversation became melancholy, Napoleon often changed the subject "to talk of Corsica, of his old great uncle Lucien, of his youth, of you, and of all the rest of the family."[13]

In his great poem *Childe Harold's Pilgrimage*, Byron summed up Napoleon's proud but ignominious end:

> *When the whole host of hatred stood*
> > *hard by,*
> *To watch and mock thee shrinking,*
> > *thou hast smiled*
> *With a sedate and all-enduring eye;—*
> *When Fortune fled her spoil'd and*
> > *favourite child,*
> *He stood unbow'd beneath the ill upon*
> > *him piled.*[14]

Joseph was severely depressed all that fall. In a letter to his friend Charles Ingersoll in November, he says he has been touched by the expressions in Ingersoll's letter of condolence about his brother and hopes that "posterity will ratify" Ingersoll's judgment "as well as other intelligent men of good faith who do not demand that a man be perfect in a way that is beyond human nature." To Joseph Hopkinson, a month later, he says that he has been suffering from a long illness, perhaps a combination of nephritis and depressed spirits. He no longer doubts that his brother was a victim of the villainy of his enemies, and believes that without this treachery he would now be living in the United States as healthy as Joseph, who was older and of a less robust constitution. He describes Napoleon as "always greater than his fate and superior to his glory," and, like Julius Caesar, the emperor believed his enemies incapable of a great crime. Is he suggesting that Napoleon was murdered? Rather than arsenic poisoning, he is probably referring to hepatitis brought on by the iniquity of the English in keeping his brother in such an unhealthy place. *Niles Weekly Register* reported four years later, "It is stated, in an English paper, that the house in which the ex-emperor of France was imprisoned, has been converted into a barn; and that, in the room in which he breathed his last, there is now a machine for threshing corn."[15]

Joseph wrote Zénaïde, who was planning her wedding to her cousin Charles-Lucien, that after being so absorbed with the sad events of St. Helena, hearing of her marriage plans now brought him happiness. He had talked about her with the emperor during "the hundred days," and during his last weeks Napoleon had been troubled (*affligé*) with thoughts of her future.[16] Because of her impending marriage, Zénaïde would not be the first to join her father in America; that role would be relegated to her younger sister Charlotte. If depression for some months had beset the Count de Survilliers over the death of his brother, in spite of the presence of Anna ensconced a short way up the Delaware, it would soon be nearly dissipated by the arrival of nineteen-year-old Charlotte. She had embarked from Anvers aboard the *Ruth and Mary* and arrived in Philadelphia forty-six days later on 21 December 1821 amid great fanfare. Her delighted father was on the quay to meet her.

Chapter 8

CHARLOTTE

The Count and Princess are most kindly, polite and attentive to me,
which renders my stay here very pleasant. I admire and love her more
every day, she is so accomplished, mild, and amiable.
—Caroline-Eleanore Girard to Stephen Girard,
Point Breeze, 4 April 1822

*W*hen the *Ruth and Mary* with Charlotte Bonaparte aboard sailed up the Delaware and docked in Philadelphia, Clara Mickle, niece of the captain, was also on the wharf. In a letter, young Clara described the thrill of witnessing, with a host of other sightseers, a real princess step down a gangplank carpeted all the way to her waiting carriage. (Charlotte and Zénaïde both had the title of princess since their father had been a king.) To her observer, Charlotte appeared very young (perhaps because she was so petite), vivacious, and delighted to see such a welcoming crowd (fig. 20). Clara guessed she was probably also glad after such a long voyage—it had been forty-six days from Brighton—to be soon free of her duenna and her physician, Dr. John Stockoë, who had cared for Napoleon on St. Helena. In order to return the enthusiastic greetings of the spectators, Charlotte vigorously waved the fur hat she had worn during the crossing, inadvertently dropping it over the side of the ship. It caught on something, was quickly retrieved, and holding it on her head and laughing she proceeded to the carriage.[1]

Charlotte had been enchanted by the ship's handsome young captain, whose half-length portrait she drew sometime during the voyage. She pictured him seated with a book in his lap with the caption: "Captain Mickle reading Hervey's Meditations." Upon leaving the ship she presented him with a beautiful diamond breast-pin and left him all the fine wines put aboard for her use.[2]

What emotion Joseph must have felt when he greeted his younger daughter. She

20. **Charlotte Bonaparte** *by Charles Lawrence, 1823. Oil on canvas. Athenaeum of Philadelphia.*

was the first member of his immediate family he had seen for six years, the first one to dare the hazardous voyage across the Atlantic in order to be with him. Her courage and obvious demonstration of love were deeply gratifying. Charlotte, like her mother petite, thin, and somewhat plain in looks, nevertheless had enormous dark eyes that betrayed a passionate soul beneath her otherwise unprepossessing exterior. Her *joie de vivre* was much more that of her father than of her mother, who was so often ailing and seemingly depressed. Intelligent and well educated, Charlotte was devoted to literature and had a decided talent for drawing. In Brussels, where she had been living for nearly two years, having moved with her mother and sister from Frankfurt in 1820, she had taken lessons from Jacques-Louis David, Napoleon's official court painter. David had moved to Brussels in self-appointed exile after the emperor's abdication. Charlotte and Zénaïde had posed for the artist less than a year earlier for a double portrait, a gift to their father (fig. 21).

In the painting, the sisters are sitting together on a red velvet sofa embossed with golden Napoleonic bees each with an arm affectionately around the other. They are elegantly dressed, Charlotte in gray taffeta with delicate ruching around the neck and Zénaïde in décolleté black velvet draped with a costly Kashmir shawl, both with jeweled tiaras on their curly dark hair. Charlotte, the smaller of the two, leans over with an expression somewhat wistful and diffident, while Zénaïde, full bosomed and erect, has an air of confidence that is slightly severe. Zénaïde, very much a Bonaparte in looks, holds a letter, presumably from their father, as "Philadelphie" and "chéres petites" are visible at the top of the paper. David made several copies of this picture. The original was sent to Joseph in America, a copy dispatched to Charles-Lucien in Rome to acquaint him with his betrothed (whom he had not met), while the second copy stayed with Julie in Brussels.[3]

As much as Charlotte loved and respected her father, the knowledge of his extramarital affair must have been difficult to accept because of loyalty to her mother. Soon after her arrival, she undoubtedly found out about Joseph's liaison with Anna Savage, scarcely a year older than herself, and the establishment at Pine Grove, a new house that Joseph had moved Anna to in Lamberton. Only a few weeks later Anna had a second daughter, Caroline Charlotte. Her first child by Joseph, Pauline Josephe Ann, was then two years old. One wonders if naming both children after Joseph's sisters was Anna's idea in order to anchor a claim on her lover. Surely if the Count de Survilliers had wanted to keep his affair anonymous he would not have suggested such an obvious link. As for Charlotte, she may have quietly disapproved of her father's life of a *bon vivant*, but she, too, in later years would defy convention for the sake of love.

21. **The Sisters Zénaïde and Charlotte Bonaparte** *by Jacques-Louis David, 1821. Oil on canvas. J. Paul Getty Museum, Los Angeles. © J. Paul Getty Museum.*

Delighted to have his charming daughter in America, even though he must have disappeared frequently to spend time with Anna, Pauline, and Caroline, the Count de Survilliers planned to give Lolotte every opportunity to enjoy her time with him. In order that she not lack for female companionship her own age—of course it was not possible for her to meet Anna—he invited one of Stephen Girard's three orphaned nieces, Caroline-Eleanore, to Point Breeze in the spring of 1822 for an extended visit. "I have scarcely had a moment to devote to my pen ere now," Caroline-Eleanore wrote Girard, with whom she lived, "I have spent all yesterday with the Princess. I have dined with her every day since I left you. She is one of the most amiable beings I ever knew. The Count's place is much improved since I last saw it and he wishes very much you would come see it. I believe, dear uncle, you have no idea the Count's place yields as abundantly as it does—he made last season 150 barrels of excellent cider, besides 400 *choice* apples for his table."[4] The next day she wrote again, even more enthusiastic about Charlotte: "The Count and Princess are most kindly, polite and attentive to me, which renders my stay here very pleasant. I admire and love her more every day, she is so accomplished, mild and amiable."[5]

In addition to providing friends, Joseph also gave Charlotte every opportunity to see the beautiful sights of the country, especially so she could draw them. There was Point Breeze itself with its many lovely vistas, the lake with the swans, the trees and the wildflowers. The surrounding countryside as well offered many scenes for her to sketch and paint (fig. 22). In December she wrote her mother that she had just painted a small landscape, her first one in oil, which was the view of Point Breeze from her window. "The last winter I spent in Brussels I felt I made some progress," she said, "Monsieur David having promised to supervise me."[6]

Joseph Hopkinson, as president of the Pennsylvania Academy of the Fine Arts, had often solicited his friend, the count, to lend his paintings and sculptures to the academy's annual exhibits, thus Charlotte had the perfect place to show her work. In the spring of 1822 she submitted a painting entitled *Landscape and Waterfall*, the first of many landscapes and studies of flowers in oil she would exhibit for the next several years as "the Countess, Charlotte de Survilliers." Later her pictures would be lithographed and published by Joubert in Paris as *Vues pittoresques d'Amérique*. Included would be scenes drawn at the many places she visited with her father: views from the park at Point Breeze, the falls of the Passaic, and the property in northern New York State, including Lake Diana. She painted the entrance to Lake Ontario from Niagara Falls, Lake George, and the North River near the little town of Clermont.[7]

Charlotte was in excellent company for her first exhibit in 1822. Not only were Americans represented, such as Thomas Sully, Washington Allston, George Catlin,

22. **Small landscape** *by Charlotte Bonaparte, graphite on wove paper, 1823. Inscribed on back of sketch: "20 Juillet 1833/ un Souvenir de Joseph Bonaparte a son ami Short/ Peintre/ par Charlotte fi." Athenaeum of Philadelphia.*

and Titian Peale (with four drawings of western animals from his recent expedition to the Rocky Mountains), but also European masters of former centuries like Salvator Rosa, Paul Brill, Rembrandt, and Murillo. And listed just before Charlotte's painting in the academy catalog of that same year is one by her teacher, David: the enormous oil of *Napoleon Crossing the Alps at the Great St. Bernard* (fig. 23).[8]

This picture, transported across the Atlantic to hang in New Jersey, was the original version of the work commissioned by Charles IV of Spain sometime between September 1799 and August 1800, after signing the Treaty of San Ildefonso, giving Louisiana back to France. Napoleon's feat of leading his army through the pass of the Great St. Bernard in May 1800 suggested to David his historic theme. In actuality, Napoleon crossed the Alps on a mule and is said to have posed for David sitting on Josephine's lap at the palace of St. Cloud. One must applaud David's imagination in transforming the scene of an ordinary general on a mule into a heroic allegory by evoking an equestrian statue and showing Napoleon pointing to a great future rather than to an invisible summit and inviting the French spectator, even more than the army, to follow him. Inscribed on rocks in the foreground are the names of Hannibal and Charlemagne, equating Napoleon with these dynamic heroes of the past. David may have taken his ideas for his icon from the painting of Don Gaspar de Guzman by Velázquez that had just entered the Spanish Bourbon collection.[9] In 1808, when

23. **Napoleon Crossing the Alps at the Great St. Bernard** *by Jacques-Louis David, 1801. Oil on canvas. Château de Malmaison, Photo: Erich Lessing, Art Resource, NY.*

Joseph Bonaparte replaced the Spanish king, he subsequently claimed his brother's portrait as his own property.

Two years earlier the academy had formally requested a loan of the David for its annual exhibit, but Joseph had declined to lend it. A letter from the count read at a special academy meeting on 2 June 1820, says that he deeply regrets being unable to loan the work, especially as the subject has been of much curiosity in Bordentown. The painting is of such large dimensions, he explains, that it could not be transported without removing it from its frame. Where it had been in the past (the royal palace in Madrid) the doors were so large that it could easily be taken out and placed in a carriage, but where it now is the doors are too small to let it pass. Instead, he offers a group of paintings that are at his house in Philadelphia, a Luca Giordano, several by David Teniers (probably *Mill and Landscape, with Gypsies Telling Fortunes*), and "a large and beautiful Flemish work."[10] By 1822, however, no doubt after much persuasion by Joseph Hopkinson, Joseph agreed to lend the enormous David after all. He continued to loan it for the next seven years, perhaps under Charlotte's influence.

*   *   *

In the summer months Joseph took his daughter on many excursions for fresh air and a cooler climate, as well as for the dramatic scenery. It was no longer possible to take Anna with him, which must have caused a certain friction with her. In June he took Charlotte to stay at the fashionable Bellmont Hall at Schooley's Mountain Springs, a New Jersey mountain resort much frequented at the time. By the first of August they were at Niagara Falls, which Charlotte found thrilling to sketch, as she thought the sight had no equal in Europe. A week later they arrived at the Sans-Souci House in Ballston Spa, near Saratoga, New York, described by a visitor a few years before as "one of the largest establishments [of its kind] in the United States and exceeds anything for gaiety and dissipation."[11] He had taken Anna there in former years, and the other guests were perhaps surprised—or maybe not—that she was no longer with the count.

The following year Joseph took Charlotte to the Bath Hotel in Long Branch, New Jersey, a fashionable beach resort. These journeys were always lively, as the count's retinue invariably included a party of friends and servants. That summer of 1822, Joseph and Charlotte were accompanied by Captain Jean-Mathieu Alexandre Sari, who had been part of the count's household for six or seven years. The thirty-year-old Sari, a fellow Corsican, had been second in command of the *Inconstant*, the ship that carried Napoleon on his great escape from Elba. Sari had arrived in the United States in 1817, sent to Joseph at the suggestion of Madame Mère, who had taken a great liking to him while he was living in Rome, perhaps because he was a native Corsican like herself. Sari had been particularly helpful to Joseph in handling the affairs of his Black River lands.

Though Charlotte was of marriageable age and her family sought to find her a suitable husband, a Corsican naval captain with an unimpressive family background was not to be considered. Ever since she was a child her father had had it in mind that to keep the imperial succession alive, his children must marry Bonapartes. The previous April, Charlotte's cousin Jérôme-Napoleon Patterson (fig. 24) had arrived at Point Breeze, instructed by his mother to court Charlotte. Although not quite seventeen, the young man, the son of Joseph's younger brother Jérôme and his American wife Elizabeth Patterson, was tall and handsome. Some twenty years earlier, Jérôme-Napoleon's father, on a visit to the United States with his naval squadron, had fallen in love with a beautiful belle of Baltimore, daughter of a wealthy merchant, and had married her in a full Catholic ceremony. When Napoleon heard of the marriage, he was infuriated that his brother should marry an American and not one of

24. **Jérôme Napoleon Patterson-Bonaparte** *by François Gérard. Oil on canvas. Collection of Christopher Forbes.*

the young women of European royalty for whom the emperor had intended him. This first Jérôme was persuaded to capitulate and Napoleon annulled the marriage, although Pope Pius VII refused to agree. Jérôme subsequently married Catherine of Württemberg, much to Napoleon's satisfaction.

Jérôme-Napoleon, Elizabeth Patterson's son, visited Rome as a young man and was made much of by his grandmother, Madame Mère, and by his aunt Pauline Borghese, who was invariably drawn to handsome men. In 1819, Joseph himself had been much impressed on meeting his nephew. He wrote Julie from New York: "I have with me the son of Jérôme—he is fourteen years old, strong, sweet and *fort gai*—large and well made."[12] Ten days later, back in Philadelphia, Joseph told Julie the young man had been with him for a month, and that, "He speaks better American than French, he is strong, well brought up, and I like him very much."[13] Joseph added that he resembled himself quite a lot.

But an American without valid Bonaparte credentials (that is, not accepted by

Napoleon) was not what Joseph had in mind for Charlotte, and whether she was simply a dutiful daughter or was actually not attracted to the younger Jérôme-Napoleon, the young man's suit was never taken seriously. A friend of his mother's who lived in Philadelphia and often encountered the Count de Survilliers, attempted to assuage Elizabeth Patterson's anger by reporting that Charlotte was *"très petite et très vilaine"* (very small and very unattractive) and that Jérôme-Napoleon was much too good for her. But this was not balm enough for Elizabeth who saw the arrival at Point Breeze of Joseph's nephew, Lucien Murat, in the same month as the aggravating reason for the ruin of her son's prospects. Eight years later, in 1829, much to his mother's disgust, Jérôme-Napoleon married a well-to-do American from Baltimore, Susan Mary Williams, with whom he would be very happy. One of his sons, Charles Joseph Bonaparte, would serve in Theodore Roosevelt's cabinet. Perhaps this Charles's middle name was in honor of his father's attachment to his Uncle Joseph.

Lucien Murat, the son of Joseph's youngest sister Caroline and Joachim Murat, a marshal in the Grande Armée and Joseph's successor as king of Naples, was a large, raw-boned, blustering fellow with none of the qualities that would have appealed to Charlotte. A visitor to Point Breeze described him as "unreserved—full of spirits—ready to laugh—he sat carelessly & acted without regard to gentility. He had his Shirt collar uncovered & neck exposed for purposes of comfort in the warm weather—he wore a peculiarly low crowned hat, & big brim of white fur."[14] There was no question of him as a possible husband. The cousin who Joseph thought was best suited to his youngest daughter was Napoleon-Louis, the oldest son of his brother Louis, one-time king of Holland, and Hortense Beauharnais, the daughter of Napoleon's wife Josephine by an earlier marriage. But with Napoleon-Louis in Europe, for now Charlotte was to enjoy her stay as her father's daughter and be the hostess of his house.

A young college student from Yale, James Holmes, tells how he often saw Charlotte in Philadelphia with the count at the Athenaeum, where they went to read the news of Europe. Holmes was introduced to father and daughter by his guardian, Mr. Chauncey, aboard the steamboat to Bordentown. The two men were then invited to visit. At Point Breeze, Mr. Chauncey, being a friend and neighbor, was soon deep in conversation with Joseph on local topics, leaving Charlotte and her companion to amuse each other. As neither spoke the other's language with any proficiency, Charlotte suggested they play billiards. "The young lady played with a mace, and I soon found that no politeness was necessary to allow her to beat me," her opponent recorded, "and I was not an indifferent player myself. She won fairly and rather easily." At the end of the match a waiter appeared, holding a silver tray under his arm and announced in English: "lunch." The young man said this repast consisted of "a half-dozen dishes all having the odour of wine and spices; one in particular looked like the hind legs of a frog, but it proved to be two small tongues (calves' possibly) redolent of spices and floating in claret." The diarist concluded that everything was new and interesting to him, and the visit was a "grand event" in his life.[15]

Charlotte loved to ride horseback with her father, but much to the consternation of the local Quakers, according to one of their descendants, she adopted the Quaker garb as a riding habit, especially the "sugar scoop" bonnet to protect her face from the sun. Even more to the Quakers' amazement was the Sunday morning when the entire Bonaparte household, including maids and valets carrying kneeling cushions used in the Catholic service, showed up at Quaker meeting. The congregation, alerted ahead of time that Isaac Thorn, a Bonaparte neighbor, had invited the family, crowded the meeting room. The members of all ages were full of anticipation when the Count de Survilliers's handsome carriage drove up. At that time, women sat on one side of the aisle and men on the other. Unaware of this Quaker custom, the entourage piled in on the men's side, causing a noticeable titter among the younger members of the meeting. When that issue was finally straightened out, one of the Friends "felt moved by the spirit" to preach against war. "My grandfather was very uncomfortable," recounts the narrator of the anecdote, "for he was afraid the Bonapartes would take it as an insult, since their brother Napoleon had been the greatest and bloodiest warrior in history, but Isaac Thorn concluded from the very affable manner of his guests after meeting, that they had not understood enough English to comprehend what would have been very offensive to them if they had fully understood all that was said."[16]

In January 1823, Joseph wrote Julie that he had been living in Philadelphia since the beginning of the year because the cold had really begun in earnest. He had been to an assembly "*assez brillante*, such that rarely occurs" (in staid Philadelphia, that is). Probably this was the "very splendid ball" given at the time by Philip Syng Physick in his house at 123 South Fourth Street in Philadelphia (a present-day house museum) where, as the doctor's daughter Susan recorded, one of the guests was her "old acquaintance, Joseph Bonaparte together with all the elite of our city of Philadelphia."[17] He says that Lolotte works all the time on her painting, and he hopes Julie's health will permit her to join them with Zénaïde and her husband.[18]

At this point, Joseph was somewhat worried about money. He wrote toward the end of the month that business in America was very bad, there were many bankruptcies, but he assured his wife there was no danger for them. "I know that next year I can count on the revenues from M. le Ray de Chaumont, and the land I will preserve for our children. Someday the lands that I bought for 2, 3, 4 pounds an acre will increase in value." Also thinking of real estate, he remembers that in 1808 or 1809, Count Miot de Melito (his old friend from Corsica and head of his Spanish royal household) had executed a contract whereby, Joseph says, "I became the owner of the house and gardens of the Marquis de Montehermoso at Vitoria—it was paid for, if I am right, in cash by Monsieur de Melito!"[19] One wonders if Julie knew any of the details of this purchase. Perhaps she did not at the time, but she would learn about Joseph's affair with the marquis's wife and why Joseph bought the marquis's house for three times its worth when Stanislas de Girardin, his so-called best friend, published his memoirs in 1829 revealing the embarrassing details.

The next month, Joseph assures Julie that he has no need for any more pictures at Point Breeze, and they should sell those that are still in Europe. "I send you my portrait and that of Lolotte. Tell me about poor David—you must profit by your stay in Brussels to have David paint your portrait." [20] Knowing that he is perfectly safe in encouraging her, for she will never come, he says, "If you could come here it would be the best for our happiness and tranquillity." Julie has apparently argued that his brother Jérôme is living comfortably in Trieste and goes back and forth to Rome and therefore he could do the same. However, Joseph has heard an opposite view from his brother. "Jérôme does not hide from me that he has always been a prisoner in Trieste and that it is with much difficulty that he obtains passports for Rome. I am in a very different position from Jérôme for going back to Rome—do you forget that I have been king of Naples and Spain? Is it the moment to hope that I could live free and tranquil on the border of the kingdom of Naples? I don't think there would be any possibility of that, and I don't think our enemies would appreciate it should the people feel I had ruled better than the government of today. I repeat that I could only leave here for a free country. I could only go to Europe at the mercy of the Triple Alliance."[21]

At this point Joseph was still much involved with Anna, even if the birth of their first daughter had caused the landlord, De Klyn, at Bow Hill, to regret allowing his house to be stigmatized by this bastard birth and to have canceled the lease, forcing Joseph to find a new house for his mistress.[22] Sometime in 1819 or 1820, De Klyn had persuaded his son-in-law to sell Anna and her mother, Margaret Savage, the old Elijah Bond house in Lamberton for $6,000, with funds no doubt provided by the Count de Survilliers.[23] The house, called Pine Grove, was high on a bluff across the

25. **Pine Grove in Lamberton, New Jersey, from** *South Jersey: A History,*
1664–1924, *ed. Alfred M. Heston (New York: Lewis Historical Publishing, 1924–[27?]).*

Delaware River to the north of Point Breeze (fig. 25). From the top of his belvedere
Joseph may even have seen a candle burning in Anna's window. Just below the house
was an ancient Quaker burial ground, perhaps the source of the erroneous legend
that Anna was a Quaker. Before moving in with her mother, Margaret, and three
servants in the early 1820s, Anna made major renovations and added on to the house.
But Pine Grove, too, was uncomfortably close to Bordentown and Joseph thought to
move Anna entirely away from the sphere of Philadelphia. For some five years she
had been accompanying him on his annual summer visits to the Black River country,
where, no doubt to her delight, she had been known as Mrs. Bonaparte. Perhaps she
would be happier in New York State. It is difficult to discern exactly when Joseph
had thought to move Anna and her daughters and to build a house for them at
Natural Bridge, near Watertown. Northern New York had the advantage of being far
away from the disapproval of Philadelphia and Trenton society.

   In any case, in the summer of 1823, Joseph commissioned a portrait of Anna
and their two daughters (see plate 3) from the Philadelphia painter Bass Otis (1784–
1861). Otis had painted Nicholas Biddle's wife, Jane, in 1814, which may have influenced Joseph in the choice of an artist. In the painting Anna is placed in a rural
setting against the backdrop of a large rock, a gnarled tree, and a river winding off in
the distance. The location is probably Pine Grove on the bluff above the Delaware,

looking south from Lamberton with Duck Island on the left side of the river and Point Breeze implied, but not shown, in the distance.[24] Anna is depicted as a buxom young woman, fashionably dressed in a high-waisted empire-style lace gown with a décolleté neckline, pearls around her neck and wrists and at her ears, and a rose-like ornament in her black hair. A large flowered hat is on a rock beside her. She is looking wistfully into the distance. Pauline kneels at her mother's left holding a rose branch and gazing calmly at the viewer. Before the year was out, this child would die in a tragic accident. Caroline Charlotte, dressed identically to her sister, her arm around her mother's neck, is just removing a wide-brimmed beribboned hat from her short, dark hair.

Otis may have taken his inspiration, possibly at Anna's suggestion, from a por- trait he could have seen at Point Breeze, executed some fifteen years earlier by Baron François Gérard, of Julie Bonaparte as Queen of Spain with her two daughters Zén- aïde and Charlotte (see plate 2). There are many details of Gérard's painting that Otis might have copied, including those of fashion and iconography. Julie wears a dress with low-cut neckline, filmy ruching above the sleeves, pearls at her neck and ears, and roses in her coifed dark hair. The children, dressed alike, with the same slippers as their mother, are placed either side of her. Although Julie, unlike Anna, is shown seated in an elegant armchair, her slippered feet on a velvet cushion, there is also water in the background in the form of a tree-lined lake seen from an open window filling half the picture space. The lake was more than likely at Joseph's estate of Mortefontaine, since Julie was in Paris at the time Gérard painted her. Like Anna, Julie, too, has a sad, reflective expression, perhaps just the melancholy typical of romantic portraiture. Then again, she may have been aware at the time, 1808, that her husband had just fathered a son by the Duchess d'Atri in Naples.

Chapter 9 ZÉNAÏDE AND CHARLES

My uncle has given us a house that he built and fitted up expressly for us on the edge of a lovely artificial lake.
—Charles-Lucien Bonaparte to Alexandrine
Bonaparte, Point Breeze, 1 November 1823

*R*egardless of her husband's pro forma entreaties, Julie was not with Zénaïde when, on 8 September, she arrived in New York aboard the American ship *Falcon* with her new husband and a suite of eight persons. Her husband was also her first cousin, Charles-Lucien Bonaparte, Lucien's son. The couple had been married in Brussels a year earlier on 29 June 1822 and then had spent most of the year in Rome (fig. 26). The ocean crossing from Antwerp to New York had been long and turbulent and Zénaïde had suffered a great deal, especially because she was four months pregnant. Charles-Lucien described the voyage to a friend in Holland as "frightful," as it took seventy-five days. "We were in Plymouth for 11 days," he said, "but had 51 days of *tribulations* from Plymouth to New York—we had altogether 3 or 4 tempests. It did not bother me but my wife suffered constantly so you can judge my sad situation aboard the ship."[1] Zénaïde, though ill and exhausted, was happy to touch solid ground at last and joyful to see her father after eight years. Joseph was no doubt amazed by the change in his oldest daughter. He had last seen a fourteen-year-old and now he welcomed a mature married woman of twenty-two carrying her first child. Perhaps it made him feel exceptionally young for his age, considering that he had two young children of his own, besides this pregnant daughter. After several days at the City Hotel so that Zénaïde could recover her strength, the party proceeded to Point Breeze.

26. **Charles-Lucien with Zénaïde at the Harp** *by Charles de Châtillon. Pencil drawing. Collection of Giuseppe Primoli, courtesy of the Museo Napoleonico, Rome.*

Sad news awaited them: Henriette Girard's husband, Henri Lallemand, who had been very ill in Bordentown, died while Joseph was in New York. The count called on Henriette at once and invited the young widow with her small daughter to stay at his house. Henriette wrote her uncle from Point Breeze to accept Girard's offer of making her permanent home with him. "The good count and family have also shown me the kindest attentions for which I can never be too grateful," she reported. "He has behaved like a parent, I am most happy in possessing such a friend." She then adds, in regard to proper mourning attire, "Be so kind dear Uncle as to get Miss Polly to send me a complete dress becoming my situation as it is impossible for me to procure them here, at least a hat and shawl."[2] Henriette, like her younger sister Caroline-Eleanore, would become close friends with Zénaïde as she already was with Charlotte.

For the accommodation of Zénaïde and Charles, Joseph had built the Lake House and decorated it with the same elegance as his mansion. Three years later, John Fanning Watson, a visitor to the Lake House with Reuben Haines, a Quaker naturalist with a large farm and impressive manor house in Germantown and a friend of Charles's, would describe "Prince Charles's house" as being three stories high with two or more large rooms to a floor. He said that a "porter" admitted them to a luxurious parlor with richly carpeted floors and walls hung with "large & expensive" paintings by the European masters. Unaccustomed to seeing nudes in art, as were most Americans in the early nineteenth century, Watson was surprised at the subject matter of these works. He noted that the largest of the paintings was the "Escape of Europa drawn in great spirit, but with little regard for female modesty." What surprised him even more was not only the presence of a large canopied bed in the same room, but "its usual accompaniment [the chamber pot], not grateful to my eyes[,] occupied a corner without a disguise! I wondered indeed if it was an *accident*!"

When Charles appeared, he invited them into his study where all around the high walls were beautiful glass cases filled with birds and reptiles stuffed by the prince, and on tables, spread out in glass plates, was a superb collection of butterflies. Watson described Charles as "very affable, republican, & frank in his manners; & puts his Plebian acquaintance quite at their ease." As to his appearance, he said that "the prince" was of medium height with "a general fatness on small bones—broad shoulders—features and face possessing that round plumpness which marked Napoleon's pictures when he became corpulent—The eyes of Prince Charles are dark, full and expressive—fine teeth and a pleasing smile—He wears his beard on his upper lip."[3] Charles's father, Lucien, had been given a papal title, Prince of Canino, because of land he bought from the Holy See, and the pope had designated Charles-Lucien Prince of Musignano.

The sophisticated young Bonaparte, who had grown up in Rome because of his father's falling out with Napoleon early on in his rise to power, ironically resembled the emperor to a marked degree. He had already established himself in Europe as an ornithologist of note by writing a book on the birds of Rome, *Ornitologia Romana*. Unable to identify an unusual bird he had shot in the campagna Romana, he had sent it to a famous ornithologist in Leiden, Holland, Conraad Jacob Temminck. The species, the moustached warbler, was new to science, and Temminck credited Charles with the discovery in a book published in 1823, just months before the budding naturalist sailed for America. He would go on to make quite a name for himself in the world of natural history.

At Point Breeze, Charles would make detailed lists of the property's trees, shrubs, and wildflowers, all with their Latin names, but he particularly collected and studied the birds. He was an accomplished horseman and crack shot who delighted in accompanying his father-in-law in hunting forays, and it was often from these outings that he discovered birds and animals new to him. These were fauna indigenous to the United States, such as the rattlesnake (*serpente a sonagli*, as he described it in his memoirs, written in Italian) and the skunk. Once while out riding, he spied a small black-and-white animal scurrying along the path before him and instantly leapt off his horse and grabbed the creature by its tail. In his journal he later recorded that nothing he did would remove the smell, no amount of bathing, or perfume, not even cutting off his hair.[4] But once the evil odor was overcome, Charles, who had a good sense of humor in spite of his temper, may have amused his father-in-law and his guests with this unfortunate escapade.

In the park at Point Breeze, carriage roads and bridle paths wound through stately pines and oaks and over stone bridges, past rustic gazebos and benches, sheltered springs, and strategically placed statuary. Reuben Haines would describe his visit to Point Breeze two years later in a letter to his cousin: after an elegant dinner he had accompanied the prince and princess (Charles and Zénaïde) in a carriage "drawn by two *Elegant Horses* along the ever varying roads of the park amidst splendid Rhododendrons on the margin of the artificial lake on whose smooth surface gently glided the majestic European swans. Stopping to visit the Aviary enlivened by the most beautiful English Pheasants, passing by alcoves ornamented with statues and busts of Parian marble, our course enlivened by the footsteps of the tame deer and the flight of the Woodcock, and when alighting stopping to admire the graceful form of two splendid Etruscan vases of Porphyry 3 ft. high & 2 in diameter presented by the Queen of Sweden."[5]

Haines's visit took place in July, but he would have had an equally delightful time in December. A former servant at Point Breeze once reminisced that, "The day before Christmas was a great day at the Park. The Princess Zénaïde had a sleigh made in the shape of a swan, and she would drive up and down the length of the lake, throwing out sugarplums and toys to be scrambled for, and the count would look on, and laugh and laugh."[6]

Outside the immediate family sphere, it was barely three months after Charles and Zénaïde arrived at Point Breeze that a tragedy occurred at Pine Grove. In December 1823, Anna's oldest daughter, little Pauline, was struck and killed by a falling jardinière. Anna was naturally bereft. On the child's tombstone in St. Michael's Churchyard in Trenton she had these words carved:

> *Pauline, your rest is now secure*
>
> *A loving Saviour called thee hence*
>
> *Knowing thy gentleness could ill endure*
>
> *The World's unbelieving malevolence.*[7]

The child's sudden death and the repercussions of this horrible accident may have hastened the end of Joseph's affair with Anna, perhaps as the result of blame being fixed on one by the other. Also, Anna's resentment at being shoved aside by the arrival of Joseph's daughters may have smothered their romance.

Joseph had planned to move Anna and her daughters to his Black River lands, But after Pauline's death, an even better idea was to send her to Paris where the excitement of a new life in that beautiful city would make up for her disappointments and help to distract her from the loss of her daughter. He could justify it to himself that if he had found a new life in America, perhaps she could find one in France, the place he ever longed to be. The presence of Charlotte and Zénaïde and the pleasure Joseph derived from their companionship, may indeed have diminished his affection for Anna, but there was a further complication to Joseph's already compartmentalized life.

Félix Lacoste was a young Frenchman who, after Napoleon's abdication had gone to Saint Domingue (Haiti) to found a commercial establishment with two partners.

In the fall of 1821, after a trip back to Paris, he came to the United States in the fall of 1821 with his beautiful wife, Emilie, and their infant son, Léon. Shortly afterward, Félix returned to Saint Domingue to handle his business affairs and left Emilie in Philadelphia. It was there she first met Charlotte Bonaparte accompanied by her father, probably at a social engagement, since French émigrés were invariably in touch with one another. Emilie Hémart, born in 1798 in Paris, was only five years older than Charlotte and the two young women quickly became close friends. Emilie was soon frequenting Point Breeze on a regular basis. The life she had led in Paris while Félix was in Saint Domingue, particularly at the salon of her wealthy aunt, Fanny Davillier, had been lively and sophisticated in the company of novelists such as Prosper Mérimée and poets like Jean Pierre de Béranger. For Charlotte, Emilie was a delightful new acquaintance from her own milieu. As for the Count de Survilliers, the comparison between the urbane Emilie and Anna was not favorable for the latter. In 1824, when Félix again returned to Saint Domingue, he left Emilie in residence at Point Breeze as a companion for Charlotte and Zénaïde.

Somewhat earlier, perhaps in the summer of 1823, Charlotte painted Emilie's portrait (see plate 4) sitting in a chair above a lake. The scene is probably in the north country, where she must have accompanied the Bonapartes, since there are spruce trees in the middle ground and a range of mountains in the distance. It is interesting how much Emilie looks like Anna (see plate 3), with large brown eyes and her dark hair arranged in the same elegant fashion. But there is a knowing sophistication in Emilie's rather tight-lipped expression that is missing in the younger Anna.

That December, Joseph, as usual, moved his entire household to Philadelphia for the winter to the elegant mansion he rented from Stephen Girard. Two months later, on 12 February, Zénaïde gave birth to Joseph-Lucien-Charles-Napoleon. The baby's name embodied practically the entire older generation of male Bonapartes: only Louis and Jérôme were left out. Joseph was elated over the arrival of his first grandchild. At last he had a legitimate male heir. The Roman Catholic bishop of Philadelphia, the Right Reverend Henry Conwell, baptized the infant at St. Joseph's Church in Willing's Alley, the Count de Survillier's house of worship, where he had his private high-backed pew and, so the story goes, often brought along his enormous Newfoundland dog.[8] In gratitude for the baptism, Joseph gave the bishop a large ornate ring that had once belonged to Cardinal Francisco Jiménez de Cisneros (1437–1517), confessor to Queen Isabella of Spain, sponsor of Columbus; this was no doubt another souvenir from Joseph's time on the Spanish throne.[9]

Life was full for Joseph with both his daughters and his son-in-law living with him. Charles wrote his mother, Alexandrine, of his uncle's love of the great literary tragedies and how often after dinner they would each take a part in reading Racine, Corneille, or Voltaire. He told her that one recent evening before a group of Americans assembled at Point Breeze, he had read part of his father's ode on America. Among the guests was "Madame Adams," wife of the minister of foreign affairs John Quincy Adams himself a candidate for the presidency the next year. His audience was "enchanted," Charles says, especially Madame Adams, who had heard his father's name among those of "the heroes of independence."[10] Lucien had always believed strongly in the ideas of the French Revolution.

Aside from all the entertaining at Point Breeze, there was the usual round of balls and tea parties in Philadelphia, in addition to the wedding of Joseph's assistant, Jean-Mathieu Sari, to Emma St. Georges, a beautiful sixteen-year-old Creole from Cuba. Sari was then thirty-two. Charles served as a witness as did the physician Dr. Stockoë. Joseph gave a gala dinner for the young couple several nights later. But Emma Sari's introduction to the family circle would prove difficult at best.

Apart from the social, familial, and amorous components of Joseph's existence, there was a decidedly intellectual one. He regularly attended meetings of the prestigious American Philosophical Society, founded by Benjamin Franklin in the mideighteenth century, to which he had been elected on 16 April 1823. Coincidentally, at the same meeting, his brother Lucien was also elected to membership. Lucien was in the process of excavating a large number of Etruscan artifacts on his property outside Rome and would write a learned work, *Muséum Étrusque de Lucien Bonaparte, Prince de Canino* (1829), that he would send the society. It was at the gatherings of this institution that Joseph would extend his acquaintance with the city's intelligentsia, many of whom, such as Nicholas Biddle and Charles Ingersoll, he had already known since his arrival in the United States eight years before. That spring of 1824, Charles also became a member of the society and accompanied his father-in-law to meetings.

Because of his scientific interests, Charles was admitted to the Academy of Natural Sciences as well. Joseph would meet the important naturalists of the day when they visited his son-in-law at Point Breeze; men such as "the father of American entomology," Thomas Say, who had been the first scientist to reach the Rocky Mountains on the Stephen Long Expedition of 1819–1820, and Charles Alexandre Lesueur, a naturalist and artist, once on a pioneering expedition to New Holland (Australia) sent out by Napoleon, who would give Zénaïde lessons in art and perhaps introduced Charlotte to lithography. According to Madame St. Georges, the mother of Emma

Sari, Lesueur came every day at two o'clock to Joseph Bonaparte's house in Philadelphia to give Zénaïde drawing lessons. In February or March 1825, after Charlotte had
returned to Europe, Lesueur showed Madame St. Georges many *gravures* (engravings) from pictures drawn by "Princess Charlotte" of scenes from her trip to the
Black River.[11] It is entirely possible that these reproductions were lithographs. Lesueur
was one of the first artists in the United States to use lithography as a means of
reproduction, a process that would soon reach such heights with John James Audubon's octavo edition of *The Birds of America.*

Audubon, too, would be a friend of Charles-Lucien. At first the artist was quite
awed by "Prince Charles." But in time, Audubon would honor Charles-Lucien more
for his knowledge than his title: "To no one on Earth have I spoken so openly as I
now do to you . . . yourself knows better than any Man [,] being the best judge, that
I am not a Learned Naturalist . . . I am no Scholar of any kind and I have no
Pretension."[12] But in spite of Audubon's appreciation of Charles as a scientist and
"best judge," the two men were often at odds, perhaps because both had such large
egos.

There is no record of Audubon having visited Point Breeze, but another naturalist friend of Charles that Joseph would have met was an older man, William Maclure,
who occasionally sailed up the Delaware from Philadelphia to visit him with Reuben
Haines, secretary of the Academy of Natural Sciences of Philadelphia where Charles
made most of his friends. Maclure, a pioneering geologist originally from Scotland,
was also a philanthropist and social reformer, who joined the Welshman Robert
Owen in his "utopian" venture of New Harmony, Indiana. Maclure's interest was in
education, while Owen planned to reorganize society according to his own ideas of
equality and mutual benefit, what he called "a new moral world." This new moral
world, whose philosophy also attracted the English reformer Frances Wright, would
come under attack when Owen advocated free love and the banning of marriage.

Owen visited Point Breeze in early July 1825. A young man who went with him
recorded in his journal that Joseph Bonaparte had been most anxious to make
Owen's acquaintance and had "sent his carriage down to the landing place on the
banks of the Delaware to receive him." The journalist added, "Mr. Owen was accompanied by Mr. Say the naturalist. They sat inside the carriage & Lucien & Murat's
sons [Charles Bonaparte and Lucien Murat] on the box, one driving & the other
opening the gates." He concluded that the party was "much interested and delighted"
with Owen's plans and promised to visit New Harmony the following year.[13]

This they never did. The small town on the frontier was an arduous journey
from Bordentown, New Jersey, and, in any case, the experiment in community living

scarcely lasted two years. Philadelphian Deborah Logan noted that she had seen in the papers a notice of Owen's Fourth of July "impious rhodomontade . . . with some proper strictures upon its poisonous doctrines. How any woman of piety and good feeling can bring herself to stay at his odious establishment, I know not. But I think he has now completely thrown aside the vail which has covered his deformity."[14]

New Harmony did, however, continue as a town. Joseph, familiar as he was with the plight of Charles and Henri Lallemand's Champ d'Asile in Texas, may have had his doubts about the prospects of another questionable settlement in the wild. But plans for utopian communities were rife in the nineteenth century, and some, like Brook Farm in New England, became famous for attracting great writers like Nathaniel Hawthorne. In any case, Point Breeze served as a meeting place for talented individuals, all of whom were making a contribution in one way or another.

Charles would make a significant mark on American ornithology. The large collection of western birds that Thomas Say had brought back from the Long Expedition to the Rocky Mountains in 1820 was still undescribed for science when Charles arrived in the United States three years later. What perfect luck for a budding, mostly self-taught ornithologist to have such a rich collection at his disposal waiting to be scientifically described. In 1825, he would publish the first of three volumes, entitled *American Ornithology; or, The Natural History of Birds Inhabiting the United States, not given by Wilson.* Alexander Wilson had brought out the first book on American birds published by an American, beginning in 1808, but he had died in 1813.

While hunting in the woods at Point Breeze, Charles was not shooting birds for sport, but for science. These specimens he would stuff himself, or else give them to Titian Peale, Charles Willson Peale's naturalist son, who was not only a taxidermist but an artist as well. He would draw most of the illustrations for Charles's book.

In later years, Charles Bonaparte would be considered the father of descriptive ornithology in America because of his book's scientific approach—surprisingly, since he was a foreigner who needed help with the English language. A Philadelphia scientist would write in 1899: "As an ornithologist Bonaparte was by far the most celebrated [of his day], and though only twenty-two . . . had already published the first volume of American Ornithology and laid the foundations for the study of nomenclature and synonymy which has to this day developed to such formidable proportions."[15]

In 1830, an English ornithologist, William Swainson, would honor Charles by naming a bird after him. Swainson wrote that it gave him "great pleasure" to name a small black-headed gull that had recently been discovered on a British expedition to the Arctic, *Larus bonapartii* (Bonaparte's gull).[16] Charles would later immortalize his wife in the designation of a more common bird. The scientific name for the ubiquitous mourning dove is *Zenaida macroura*. In 1849, he would write to her: "Zénaïde lives! . . . It is at all times so delightful to think that a thousand years from now this mark of my esteem and of my tenderness will live on with this lovely species."[17]

Along with his brilliant son-in-law, Joseph's two gifted daughters—Charlotte with her art and Zénaïde with her musical ability, for she was quite a harpist, and also a linguist who translated the works of Schiller into French—enhanced his life with their acquaintances and connections, especially their bewitching new friend from Paris.

Chapter 10 EMILIE

*We understand each other so well! We would be so happy living
together, we could see each other to the end of the world!*
—Joseph Bonaparte to Emilie Lacoste, Point
Breeze, 8 July 1826

The first of August 1824, Charlotte boarded the American ship *Crisis* bound
for London. From there she would go on to Brussels. Much to her regret at
leaving the lively, stimulating household at Point Breeze, Charlotte had two reasons
for returning to Europe: her duty to her mother, whose health was as unsteady as
ever, and her impending marriage to her cousin Napoleon-Louis Bonaparte. Joseph
must have particularly regretted her leaving, perhaps because she had a more adven-
turesome and romantic temperament than Zénaïde. After all, she had been the first
to risk crossing the Atlantic, without family, in the uncomfortable and hazardous
sailing vessel of those days, and had fallen in love with the handsome captain. Thus
she may have understood her father's romantic entanglements better than her somewhat straight-laced sister, whose rigidity is well depicted in Jacques-Louis David's
portrait of the two women.

The day of Charlotte's departure, Joseph wrote a letter to her mentor, David, to
be delivered by Charlotte on her arrival in Brussels. David was then seventy-five and
would live for another year and a half. "I cannot see my daughter leave for Brussels,"
Joseph said, "without remembering all the interest with which you have motivated
her and without expressing my gratitude to you. She will tell you that your fame had
crossed the Atlantic before us, but it has only been since our arrival that your works
have been here [his own collection] and could justify your *gloire*."[1]

A year earlier, Joseph had heard from David: "My Prince, I have received the
letter with which you have honored me; it was brought to me by the countess, your

wife. I will keep it as a precious witness of the esteem you have for me." He said Joseph had made him aware that his works were admired in the New World, but he takes only a modest part of this credit and "leaves all the glory to those illustrious persons who have represented it." Referring to Charlotte, he said, "I often think of her and of her fine aptitude [*heureuses dispositions*], that I would have had great pleasure in cultivating if she had stayed near me. But alas! All that recalls to me those days of triumph and glory are far away and I only live with memories; but they will be embellished by the certainty that you remember me with interest and that you believe me, with the most profound respect, etc."[2] David would be best known in America for his enormous painting of Napoleon's coronation, which toured the country in 1826 and 1827.[3] It is probable that the arch-republican David was closer to Joseph than to Napoleon. David's depiction of classical heroes from the time of Rome's Republic with their Spartan austerity, severity, and self-sacrifice were intrinsically subversive of the imperial ethos. Joseph would have been sympathetic with David's republicanism, while Napoleon preferred the outright propaganda of David's students, François Gérard, Antoine Gros, and Jean-Auguste Ingres.

Joseph had no idea when he would see Lolotte again, and there was something ominous and troubling in the vessel's name of *Crisis*. Emma and Mathieu Sari were sent along to accompany Charlotte on the trip. The Saris' assignment, in addition to serving as traveling companions, was to attend to the sale of Joseph's château in Switzerland. Zénaïde's dowry, an exorbitant amount of 700,000 francs demanded by the avaricious Lucien, had depleted Joseph's coffers, and he now needed to raise money for Charlotte's dowry. Julie had put the estate on the market in 1821 for 500,000 francs, but it had not yet sold.

The château of Prangins had been a refuge when Joseph bought it in late June 1814, after Napoleon's exile to Elba when it was unsafe for the ex-king of Spain to remain in France. While Julie was still in Paris with the children, Joseph stayed at a friend's château, Allaman, near Lausanne. When Joseph was unable to buy Allaman, he considered purchasing the château of Prangins instead (fig. 27). He had still not decided on this sale when he wrote Julie laying out the various alternatives open to them. "I have always thought of Florence as a possibility," he had stated, prophetically. "The future events of Naples are uncertain and the nearness of Rome does not render our stay there convenient, it is thus of Florence, or Venice we must think." But, he says, they must consider the fact that the Bourbons would not allow him to be so near France. And her health and the children's would not permit them to live at Mortefontaine during the winter because of the cold. Therefore, he suggests they acquire Prangins, where he would be content with a domain on the border of the

27. **Le Château de Prangins,** *vu du village,* artist unknown, c. 1820. Château de Prangins, Switzerland.

lake of Geneva, a place where he could walk every day.[4] But Joseph had lived at Prangins for less than a year when Napoleon escaped from Elba and Joseph joined him in Paris. Julie stayed on with her children before returning to Paris to be with her sister Désirée. She subsequently moved to Frankfurt, then Brussels. Now she was thinking of moving to Florence because of the milder climate and because other Bonapartes were there, particularly Louis and his son, Charlotte's intended.

Soon after Charlotte's reunion with her mother in Brussels, she and Julie obtained passports for Italy from Chateaubriand, minister of foreign affairs, at the request of Julie's friend Madame Recamier. In Rome, mother and daughter established themselves at the beautiful Villa Paolina that Pauline Borghese, who died the year before, had willed to Napoleon-Louis, knowing he would marry Charlotte. It was there Charlotte first met her fiancé.

At first she was not pleased with him. He seemed immature, and he confused her with banter and teasing that she at times found insufferable. For his part, he found Charlotte especially defensive, seeming to wish to receive love more than to give it, and lacking a sense of humor. In a letter to a cousin where he declared himself a republican and made fun of his father's ex-royalty (Louis Bonaparte had been king of Holland), he showed a light-heartedness that Charlotte, so proud of her Bonaparte name, would not have appreciated.[5]

The marriage contract was signed by the two parents, Julie and Louis, in June 1825, but Charlotte delayed the wedding for an entire year and did not hide her reasons. She continued to find Napoleon-Louis too young (he was two years younger than she), and his appearance reminded her of their mutual cousin, Achille Murat. This was distinctly unflattering since Zénaïde, in Philadelphia, had once described Achille to her mother as having the face of a monkey and the manners of a pig (*la figure d'un singe et les manières d'un cochon*).[6] According to one no doubt biased account, Achille, who lived in Florida, never washed, ate alligators and turkey buzzards, and used his shaggy dog as a spittoon.[7]

Finally in early 1826, Charlotte agreed to visit Louis and his son—who was actually very different from his cousin Achille—in Florence with her mother, but first she insisted on taking the baths at Pisa. Napoleon-Louis met them there and the betrothed young couple changed their minds about each other. Joseph must have been pleased to hear that the wedding had at last taken place in July.

As sad as Joseph was to see his younger daughter depart America, there was a decided compensation not only in the presence of Zénaïde, Charles, and little Joseph, but also in the person of Emilie Lacoste. Though Joseph, at fifty-five, no longer had the slim figure of his youth, he still had a young face, Old World elegance, and *savoir faire*. These attributes, combined with a dramatic past history, royal titles, and the prestige of his name, entirely seduced the vivacious Emilie. Zénaïde and Charles were conveniently removed in the Maison du Lac and completely occupied with their own lives, Zénaïde raising little Joseph and practicing the harp, and Charles writing a book on American birds in which he was struggling to express himself in English.[8] He had so little in common with his father-in-law that they would not have spent time together except perhaps for hunting and attending meetings at the American Philosophical Society. Félix Lacoste was safely in Saint Domingue attending to his business interests. And Anna, at this point, may have gone to Paris with her little daughter, Caroline Charlotte, to find a new life; perhaps equipped with an introduction to the man she would soon marry. Thus the debonair Count de Survilliers was quite free to pursue his affair with Félix Lacoste's attractive wife.

Two months after Charlotte's departure, on 26 September 1824, a special event took place at Point Breeze. General Lafayette, renowned hero of the American Revolution, on his triumphal tour of the United States as a guest of the government, paid

Joseph Bonaparte a visit. Accompanied only by the governor of New Jersey and his secretary, Lafayette arrived by carriage without escort after having spent the night in Trenton. (He would arrive with much more ceremony the following July.) How delighted the general must have been to encounter the sparkling Emilie Lacoste, whom he had often met in Paris at her aunt's soirees. Though Zénaïde was Joseph's official hostess, it was decidedly Emilie who charmed the general and brought off the visit with great success.

Was it beginning to show, however, that Emilie was four months pregnant, especially since she was destined to have twins? And did Lafayette wonder how long her husband had been in Saint Domingue? Emilie, on first discovering her pregnancy, had called her husband back briefly from the Caribbean, ostensibly to discuss business with the count, so there had been no suspicion cast on her host.[9]

In any event, the ex-king and the famous general and statesman had much to discuss concerning the situation in France. Lafayette had opposed the empire of Napoleon—as had Joseph himself—and after Waterloo had called for Napoleon's abdication, stating in the Chamber of Deputies that since 1805 Napoleon had caused the deaths of three million Frenchmen. But he had since changed his mind about the Bourbons and expressed to Joseph his regret at having concurred with the restoration. The monarchy of Louis XVIII had proved repressive and retrograde in every way, and after all, Lafayette, a republican, had fought in the American Revolution against a king, George III of England. At the time Joseph and Lafayette were conferring on the future of France, Louis XVIII, brother of the beheaded Louis XVI, was recently dead, but the news had not yet reached the United States. His younger brother, Charles X, succeeded him. When Lafayette returned to Point Breeze the next summer there would be even more to talk about.

The following July, Lafayette would express his belief that the dynasty of the Bourbons could not survive. He told Joseph that all were persuaded in France that only Napoleon's son, the Duke of Reichstadt, then thirteen and living with his grandfather, the Emperor of Austria, in Vienna, could represent the interests of the French Revolution. If Joseph would place two million francs at the disposal of his committee, Lafayette promised that in two years Napoleon II would be on the throne of France. But Joseph refused, thinking the Bourbon monarchy too firmly ensconced and the time not ripe to restore popular rights for the French.[10] In five years the situation would be very different and both men's ideas would change dramatically.

In early March 1825 Joseph met with a nasty accident that laid him up for months. He was traveling to Trenton when his horses suddenly bolted, overturning the carriage and throwing him to the road. When he tried to stand, he fainted, for his knee was badly fractured. By chance, a doctor was passing in his cabriolet and took him at once to the nearby Delaware Hotel where he stayed until June.[11] It must have been disconcerting for Joseph to be laid up in bed for months so near the recent passionate and tragic scenes at Bow Hill and Pine Grove of his past love. But that affair was all over now and Anna, totally estranged from the count, was in Paris with certain introductions, money to live on, and a quantity of jewelry that he had given her.[12] Joseph must have felt it particularly unfortunate to be away from home just then because Emilie's pregnancy was nearing term.

On 22 March 1825, in Philadelphia, where Joseph's entire entourage was spending the winter, Emilie gave birth to twin boys. Since her husband was at Port au Prince and would not return until the beginning of May, perhaps it was just as well that the Count de Survilliers was confined to Trenton. Yet no one seems to have suspected that Joseph was the father, at least no one outside the family. There is no indication that Zénaïde had any idea that her father had sired her friend Emilie's babies. Emma Sari's mother, Madame St. Georges, made no allusion to such suspicion when she wrote to her daughter Emma in Europe about her visit to see "Mme Lacoste" and the twins on 17 April. Had she known, this would have been an irresistible bit of gossip. She reported only that the two large babies were sleeping in the same cradle, one at the head and the other at the foot.[13] But in Emilie's correspondence to Joseph and to Mailliard, she would make the paternity quite clear. In a letter to Mailliard some years later when Joseph had returned to America from a stay in England, Emilie expressed her concern that Joseph would never return to Europe: "I would then lose all hope of seeing him again and of speaking to him of his son."[14] Only one twin survived, however. He was christened Félix-Joseph, the child's second name given in deference to his godfather, the Count de Survilliers.

During the summer months of 1825, the Lacostes, with their children—Léon, then about five years old, and the infant Félix-Joseph—stayed at Point Breeze while the count with Zénaïde and Charles, after Lafayette's visit, journeyed to the spas at Saratoga and Ballston, as well as to the count's Black River lands.

Toward the end of 1825 the Lacoste family moved to New York City. Perhaps to celebrate the New Year, Joseph wrote to Félix at the end of December to make arrangements at a boardinghouse for himself, Zénaïde and Charles, and his guest Count Miot de Melito, a statesman who had been attached to Joseph since 1806 and his guest at Point Breeze since the previous summer. He said he was sending ahead his chef, François, and that the dining room should be on the first floor near the stairs. He continued with instructions for Félix on the distribution of the rooms and sent his kind regards (*amitiés*) to "Madame" and "M. Léon."[15] But something must have gone wrong because he informed Zénaïde from New York that he was not happy with the arrangements for her. He and Monsieur Melito were not finding things to their satisfaction in New York and he planned to leave the next day if his carriage was ready.[16]

Back at Point Breeze several weeks later, he again wrote Zénaïde, who was pregnant and staying at his townhouse in Philadelphia. In the letter he is very concerned with her health and says it pains him that she was not well when he had left her, presumably on his return from New York. "All that I said and wrote to you stemmed from my fatherly love for you," he explains with true concern. "It is not good timing for you to be pregnant three times in one year. I must repeat to you what I already said a few months ago about what your husband asks of you. At your age you should begin to think of yourself, of your own *conservation*—your husband has his passions that need to be regulated in accordance with the need to maintain your health. This means that you must grow up a bit yourself, because it is the nature of the passions one has for the woman one loves to pursue her always in order to show her one's affection."[17] Charles no doubt saw this letter because he and Zénaïde were particularly close early in their marriage, or even if she had only referred to it in some way, it would certainly have infuriated him, since he was not on the best of terms with his father-in-law to begin with and he would have seen Joseph's admonitions to his daughter as interference in his marriage. Charles was at all times touchy and hot-headed and did not take criticism easily. And, according to Joseph's letter, this was not the first time he had admonished his son-in-law for his "passion."

Joseph's advice to Zénaïde comes from the heart, however. Not only is it dictated by his love for his daughter, who had given birth to a weak baby girl the previous June, but also from his own situation: He was himself in the throes of passion. The "kind regards" he had sent to Madame Lacoste was hardly the expression for what he was feeling about Emilie.

The following July he wrote to apologize for sending her a love letter that Félix had apparently seen. (He had thought Félix was in Saint Domingue.) Yet Joseph could not resist placing some of the blame on Emilie herself, for she has the bad habit of letting her husband unseal her letters. But he admits there are things he should not have written her since their separation. He was only answering what she had asked in her confidential letter to him, and he had waited twenty days at least, having guessed that Félix had seen an earlier imprudent missive. He will write to her again using the pretext of the return of Monsieur Melito, who has already been there for eight days. "I hope that will succeed in calming the jealousy and pride of your husband who I am distressed to have injured [*d'avoir affligé*], although to tell the truth,

I do not recall having pushed things to such a point." He continues, "Four years ago I would have said many things that I no longer dare to say to you today. You assure me that I exercised much power over you; that you could have loved me. I have done better than that and truly say to you, though you have not perhaps preserved the memory, that I believe you have not been sorry and that you did all that was possible to bewitch me. I have been horribly upset by your departure . . . ah! That you are not still beside me! We understand each other so well! We would be so happy living together, we could see each other to the end of the world!"

Now that she has children, new loves have distracted her and all has changed.

> You see another heaven . . . another earth, while I stay where I am, where I knew you, where I loved you, where I am reminded every instant of you by all that surrounds me. Ah! I tell you all that is still with me! But it no longer means anything to you. Four years ago you found me charming but now we are separated forever. I will not see you any more—fate has decided it. You will stay where you are, or you will only return when I am no more. Keep at least some memory of your friend. Remember the hours, the entire days together. How short they were for me! They were my last beautiful days, though I grow old one could still have some flirtations, but your memory will shield my poor heart. I cannot let go in spite of myself of a sentiment that must appear ridiculous to you today. Adieu, dear Emily, think of me sometimes, and pardon the involuntary pain that I have caused you. But above all, do not let this letter lie about. I would not be the guilty one this time. I kiss you with all my heart.[18]

This is certainly the letter of an aging lover who mourns not only the loss of his *amour,* but of his youth and vigor as well. But Joseph was only fifty-eight, and one wonders if there is not hyperbole in his sentiments. He had always had a flair for the dramatic and had enjoyed declaiming the classics in a stirring voice. The ex-king had a long history of mistresses and no doubt had grown adept at passionate love letters. His own brother Napoleon was quoted as saying that Joseph had "an evil reputation with women."[19] And there is such an abrupt switch in tone in his closing admonition to Emilie not to be careless with this letter so that Félix sees it, that one gets a glimpse of the practical man who does not want any unpleasantness. Although his affair with Emilie was ending, he did not want to disrupt his friendship with Félix, who handled certain business transactions for him. Félix's affairs in Saint Dominigue had taken a bad turn and he would be forced to close his establishment in 1826. Joseph had set him up financially in a New York commercial house and their friendship would continue until the count's death. Félix apparently never suspected that the Count de Survilliers was the father of his second son.

Since Emilie could no longer remain at Point Breeze and New York did not offer her the stimulating life she had led in Paris, she longed to return to France. She wrote her friend, Béranger, whom she had known at her aunt's soirées in Paris, that she must return home in the spring or else she would die from the pain of being away.[20] Toward the end of April 1827, Emilie, Félix, and their young son Félix-Joseph embarked for Le Havre. They left the eight-year-old Léon in a boarding school in New York with Joseph's promise to look after him.

Joseph wrote Emilie upon her arrival in France that he hoped her stay in her native land would not make her forget "*modeste* Jersey" and that she would preserve those sentiments she had shown him in her letter and that he had always known she had for him. He says there have been many visitors since her departure but none have replaced the friendships of five years. Achille (Murat) has been there for a month with this wife, and although she is sweet and charming she does not speak a word of French and her family of six or seven persons who have visited for ten days do not speak French either, "so you can see that our conversations are not very spirited [*animées*]."[21]

He mentions the songs of Béranger, to whom Joseph's brother, Lucien, had once given a small pension early in his career. "We admire your friend every evening for his truly original genius," he says, "since we read two or three of his charming songs from the collection you gave Zénaïde." When the group gathered in the salon after dinner to sing Béranger's works, Zénaïde must have provided accompaniment on the harp.[22]

To Félix, Joseph wrote in September that he was afraid Zénaïde would be leaving on the first ship for either Livorno or Liverpool and thus he would be more alone than ever. Charles, who had been in Europe pursuing his research in natural science since the previous fall, had just returned and was anxious to take his family back to Italy as soon as possible. Joseph, dreading this impending departure, wrote unabashedly to Félix: "If you think [Emilie] would not miss Paris too much, I would be delighted if your affairs and also your pleasure brought you back to Point Breeze." And to Emilie he wrote the same day: "Monsieur Lacoste allows me to hope that you

will not wait long in returning to America." To entice her, he suggests she bring
Béranger with her. "His society would be as agreeable as yours. And if my place
makes him feel that he is too far from Paris, *eh bien!* When he returns he will see it
with more joy. Knowing what I do of him, I hope he will not be too discontented
with Point Breeze, and at least he will be enchanted by your singing his songs."[23] The
old seductive charm is still much in evidence.

But Emilie was in her element in Paris, and without a backward glance at Point
Breeze she promptly resumed the festive existence she had led prior to her sojourn
in the United States. Félix was shortly called to London on business, and in his absence Emilie abandoned herself to the attentions of her old friend, the writer Prosper
Mérimée. At the beginning of 1828, Félix returned to Paris, discovered his wife's
affair, and challenged Mérimée to a duel. Félix was unhurt, but he shot Mérimée in
the left arm. (The writer had requested that Félix aim for his left rather than his right
arm, and being a gentleman, Félix had complied.)[24] This was virtually the end of the
Lacostes' marriage. They separated, Félix returned to London, and Emilie continued
her affair with Mérimée even more intensely.

She was still corresponding with Joseph and wrote to him the following April in
answer to a letter from him in February; this time with more tender feelings toward
him than she had had since quitting the United States, because her life had recently
taken a downward turn: "You now know of the storm that has erupted; your good
and tender advice arrived too late. I have been relegated to my father with a pension
of 1,500 francs to take care of my little Félix and myself. If I have to live under such
strict economy, be sure that I will give up everything rather than have the poor child
lack for a thing. I love him passionately. He brings back such happy memories. His
face is charming. He resembles you. His character is yours. If you could see him you
would love him. I do not despair of bringing him to you some day. Certainly I will
see you again."[25]

However, there had definitely been a sea change in the relationship between
Emilie and the Count de Survilliers. With her marriage in ruins, her interest in Méri-
mée now fast evaporating, and her finances at low ebb, she was the one in despair.
"It seems that you must still take an interest in me," she says.

> I am perhaps under an illusion, but the past is there, I cannot
> forget it. You could write me if you wish, I am alone and totally
> free. How happy I would be to receive news of you, how much I
> wish you happiness! I have renounced it for myself; I have no de-

sires except for you and for my children. I expect Léon at the end of the month, but he will not be given to me and his father wants him as far from me as possible. I will see him however and go to his school. I am very happy that he leaves me Félix, but if he had wanted to take him away, I believe I would have told him the truth. Adieu, it is useless to assure you of my sentiments, the gratitude, the tenderness, the regrets, the remorse, all that tortures me and I have not a moment of repose. I beg you, write to me in total confidence and safety."[26]

Although the liaison with Prosper Mérimée lasted a while after the duel, in time Emilie rejected him as a lover. He suffered profoundly over the loss of her affection and in February 1830, in Paris, published a short story, *Le Vase étrusque* (*The Etruscan Vase*) with Emilie as the heroine, according to a letter from Hortense Allart to the critic Sainte-Beuve (fig. 28).[27] In the story, the hero, Saint-Clair, is killed in a duel resulting from a mistaken assumption about the faithlessness of his loved one, the countess Mathilde de Coursy, and she, innocent, dies of a broken heart.

A real-life event was the source of the scene where Saint-Clair accuses Mathilde of unfaithfulness. Mérimée, told at a party of Emilie's liaison with Joseph Bonaparte, afterward confronted her with the truth. She had represented Joseph simply as a respectable old man who had been kind to her and her husband, so he was crushed by the revelation of their love affair (fig. 29).[28] Mérimée wrote in his story: "Saint-Clair thought he heard a voice whisper in his ear: 'The special honor of being the successor . . .' He sat up on the couch and glanced wildly about him. How glad he would have been to have found someone in the room! Unquestionably he would have torn him to pieces."[29] As it turns out, Mérimée's heroine is innocent of any involvement with his suspected rival, wishful thinking on the author's part perhaps.

Félix returned to New York at the end of that year and occasionally spent time at Point Breeze with Joseph. In November 1829, with the count's patronage, he would found a journal, *Le Courrier des États-Unis*, in New York. The paper would concern itself with Joseph's political opinions, his ongoing petitions that the Bonaparte family be allowed back into France, and refutation of the many calumnies against his famous brother.

Emilie, the *femme fatale* and muse to an eminent writer, was no doubt undone by her unbounded charm and the inconstancy of her affection. But the one attachment she would hold onto for years would be to the ex-king of Spain, the father of her beloved Félix-Joseph.

28. **"Auguste Saint-
Clair and the
Countess Mathilde
de Coursy,"** *from Le
vase étrusque* by Prosper
Mérimée (Paris: Henry
Babou, 1930). Photo: Lisa
Tyson Ennis.

29. **"Saint-Clair after learning about the older man in Mathilde de Coursy's life,"** *from* Le vase étrusque *by* Prosper Mérimée. Photo: Lisa Tyson Ennis.

Chapter 11 CONNOISSEUR AND
COLLECTOR

Roaming through the different apartments of the mansion through a
suite of rooms 15 ft. in [height] decorated with the finest productions
of the pencils of Coregeo Titian! Rubens! Vandyke! Vernet! Tenniers
and Paul Potter and a library of the most splendid books I ever beheld.
—Reuben Haines to Ann Haines, Wyck,
Germantown, 3 July 1825

A Philadelphia newspaper reported in March 1827 that Joseph Bonaparte
had contributed one thousand francs for a monument to Jacques-Louis
David, who had died near the end of 1825. Joseph was a grateful admirer of David,
not only for outstanding services to his brother but also for the beautiful painting of
his two daughters and the art instruction he had given them in Brussels. Joseph's
patronage of the arts was an important aspect of his life in the New World and no
doubt his greatest contribution to the culture of the young republic.

The masterpieces of European art he had collected in France, and particularly in
Spain (see plate 10), were openly displayed at Point Breeze. At that time the general
public did not understand the value of such great works of art. As Joseph had told
his brother Lucien, "one could not buy a Raphael for one hundred dollars or a Titian
for ten thousand." Samuel F. B. Morse wrote to his wife from New York in 1814 that
"A fine painting or a marble statue is very rare in the houses of the rich in this city
. . . individuals who would not pay fifty pounds for either expend double that sum
to vie with a neighbor for a piece of furniture."[1] Fortunately, there would have been
no underground market for such paintings as Joseph Bonaparte possessed, even had
the value of them been understood. The Count de Survilliers welcomed artists, profes-

sional and amateur, as well as interested friends, neighbors, and sightseers from Philadelphia to view his collections of paintings and sculpture. And he was more than generous in loaning his works year after year to the annual exhibitions of the Pennsylvania Academy of the Fine Arts. Not only was there risk of damage, but he also had to live with the empty walls usually occupied by such monumental paintings as the David of *Napoleon Crossing the Alps*, the huge Snyders of *Young Lions and a Fawn*, and the two full-length portraits of Joseph and of Julie with her daughters by Gérard. All four of these pictures were listed in the academy's exhibition of May 1826, as well as marble busts by Antonio Canova of Madame Mère, Napoleon, and Pauline Borghese. And Joseph was in residence at Point Breeze in May when these works were loaned, having moved from his winter abode in Philadelphia and not yet departed for his northern lands, or to the Saratoga and Ballston spas.

The month before the Pennsylvania Academy's 1826 exhibition opening, the highly regarded Philadelphia artist Thomas Sully visited Point Breeze to see the count's art collection. No doubt what he saw influenced his own work. On viewing Joseph's several Titians, Sully noted in his journal: "Titian's plan does not appear to me to produce splendour of colouring by employing the brightest colours, but by the judicious and artful use of sober tints, and the practice of toning and glazing them. I am now speaking of the impression made upon me by an inspection of those [paintings] examined on this occasion." After technical remarks on flesh tones, he went on to jot down his ideas on the mythological *Tarquin and Lucretia* (see plate 9), originally bought in 1571 by Philip II of Spain. The painting had hung in the Alcazar in Madrid for two hundred years, then in two other royal palaces in Madrid before being taken to Paris in 1813 by Joseph and subsequently shipped to the United States: "It is remarkable how much glazing has been used in the Lucretia, which I examined closely, even the whole drapery has been glazed or toned down. The effect is a subdued splendour, far preferable to the oily smoothness of the opposite system. Absorbent canvas seems to have been used; the colours much loaded." Sully noticed that, "in large pictures very sober colours may be employed to produce richness of effect."

In examining a "deer-chase" by Velázquez, Sully observed that the picture had "very much the aspect of a Titian, but there is not so much display of glazing and process; the unity of the tone seemed effected by beginning the whole picture with one colour for the shade, and one for the light, which are afterwards finished upon." Of a Murillo, he thought it looked "dirty and clouded in the tone and in the flesh; except in small pictures of a portrait size, *there* the flesh was rich and natural." And a Guido Reni to him looked "hard and liny after Titian, and very cold and weak." He added that, "The large pictures of Rubens have much of Titian's good colour in them, although generally of a higher scale.”[2] In 1809 Sully had been to London, where he was befriended by the distinguished American expatriate painter Benjamin West and had studied many masterpieces in galleries and private collections, so he was well acquainted with great works of art with which to compare those of the Count de Survilliers.

The count not only welcomed established artists to his house, but encouraged unknowns as well. George Robert Bonfield (1805-1898), apprenticed as a young man to a marble cutter, was once sent to Point Breeze on an assignment. At times he stole a few moments to study and sketch the magnificent paintings that surrounded him. One day as he was drawing a detail of Claude-Joseph Vernet's *Shipwreck*, Joseph discovered him and asked to see the notebook the young man hastily tried to hide. Impressed by the stonecutter's talent, Joseph gave him permission to sketch whatever he liked.[3]

The Count de Survilliers's art collection had come from many sources. Certain paintings, particularly French, had been bought in Paris during the consulate and empire periods, others had been gifts for services and favors rendered to Spanish grandees sympathetic to France, but a majority of his finest masterpieces Joseph, as king, must have taken from the Spanish royal collections. According to art historian Isadora Rose de Viejo, in January 1808 when Joseph ascended the throne there were 1,100 paintings in the royal palace in Madrid, while in October 1813, after his departure, only 381 remained.[4] However, before he was forced to leave Spain, Joseph had sincerely tried to foster the arts there, he had recognized the genius of Goya and had even persuaded him to direct a future museum. Goya was an *afrancesado* (a person sympathetic to the French) who accepted Joseph's patronage as willingly as he had accepted that of Joseph's predecessor Charles IV. Legend has it that instigated by King Joseph, Goya designed the "suit of lights," the traditional matador costume worn up to the present. Certainly Joseph would have sympathized with Goya's attitude toward war depicted some years later in the artist's devastating series of prints, *Los desastres de la guerra*.[5] One can only wonder why Joseph had no works by Goya in his own collections.

As for the masterpieces of world art Joseph attempted to spirit out of Spain, the English nation would have to be indirectly grateful to him because of his defeat at the battle of Vitoria in northern Spain on 21 June 1813. For when the Duke of Wellington, as head of the English forces assisting Spanish resistors to drive out the occupying French, captured Joseph's abandoned wagon train as the ex-king escaped on horseback, one of the coaches was found stuffed not only with state papers, a few love letters, and a sterling silver chamber pot, but also with more than two hundred paintings taken from the royal palaces, cut from their stretchers and rolled up for easier transport to France. In addition, there were a number of drawings and engravings. All these works of art the "Iron Duke" sent back to England. The keeper of the Royal Picture Galleries drew up a catalog of the principal paintings and wrote Wellington that it was "a most valuable collection of pictures, one which you could not have conceived." Benjamin West was among the experts who examined the collection and declared many of the paintings of "inestimable" value.[6] Among the works were Jan Bruegel's *Travellers on a Country Road with Pigs and Cattle*, Correggio's *Agony in the Garden*, Velázquez's *Two Men at a Humble Table* and *The Waterseller of Seville*, Vernet's *Sunset: View over a Bay with Figures*, and Titian's *Portrait of a Lady*, as well as, ironically, a portrait of Joseph Bonaparte by Gérard.[7] Wellington subsequently offered to return to Spain the pictures he had sent to England, but the Spanish minister replied that the paintings had been captured fairly in war and the duke should keep them in gratitude for his aide in expelling the French. To this day, these paintings hang at Apsley House, the Duke of Wellington's mansion in Hyde Park, London. One must give Joseph the benefit of the doubt that aside from the Prado Museum in Madrid, the other loser of this large collection was not the ex-king himself, but the Louvre, where one hopes he would have deposited them.

However many masterpieces Joseph lost in the battle, he did manage to elude the capture of his apparent favorites, five Raphaels, a Titian *Venus*, a Guido Reni *Madonna*, a Murillo *Holy Family* and some five others which he got back to Paris. Ironically for Joseph, only two Raphaels were actually by the artist, the other three being entirely of studio execution. He missed the most important Raphael, a small portrait of a cardinal, at the time attributed to a lesser artist.[8] In addition to those paintings removed from Spain, Joseph had Julie and his agents send his personal collection from Mortefontaine outside Paris, such as *Parc de la Mortefontaine*, which he commissioned from Jean-Joseph-Xavier Bidauld in 1806,[9] and others from Prangins, to him in the United States.

Even before Joseph's defeat at Vitoria, the French had taken a large number of works of art from Spain. In 1809, Vivant Denon, the artist who had been to Egypt with Napoleon and was the first director of the Musée Napoleon, the future Louvre, visited Spain and persuaded Joseph Bonaparte to appropriate fifty Spanish masterpieces from the royal collections and from nobles who sided with the exiled king, Ferdinand VII, and send them to France. After Denon's departure, King Joseph issued a decree (20 December 1809) for founding a national gallery in Madrid. But it would be another ten years before the museum would open, and under different auspices.[10] The decree of 1809 also included a provision for sending a collection of

Spanish art to "our august brother, the Emperor of France." Nine months later, the French ambassador in Madrid, the Count de La Forest, wrote that King Joseph had permitted pictures to be taken from the royal palaces in Seville and Cordoba, but not from his palace in Madrid. It would be four years later, in September 1813, that 250 confiscated pictures would arrive at Paris. As they had mostly been selected by the Spanish themselves they were, understandably, not of the first quality.[11]

Several of the masterpieces taken by Joseph are apparently lost. Titian's *St. Sebastian*, said to be life-sized, was recorded as sent by Joseph Bonaparte in 1810 to the palace of San Ildefonso at La Granja, the royal Spanish summer palace in the mountains outside Segovia.[12] Louis Mailliard, in his notes, wrote that on 29 September 1842, Joseph sold his nephew, François Clary, two paintings: Titian's *St. Sebastian* and Correggio's *Virgin with a Rabbit*, for the sum of 20,000 francs.[13] Could the Titian still be somewhere in France?

Another great Titian, *Mary Magdalen in Penitence*, which spent 236 years in the Sacristy of the Escorial, Joseph also sent to San Ildefonso in 1810. The painting was subsequently sold to Alexander Baring, the first Lord Ashburton, possibly some time in the 1820s, in New York, for the 25,000 francs it is listed by Joseph as being worth.[14] The painting would be destroyed by fire in the drawing room of Lord Ashburton's Bath House, Piccadilly, London, in 1873. An account of his collection at Bath House, published in the *Art Union* in 1847, states that he had purchased many pictures from the Count de Survilliers. The *Magdalen* is described in the article as having remained in the Spanish royal collections until it was "abstracted by Joseph Bonaparte, who sold it to Lord Ashburton."[15] *The Stag Hunt* by Velázquez, painted before 1629 and showing Philip IV of Spain and his courtiers hunting stags in an amphitheater before seated spectators, was taken by Joseph from the royal palace in Madrid, brought to America, and later also sold to Lord Ashburton.[16]

He loaned many of these great works of art to various institutions for exhibition where American artists, most of whom were unable to make the Grand Tour of Europe, could study them and derive inspiration. He also patronized local talent, such as Charles Lawrence who painted several pictures of Point Breeze from various aspects, and he hired Bass Otis to paint Anna Savage and their two daughters. Both artists copied the David of Napoleon crossing the Alps. Nicholas Biddle commissioned Otis to paint the David replica and it hangs today at his house, Andalusia. Biddle also hired George Catlin to copy a miniature of Napoleon that belonged to Joseph. When Antoine François Teriggi, a miniaturist who taught drawing in Philadelphia, showed two miniatures at the Pennsylvania Academy's annual exposition of

1820, one was *Tarquin and Lucretia*, no doubt copied from Joseph's painting. Four years later Teriggi exhibited a miniature portrait of Charlotte.[17]

The Pennsylvania Academy of the Fine Arts was the principal benefactor of Joseph's generosity, as was the American Academy of Fine Arts in New York, but other institutions also benefited. In July 1823, the American diplomat Joel Roberts Poinsett, wrote from Charleston, South Carolina, to the Pennsylvania Academy to say he was shipping to them a painting called *Charity*—probably by Andrea del Sarto—and asked that "the count" be thanked for loaning it to the museum in Charleston.[18] In 1825, the Count de Survilliers wrote to Joseph Hopkinson asking that the Pennsylvania Academy make available to a Mr. Robertson, secretary of the New York Academy, two paintings by Salvator Rosa that had previously been sent to "the academy at Charleston."[19]

And in the summer of 1831, he wrote Robert Gilmor, a noted collector of fine art who lived in Baltimore, that after receiving Gilmor's letter he had sent the manager of the Baltimore Museum the twelve paintings he wanted, presumably for an exhibition.[20] Gilmor had once visited Point Breeze with his wife. A card exists from the Count de Survilliers inviting the Gilmors to dine with him at Point Breeze. They are to take the boat that arrives at four o'clock in Bordentown and Point Breeze where they can see the paintings before dinner and the gardens afterward. "We dine at five o'clock," the card from Joseph stated.[21]

Elected a member of the American Academy of Fine Arts in New York in 1825, Joseph loaned many paintings to that institution for the next three years. For its annual exhibitions he sent over *Lion in a Trap* by Peter Paul Rubens; two landscapes by Rosa; and several landscapes by Vernet and others by David Teniers. A Luca Giordano entitled "Amphitrite, with the Spoils of the Ocean" may have been *The Riches of the Sea with Neptune and two Nereids* by Luca Giordano and Giuseppe Recco, a painting that since 1700 had been in the palace of Buen Retiro in Madrid. King Joseph included it in his baggage when he fled the country. This enormous work of art somehow reached the United States and hung at Point Breeze.[22]

It is difficult to identify with any certainty the pictures that were exhibited in the various academies because the descriptions are so scanty, and as an art historian has said, "it is a safe guess to infer that the attributions were 'enthusiastic.' The unscrupulous had an easy time of it in foisting rubbish with success and impunity. It was an uncritical age; dealers, collectors, and public were all more or less uninformed."[23]

In 1828, a writer for the *Evening Post* complained that the exhibit at the New York Academy was a collection of good and bad "from the rich and glowing pencils of Sir T. Lawrence and [John] Trumbull, down to the leaden caricatures of Parisen and Catlin." He lamented that "there were *huge* copies and *little* copies, and *whole* copies, and *half* copies, and *good* copies, and *bad* copies; indeed [it] is a sort of Noah's Ark, in which [are] things of every kind, *clean* and *unclean*, noble animals, and *creeping things.*"²⁴ The paintings belonging to Joseph Bonaparte were no doubt among the "noble animals" since they had, for the most part, come from Spain's royal palaces, bought by previous monarchs. And the copies, of which there were many both good and bad from Joseph's collection, were certainly part of the development of American art.

As well as the great paintings Joseph Bonaparte had at Point Breeze was a magnificent Greek amphora, probably made in Athens about 530 B.C., and given to him by Lucien, who may have dug it up at his estate in Canino outside Rome. In London, on 26 May 1833, Joseph wrote to General Thomas Cadwalader in Philadelphia to present him with the amphora, referring to it as an "Etruscan vase," no doubt described this way by Lucien.²⁵

As time went on, Joseph's expenditures multiplied in developing his house and gardens at Point Breeze, as well as in maintaining his princely lifestyle and providing large dowries for his daughters, and the constant expenses of supporting Charles and Zénaïde. For Joseph and Charles, money was a point of contention. Charles's father, Lucien, was supposed to give the young couple the interest on a mortgage he had taken out on his estate at Canino outside Rome, after keeping Zénaïde's dowry for himself, but he sent them nothing. Joseph resented the support of his son-in-law, and with good reason after the enormous dowry he had given his daughter. He apparently made it quite obvious.

In November 1824, Charles wrote his father that his uncle complains constantly (*se plait toujours*) about the expenses of his daughters and the modest amount of his fortune. Because of the huge inconvenience of Charlotte's dowry, Joseph has told them he cannot, or will not—Charles says it comes to the same thing—do more for him and Zénaïde. "What's more," Charles says, "he signified to us that while we are visiting here, if you do not pay part of the interest on the dowry that you have promised in the contract, he would want us to leave sooner rather than later." Charles says he has tried to persuade his uncle that it is inconvenient at the moment for Lucien to send money, but his uncle says that the entire world tells him Lucien doesn't intend to pay a cent while he and Zénaïde are with him. "You know my character well enough," Charles concludes, "that the day that becomes a certainty [that Lucien will never support them], I will not stay twenty-four hours with him."²⁶

The following summer he tells Lucien that he doesn't even have spending money. "You judge what our situation is, deprived of all pecuniary assistance, in spite of Zénaïde's large dowry. We are obliged to undergo privations of the most disagreeable kinds and we find ourselves in complete misery and total dependence. My uncle has given his daughter one hundred dollars in charity so we can pay our servants and some of the expenses of our little menage." He continues, even more agitated: "Do you want me to bury myself like all the others [his naturalist friends] in the forests of Indiana [New Harmony], or Missouri to live by the toil of my hands cultivating the wild land bought dirt cheap, or accept the chair of professor in some university of the United States? . . . If you can't support us here we will come to you."[27]

In addition to his money problems, Charles the serious scientist was constantly irritated by what he considered the frivolity of endless entertaining at Point Breeze and the social scene at spas. He had just returned from Saratoga Springs, from where he had written his colleague Isaac Hays that at eleven o'clock at night, "500 people below are dancing like fools! At a great rate!" For these reasons it was quite clear that Charles and Joseph were daily becoming more seriously incompatible.

Charles decided to make a trip to Europe in the late fall of 1826 to meet with ornithologists in England and the continent, to further his scientific studies by examining various collections of birds, but, most important, to confer with his father in Rome about his financial future. For Joseph, convinced that he needed to raise considerable moneys, the only method to accomplish this was to sell some of his art collection. Joseph sent with Charles a small but select group of pictures to be sold at auction by his financial agents Sampson Batard of London. Before leaving, Charles made a list of the pictures with projected prices. They included "David Teniers's *Adoration of the Magi* and *Fêtes de Village* for 2500 and 2000 pounds respectively; Van Dyck's *Christ on the Cross* for 7500 pounds; Murillo's *Virgin and Infant Jesus*, and Breughel's *Fair in a Village*, both for 2000 pounds; and a Rubens 'worth all the rest' for 12,000 pounds."[28]

These paintings suffered damage during their transatlantic voyage. Sampson Batard wrote Charles in London that the pictures had arrived in a very bad state, "much injured by injudicious packing and three of them broken from top to bottom." They should never have been sent with their frames on, and were "perfectly unsaleable" until repaired. "Besides," a letter from the firm admonished, "the prices you have fixed from what we can learn will very much impede the sale from their being so extremely high."[29]

Charles was much too busy with natural science to bother with his uncle/father-in-law's art works, which were of no interest to him. Perhaps the botched packing had been his fault. In any case, he heard from his mother-in-law, Julie, whom he admired and respected, that Joseph was angry with him. "I don't think he has anything to complain of about me," he answered Julie indignantly from Dublin, where he had gone to visit his sister Letizia, who was married to an Irish nobleman, Sir Thomas Wyse, "but perhaps [Joseph] would find it quite natural for me to stifle the rage and the torrent of complaints my pride alone makes me hold back. In every way, if he is discontented with me, we are a match for each other!" But this does not matter because he hopes they will not be "condemned to live long together!" At this point, Charles had decided to return to Europe permanently with his wife and two children.

He continues to Julie that it hurts him to open up his heart to his "chère Maman" because she is so good and she is sure to lose her esteem for him since she has always seen only good qualities in her husband—qualities that no one has rendered more justice to than he, Charles, has—the problem of their disagreements may be a cause of his own bad character. But if forced to recommence his career he would certainly do things differently. He would not accede to the false entreaties (*fausses instances*) of his uncle to rejoin him in America (clearly, he saw Joseph as insincere), but the faults of which he is accused he would commit again. "Yes, my dear Mama, I would leave you all the same at Aix la Chapelle, I would leave my mother at Bologne. . . . and above all Mme Lacoste at Point Breeze (forgive me for putting you in the same sentence). It is there that I believe are my three mortal transgressions! . . . I am far from disavowing them and above all from repenting them! . . . but my uncle, you say, has always been so good to his children!"[30] The truth about Emilie Lacoste's relationship to her husband appears to have been no secret to Julie.

And therein may lay yet another part of the antagonism between Charles and Joseph. Charles was genuinely attached to Julie, probably because Zénaïde was so close to her mother, and at least during this period, Charles was devoted to his wife and faithful to her. His father-in-law's affairs were no doubt odious to Zénaïde and therefore to Charles. And when Charles thought of Joseph's letter to Zénaïde about curbing her husband's passion, he must have scoffed at Joseph daring to say that to him.

Not only were there differences in personality between Joseph and Charles, but they also had few interests in common. Joseph's great collections of paintings and furniture were of no concern whatever to Charles, and Joseph apparently had little interest in science. When we think of Point Breeze with its walls hung with paintings by Titian, Rubens, and Salvatore Rosa, in rooms filled with great empire furniture, and compare it with the Lake House where Charles lived—there were great paintings as well, but they were all Joseph's—with his study walls supporting glass cases filled with the birds and reptiles he had stuffed himself, glass plates of butterflies spread out on tables and a chamber pot in the corner of the room, we can understand something of the difference between these two men. Charles was a dedicated scientist who saw Joseph as shallow and philandering. He did not appreciate any of his father-in-law's finer points, such as his devotion to literature and the arts, his generosity in loaning his collections, his kindness and open-handedness to those who worked for him, and the genial personality that so appealed to his friends.

Joseph had attempted to keep his daughter in America without himself having to live with Charles by proposing an alternative to Point Breeze. In mid-August 1826, while Charles was still in Europe, Zénaïde, on the way back from the Black River and the Saratoga Spa, had written her mother from New York, "I ask your advice in a private affair that has been in question for the last two days." She says that a Mr. Lafarge, after having built a superb house and acquired large woods at Black River, was ruined financially and forced to sell. (Presumably Joseph considered being the buyer.) "Papa" suggests that they could make their fortune by clearing and cultivating the land while in exchange Mr. Lafarge would go to Italy to attempt to settle their affairs. "But as for me, she confides, "the idea of fixing myself in the woods does not appeal to me [*ne me sourit pas*], however, I would love to have your advice, dear Mama. . . . I hope you will respond as soon as possible."[31] Of course, that was the last thing Julie wanted for Zénaïde. She eagerly awaited her daughter's return to Europe. And Charles would have had none of it. Nothing came of the idea.

Thus, in December 1827, Charles and Zénaïde made plans to return to Europe. Through the assistance of President John Quincy Adams they were able to book passage on the *Delaware*, a warship belonging to the United States government. Carrying a hundred guns, the *Delaware* was the largest ship that had crossed the Atlantic at the time. President Adams happened to be in Philadelphia in October when Joseph, in order to make his request, took Charles to meet him at the United States Hotel where he was staying. The president wrote Joseph Hopkinson in early November that it would be a pleasure for him to do whatever he could for the count, but it was important that Joseph make the arrangements for the *Delaware* with the Secretary of the Navy, privately, not officially. It would be necessary to know the number of individuals in the party and where they wished to disembark, as long as this would not be in any way difficult for the government. Joseph responded that, aside from his daughter and her husband, there would be a nurse, a chambermaid, a chef (*maître-d'hôtel*), and two infants. He hoped the captain would land his children in one of the

Italian ports of Livorno (Leghorn), Civittavecchia, or Genoa, and not in one of the Spanish or Neapolitan ports.[32] It was decided their destination would be Leghorn.

Joseph accompanied the young family and their retainers as far as Baltimore, where he reluctantly took leave of his beloved Zénaïde and his grandchildren, but perhaps not so reluctantly of Charles. Part of the large amount of baggage included cases of Charles's books and natural history specimens, as well as a number of paintings Joseph had given his daughter to embellish her eventual house in Rome. But, the embarking for Italy was delayed more than a month when the *Delaware* caught fire in Norfolk harbor. Zénaïde and Charles had to wait many weeks at Old Point, Virginia, while repairs were made, only to face a hazardous voyage. Charles wrote to a friend in Philadelphia from the lazaretto in Leghorn where the family was quarantined, that for the first ten days of the voyage the wind blew so hard "the heavy *Delaware* was pitching her lofty masts into the deep & though close reefed" the ship was going faster than anyone wished.[33] But then there were many times when the wind stopped altogether and they were becalmed for days. In mid-April the *Delaware* had finally anchored safely in Leghorn after an exhausting, hazardous voyage of more than six weeks.

As the months went on, Joseph sorely missed Zénaïde and her children, particularly his namesake, and forgot all the angst over money. In mid-July, just back to Point Breeze from his annual trip to the Black River, he wrote that he had received her letter and little Joseph's. "He is always present in my heart as you are my dear daughter," he says. "I cannot take a step here without remembering that you are no longer here. A lonely walk I took this morning led me to Joseph's little house near the Bridge of Savages and led me to the room where I write this" (perhaps in a summerhouse or gazebo). He mentions the situation in Spain where the partisans of his successor, King Ferdinand VII (fig. 30), have deserted the king, since he was a horror. The historian Robert Hughes describes Ferdinand as "cowardly, dim, cunning, and cruel."[34] According to Hughes, one of Goya's etchings in his series, *Los desastres*, plate 72, *Las resultas* ("The consequences"), refers to Ferdinand's return in depicting "a flock of Goya's nightmare bats, the lay and Church parasites that accompany" him and are descending on the half-alive body of "prostrate Spain."[35] Ferdinand had turned the country into a "medieval wasteland of violent repression, recrimination against anyone suspected of liberal views, and a resurgent Inquisition."[36] Referring to his own time as king of Spain, Joseph confides to Zénaïde, "It is my consolation, in this place where I am, to see that my children are not left with a memory they would need to defend."

With a thought for Charles and his natural history studies and collections, all

30. **Ferdinand VII** *by Francisco de Goya y Lucientes, c. 1814. Oil on canvas. Prado Museum, Madrid. Scala/Art Resource, NY.*

animosity apparently put aside in his absence and now that his expenses are Lucien's problem, Joseph says he has killed a loon with one shot on Lake Diana and that it is twice as large as the one he has seen at "the museum of the Peales" in New York.[37] "Monsieur Sari will prepare it so it will arrive in good state, and I will send with it the two stags when there is a favorable occasion." He concludes that he will pay all the little bills of which she speaks.[38]

But indulgent and affectionate a father as he was, Joseph could still be a strong critic of his daughter's attitude. "I am angry that you commence to dislike your beautiful villa," he wrote the following year regarding the Villa Paolina in Rome that belonged to Charlotte. "It is necessary to resist capricious tastes for the things you have. It is though I would become disgusted with Point Breeze!"[39]

Perhaps this strong reaction surfaced from an underlying feeling that he *was* becoming disenchanted with *Pointe* Breeze, as he spelled it in the French way. Without his family, without a mistress, and fewer French friends as they drifted away to other parts of the country, returned to Europe, or died, Joseph was increasingly lonely. He was feeling his exile more acutely than ever. Part of the estrangement must have been language since he had fewer and fewer of his countrymen with which to converse. Charles Ingersoll said that Joseph "could not, and seldom, if ever, attempted to speak English."[40]

Zénaïde had written her mother a few years before that she thought her father was a bit disgusted (*dégoûté*) with the United States. "If I am not mistaken," she says, "his health and the isolation he finds here, your distance from him most of all [she was wrong about that considering the presence at the time of a pregnant Emilie], and the absence of Charlotte makes him want to return to Europe. He will tell you all this himself, if I am right in my suppositions, although I am mixing myself up in what is not my business."[41] There may indeed have been an element of truth in Zénaïde's suppositions, in spite of all that then surrounded Joseph in America—family, a mistress, and splendid possessions—because he ever yearned to be back in France.

At the end of May 1829, there was a major auction of Napoleon's possessions at Malmaison. No doubt Joseph's Parisian agent, Jean-Baptiste Presle, alerted him about the sale and Joseph sent Presle to bid on various items for him. Sometime afterward, a handsome armchair carved with gold designs on a black background with red wool upholstery, one of ten from Napoleon's Council Chamber at Malmaison, reached Point Breeze (fig. 31).[42] There may have been other items as well, but only the armchair is known for sure. Seeing this faded trophy of his dead brother's past unloaded at his house in America must have recalled numerous memories of Paris, family, and friends Joseph had been forced to leave, perhaps never to see again.

31. **Napoleon's armchair from the Council Chamber at the château of Malmaison,**
made by Jacob Frères, Paris, 1800. Collection of The New-York Historical Society.

Chapter 12

LAFAYETTE CHANGES HIS POSITION

You see, my dear Count, these are the reasons why, despite my
personal regard for you, I cannot wish for the reestablishment of the
Imperial throne; the Hundred Days have demonstrated an
unremitting tendency to repeat past errors.

—Lafayette to Joseph Bonaparte, Paris,
26 November 1830

*B*y 1829 the Count de Survilliers's family was all in Italy. Julie had moved from Brussels to Florence, and Charlotte and her husband Napoleon-Louis were living with her. Napoleon-Louis's father, Joseph's brother Louis, was in a nearby villa. Zénaïde and Charles were in Rome, as was Madame Mère and her brother Cardinal Fesch. Lucien with his wife and many children were alternating between Bologna and Canino, while Jérôme was in Trieste. Joseph's sister, the beautiful Pauline Borghese, had died in 1825 of the same cancer as is thought to have killed Napoleon in 1821. At least Joseph had Canova's exquisite statue of Pauline, recumbent on a couch, with which to remember her.

With both daughters back in Europe and no possibility of their returning to America in the foreseeable future, Joseph felt his exile more keenly than ever, in spite of the fact that he had become more and more acclimated to his adopted country. By then he even "spoke English enough to be understood," according to John Fanning Watson, a visitor to Point Breeze in 1826, but this was contrary to what most people thought. Watson, who met the ex-king of Spain the July day when he and Reuben Haines had come to visit Charles, wrote in his diary: "The King had to my eye little or none of a foreign physiognomy. His person [was] of good size, of neat &

genteel form, & on the whole, such as we often see in a pretty gentleman—his head was of good proportion—his profile feature regular—a neat mouth & teeth—blue eyes and rather fair complexion. He wore a black *Coatee* & pantaloons of bombazeen—bootees under his pantaloons & white vest—hat of yellow straw & green linings & ribbon."[1]

At the time Joseph was sixty-one, still crisscrossing his land on horseback, often alone with a servant and one dog (possibly the Newfoundland who accompanied him to church), traveling frequently to New York, and every summer making the arduous trip to his northern property to hunt and fish. In June 1828, the spring after Zénaïde left, Mathieu Sari had accompanied him to his lodge on Lake Diana, but their stay had been short because Sari was anxious to return to his wife and children at Point Breeze. The count then went alone to Saratoga to take the waters.

He may have begun to think his trip to the Black River was too long and difficult to do every year. It was certainly not the same jolly excursion it had once been, since his daughters were no longer with him, and so many of his friends either were dead or had returned to Europe. Gone were the days when, after a boisterous evening of drinking and laughter at a tavern in the Mohawk Valley, he had been handed a two-hundred-dollar bill by the owner for "making in mine house one big fuss."[2]

Therefore, in the fall of 1829, when Stephen Girard made an interesting proposition to him, Joseph was definitely interested. He answered Girard:

> I have thought over the conversation we had together concerning the most convenient way for me to get a dwelling house in Philadelphia without increasing the number of land properties—already too large—that I own in this country, as my children do not think of leaving Europe. Your friendship for me leads you to offer to exchange one of the houses you own in Philadelphia for a tract of land that I own in Lewis County, state of New York. In this way I shall have a property in Philadelphia that will be of use to me every day, and you will have a large tract of land in New York that in time will be of great value but which now yields no revenue. It remains now for us to settle the prices of the house and of the land so that you will lose nothing by this transaction, taking into account that the house produces rent, while the land would be an

expense for taxes, which, however, are small in the state of New York.

He continues, responding to Girard's question of the location he would prefer, that either between Front and Twelfth Streets and between Vine Street on the north and Pine on the south would suit him, and either a single or a double house.[3] This area encompassed basically all of Philadelphia at the time.

Girard answered that he could not respond definitely before he knew the location, quality, and price of the lands Joseph wished to sell him.[4] Several months passed before Girard wrote in January 1830 to say that he had been looking at the map the count had confided to him and that it was now locked up in his bank where it would be safe from fire. He ends by saying, without further comment, that he has received advice from his friends in New York about the land "you have received from Mr. Le Ray de Chaumont."[5] And there the matter stood for a few years.

The Count de Survilliers's love life was at a total standstill. For the most part he had lost touch with Anna Savage since she had gone off to Paris four years earlier, in 1825, not having moved to the Black River country as had once been the plan. In Paris she had met and married François Alexis de la Folie, a wholesale silk merchant, in April 1826, at l'Oratoire, the French Reformed Church, with the minister Paul-Henri Marron officiating.[6] Seven months later she had had a child, Clarissa-Angélique, who apparently did not live long.

In a letter to Joseph of December 1827, Anna had written, with a strong tone of resentment, soliciting support for Caroline Charlotte, her daughter by him: "*Monsieur le comte*, it is nearly a month since I wrote you and you have not judged my letter worthy of response. Is it possible to act in this manner toward a person who in writing to you has only been guided by motives of kindness for you and for my child?" She has given Caroline Charlotte her stepfather's surname as she thinks it would be better for her and for the count if she does not use her real father's name. But she does not want her daughter to be a financial burden on her husband, with the clear indication that de la Folie is not well off, so she asks Joseph to settle a certain amount of money on Caroline Charlotte. She knows he will provide for her as he said he would, but if something should happen to him unexpectedly, it would be extremely awkward for her to deal with his relatives.

After Anna's separation from Joseph and before her move to France, she had been living in Lamberton, New Jersey, in the house Joseph had bought for $6,000 for her and her mother. She had made improvements, no doubt paid for by him, but now she wants to sell it to him for $18,000. "I can assure you that I want to leave America for good, but how can I if you won't buy my property?" she demands. "I hope you will reflect on this letter and rest assured that it is a very disagreeable thing for me to be obliged to address myself to you." She signs herself, "With respect, Anna Delafolie."[7]

Apparently Joseph did not answer her letter since there is no "R [*répondu*]" written in the upper right hand corner, as was his habit. Perhaps he was annoyed at the inflationary price Anna put on the house, because he did nothing about it for five years. Then, in May 1832, as he was preparing to depart for England, he bought it from her for the odd sum of $14,011.50.[8] Three years later, in 1835, he would give the property to his faithful chef, François Parrot, who had accompanied him to America in 1815 and had been with him ever since. But he was not unkind to his former mistress. In 1832 he conveyed to her three tracts of land in the town of Le Ray, Jefferson County, New York. On the first tract, in Evans Mills, he built a house for the Delafolies (an Anglicized spelling adopted in America). Presumably this is when Anna returned to America from France, and Joseph would provide a handsome dowry for Caroline Charlotte when she married Zebulon Howell Benton on 31 July 1839 in Watertown, New York.[9] Although she had assumed her stepfather's name, the *Public Ledger* in Philadelphia, in noting her marriage, referred to her as "Caroline Charlotte, daughter of Joseph Bonaparte, Count de Survilliers."[10] At the time this announcement was remarkable for an illegitimate child.

In April 1828, Joseph received the letter from Emilie, after she and Félix had separated, saying how much she missed the count and that she had no desires except for him and for her children. Somehow this letter had a hollow ring for Joseph. Perhaps it was the part where she regretted all the count had done financially for her husband. "Why did I not have more foresight," she lamented. "A fourth of what you gave him would be sufficient to assure me a peaceful future [*un sort tranquille*] and I would not reproach myself for your having lost so much money." Presumably this was money lent to Félix for his business ventures. She goes on to say, "Everyone in Paris is persuaded I was your mistress. It has even been said that my husband sold me to you. Now that I am nothing to him he takes the first opportunity to mortify me."[11] Surely, this kind of gossip was anathema to Joseph, who was essentially a private person.

He answered her coolly, but with dignity and reserve. "Madame, I have received your letter. You must conceive how grieved I am at a time when I counted on your near arrival. My sentiments for you and your family you have known for many years. Your misfortunes (*malheurs*) do not change them, persuaded that you have not ceased to be as estimable as I have known you. Fate has embittered your life. Monsieur Lacoste has also written me: it appears he is as unhappy as you are." Joseph then gave her news of her son Léon, still at school in New York, and said that his own children had gone to live in Italy. As for himself, he was about to leave for the Black River and would not return for two months. "In all situations, Madame," he concluded, "do not doubt my true interest and friendship." He signed simply, "Yours affectionately, Joseph, Count de Survilliers."[12] Clearly, he was disappointed in Emilie and wished to distance himself from her. Since she was no longer with Félix, Joseph did not invite her to join him in America. Félix was his friend and he planned to support him in New York as editor of *Le Courrier des États-Unis*. He hoped the journal would rally all former Bonapartists to exert their efforts on behalf of the imperial family's return to France. As much as he admired the United States, Joseph still fervently wished to go back as a French citizen, reclaiming his rights.

On 3 September 1830 the ship *Hibernia* arrived in New York harbor from Liverpool bringing news of the July Revolution in France: the repressive Bourbon monarch Charles X had been dethroned and driven into exile in England. There was much rejoicing among New York's French citizens, and in America in general, thoughts soon turned toward Joseph Bonaparte. A newspaper in New Jersey even stated that the ex-king of Spain was getting ready to leave for France.[13]

Charles X had published three ordinances on 26 July: dissolving the Chamber of Deputies, virtually abolishing freedom of the press, and reducing the electorate to only 25,000 persons, mostly landed proprietors. At once the barricades went up all over Paris; fierce street fighting broke out in the city and continued for three days. To quell the violence, the deputies, who did not disband, proclaimed Louis-Philippe, Duke of Orleans, "king of the French."

Louis-Philippe (1773–1850) had been born at the Palais Royal in Paris, the eldest son of the Duke of Chartres, later Duke of Orléans, who at the time of the Revolution, changed his name to Philippe Égalité and was elected to the National Convention. He was later executed. Following his father's death, Louis-Philippe inherited the title but had to escape to Scandinavia where he spent a year before sailing to the United States and settling in Philadelphia for two years. After that he went to England for a long period, after which, in 1809, he joined the Neapolitan royal family at Palermo, Sicily. This was only a year after Joseph Bonaparte, whom he opposed, had left as

32. **Portrait engraving of Marie-Joseph-Paul-Yves-Roch Gilbert Du Motier, Marquis de Lafayette.** *American Philosophical Society.*

king of Naples to become king of Spain. While in Sicily, Louis-Philippe married Marie Amélie, a daughter of King Ferdinand IV of Naples, by whom he would have nine children. After the first Bourbon restoration (1814) Louis-Philippe regained his family estates and forests that had not been sold after his emigration and his father's execution. Under the second restoration, he was a steady and open adherent of the liberal opposition to the crown. The July Revolution of 1830 gave him his long-awaited opportunity, and in Paris, wrapped in the tricolor flag beloved by Republicans and by Bonapartists, he went to the Hôtel de Ville where he was embraced by Lafayette (fig. 32).

Joseph Bonaparte was incensed when he heard the news from France because he did not regard Louis-Philippe as a legitimate heir to the throne. When Napoleon had been forced to abdicate in 1815 he had declared his son, Napoleon II, his heir. Joseph had deplored the restoration of the Bourbon monarchy, but he nevertheless considered it legitimate as the divine right of the kings of France—Charles X was, after all, the heir of sixty monarchs—but Louis-Philippe was not in the direct line. Joseph believed that his nephew was the only true successor.

He sent a letter with General Charles Lallemand (of Champ d'Asile fame, or infamy as the case may be) to the Chamber of Deputies proclaiming his nephew's legal right to the French throne. The ex-general left New York bound for France on 24 October 1830 bearing Joseph's letter, along with thousands of dollars. But according to Charles Ingersoll, Lallemand, "not a man of probity and high-toned fidelity," betrayed Joseph by turning his letter over to Louis-Philippe, who told him to burn it because nothing could be done by or for the Bonapartes. Besides, the king is supposed to have said, the Bonapartists and the Orleanists have common interests in France. The money was never accounted for.[14]

Joseph also wrote a long letter to Lafayette delivered by Lallemand. Speaking of the July Revolution and the expulsion of the king, Joseph said that Lallemand "will tell you with what enthusiasm the population of this country, American and French, have received the news of the glorious events [the overthrow of the king] of which Paris has been the theater. If I had not seen at the head of affairs a name [Louis-Philippe] with which mine can never be in accord, I should be with you immediately with General Lallemand. You will recall our interview [at Point Breeze] in this hospitable and free land. My sentiments are as invariable as yours and those of my family. *Everything for the French people."*[15]

He reminds Lafayette that the Chamber of Deputies had proclaimed his nephew as Napoleon II, in 1815, before "the bayonets of foreigners" had dissolved the Chamber. He thinks that should the French nation call to the head of affairs "even the most obscure family"—is he thinking of his own antecedents in Corsica?—they should acquiesce at once. He asks for the abolition of the "tyrannical law" that has kept his family in exile from France. "Adieu my dear general," he concludes. "My letter proves to you the justice I render to the sentiments [that Napoleon II should be restored] you expressed to me during the triumphal journey you made among this people [Americans], where I have seen, for fifteen years, that liberty is not a chimera, that it is a blessing which a nation, moderate and wise, can enjoy when it wishes."[16]

Joseph does not realize that things have changed and that General Lafayette, now head of the National Guard and in the forefront of French politics, no longer wants an underage emperor with Joseph as regent, but a constitutional monarch. Lafayette had decided that there should be a monarchy so as not to alarm France's neighbors, none of which were republics, but that the monarchy should be surrounded by republican institutions. With that philosophy, Lafayette had embraced Louis-Philippe on the balcony of the Hôtel de Ville before a large crowd at the end of July. Joseph's September letter was, therefore, after the fact. As one historian has said, "Lafayette had found a king who would be 'republican'; Orléans had found the leading republican to be a monarchist."[17]

Lafayette was completely candid in his reply to Joseph. He could point out, he said, that the Bonaparte dynasty was dispersed, with some in Rome, Joseph in America, and his nephew in Austria. "But," he added, "in the name of friendship, I must tell you my true thoughts. The Napoleonic system was resplendent with glory, but stamped with despotism, aristocratic pretensions and servitude. . . . Moreover, the son of your immortal brother is now an Austrian prince, and you know full well what the Austrian Cabinet is like. You see, my dear Count, these are the reasons why, despite my personal regard for you, I cannot wish for the re-establishment of the Imperial throne; the Hundred Days have demonstrated an unremitting tendency to repeat past errors."[18]

Lafayette was being true to himself because he never endorsed Napoleon's empire and during the imperial years retired to his estate of La Grange. If Joseph would likewise be true, he had never approved the empire, either. As Nicholas Biddle once quoted him, "I am a Republican more even than you Americans are. I did not wish the formation of the French Empire."[19] But he now had a serious conflict. He needed to be faithful to his dead brother, whose dearest wish was that his son succeed him as emperor of the French. Joseph's strong sense of duty and loyalty to his family, an ingrained Corsican trait, required that he suppress his own professed principles and act on behalf of Napoleon's legacy.

The ambivalence of the situation was torturous, but familial duty dictated with a firmer voice. Joseph wrote immediately to the Chamber of Deputies, the emperor of Austria, Francis I, and Marie-Louise, the emperor's daughter and the Duke of Reichstadt's mother, living in Italy, totally disregarding her adulterous behavior with her lover, General Neipperg, as soon as Napoleon had been sent to St. Helena. To the Chamber, Joseph affirmed that his nephew was the rightful heir to the imperial throne of France, having been lawfully elected by the French people in 1815. To the Austrian emperor he said, "Sire, if you will entrust to me the son of my brother, that son whom he enjoined on his death-bed, to follow my advice in returning to France,

I guarantee the success of the enterprise. Alone, with a tri-color scarf, will Napoleon II be proclaimed."

In an attempt to give the emperor confidence in his character, Joseph recalls to Francis I that once he had offered him the crown of Lombardy, but Joseph had refused, preferring to stay in France. "Today, as then, I am guided by the single sentiment of duty. My ambition limits itself to doing what I ought for France, for the memory of my brother, and to die upon my native soil a witness to the happiness of the grandson of your Majesty, which is inseparable to that of France and from the tranquillity of Europe." To Marie-Louise he wrote soliciting her help and concluding, "For a long time I have been disabused of the illusions of human grandeur; but I am more than ever the slave of that which I deem to be my duty."[20] None of them would reply to his entreaties.

He could not let Lafayette's letter go unanswered. "The portion of your letter in which you speak of the Napoleonic system as impressed with despotism and aristocracy merits, on my part, a more detailed response," he said. "While I render justice to your good intentions, I cannot but deplore the situation in which you found yourself when released from the prisons of Austria. That imprisonment [1792-1797] did not permit you to judge of the influence exerted upon the national opinion and character of the wretched Reign of Terror." Joseph was familiar with Lafayette's situation, as he had negotiated the treaty by which Lafayette was freed from the Austrian prison of Olmutz.[21] "You had only seen the liberal system of America, and you have condemned the all-powerful man [Napoleon] who did not transfer that system to France. Napoleon never doubted your good intentions. But he thought you judged too favorably of your contemporaries [the radical republicans]. He was forced into war by the English, and into the dictatorship by the war. These few words are the history of the Empire. Napoleon incessantly said to me, 'When will the peace arrive? Then only can I satisfy all, and show myself as I am.' The aristocracy of which you accuse him was only the mode of placing himself in harmony with Europe."[22] This last was in fact the same argument that Lafayette had used for advocating the monarchy of Louis-Philippe in place of a republic.

Joseph's life in the early years had often touched that of Lafayette. Both men had a devoted mutual friend in Germaine de Staël (1766–1817), who also opposed Napoleon's empire and was forced by the emperor into exile in Switzerland. Joseph, himself in exile after Napoleon's first abdication in 1814, lived near Mme. de Staël at her château, Coppet. There he may often have met Lafayette. Mme de Staël's friendship for both men was filled with warmth and loyalty. After Lafayette was freed from prison in Austria in 1797, she wrote to him: "I would like to be one of the first persons to tell you about the feelings of indignation, sadness, hope, fear, anxiety, [and] discouragement with which your fate during these five years has filled the souls of those who love you."[23] During the preliminary conferences for the Treaty of Amiens (1801) that Joseph drew up with Lord Cornwallis for peace with England, Mme de Staël wrote to him, "Look around you for one who loves you more sincerely than I do, who loves you more for yourself, without having to ask for more than your presence."[24]

But as much as Joseph respected Lafayette for his courage and for the history of their off-again on-again friendship over the years, he felt that "Lafayette misjudged French interest, welfare, and glory: once by his flight from the head of the French army in 1792; again by his acquiescence in the Bourbon restoration of 1815; and a third time when he helped the Duke of Orleans to the throne; all calamitous for his country."[25]

And yet, Lafayette was more sincere in his professed republicanism than Joseph. An aristocrat, born Marie-Joseph-Paul-Yves-Roch Gilbert, Marquis de Lafayette, he preferred to be called general, not marquis, while Joseph Bonaparte, born without a title, always insisted on his made-up one of Count de Survilliers, even in the United States.

Chapter 13 THE SIREN CALL OF EUROPE

Could you give me your opinion Monsieur, you who have lived [in England] a long time, on the welcome I could expect either from the government, or the people?

—Joseph Bonaparte to Count Charles de Flahaut,
Point Breeze, 24 September 1830

*J*oseph convinced himself that the interest, welfare, and glory of France depended on the establishment of Napoleon's son on the throne as Napoleon II. By early January 1831, he still had had no response from the Chamber of Deputies and, as he told Charles Ingersoll, he no longer expected any. But he was ready for whatever events would transpire "without too much fear, or too much joy." He was clearly suspicious of Charles Lallemand, for he said the general had no doubt arrived in England because the boat he had sailed on had returned to New York, but he had not had any direct news of his arrival in Europe. He was feeling better about Lafayette since he had received news from "highly trustworthy persons" that Lafayette, at the Hôtel de Ville, had at first proposed that all Bourbons be excluded from the government and that he had no objection to the proclamation of the young Napoleon. It was only after resisting for thirty hours that he had conceded to those who backed the Duke of Orléans.[1] This information seemed to fly in the face of Lafayette's own letter to Joseph, but the ex-king was quick to believe his well-meaning friends because it suited him.

That past September, after learning of the momentous events in France, Joseph had written a number of letters to his French friends. He wrote to one of Napoleon's generals, Jean Maxmilien Lamarque, that Louis-Philippe, by his birth and liaisons with the reigning branches of the Bourbon family, whom Louis-Philippe wished to disown, would soon be under suspicion by French patriots and Italian and Spanish liberals. It was not the French nation that had put him on the throne, but a group of rich bankers and merchants who were afraid of popular movements. "A few Parisian capitalists are not France,"² Joseph stated emphatically. He added that he expected "new treason and new disasters." How is it possible, he asks, to depend again on a prince of this house after having been betrayed by Louis XVI and by Louis XVIII, who destroyed the liberty of the press. Now Louis-Philippe only waits to do to France what Ferdinand VII did in Spain, that is, extreme repression. Joseph ignores the fact that during the empire Napoleon tightly controlled the press and shut down all newspapers critical of him.

"Is there not in France a man more worthy to take the helm of state for the time being?" he wonders, "And General Lafayette himself, who was at the head of the provisional government, has he not given to the nation and to the friends of liberty and order in two worlds, stronger guarantees than a prince of the house of Bourbon? Because in the end is Orléans [Louis-Philippe] not of Bourbon blood? I affirm that only the enemies of France could approve the Duke of Orleans!"³ He suggested to Maréchal Jourdan that one could sometimes judge great events better from a distance than nearby. The opinion in the United States had been that, following the popular uprising at the end of July, Lafayette, as head of the provisional government, should have supported it until the will of the nation had pronounced itself.⁴

To a former ambassador, charged by Napoleon to write a history of French di- plomacy, Joseph said that he had carried with him for many years the determination to see Napoleon's son in France, but he had been held back by the fear of those who only judged the Duke of Reichstadt by Napoleon's dictatorship—made necessary, he said, by the war that the enemies of France constantly made against him—and did not know his nephew. "What would France be today after a peace of eighteen years if Napoleon had continued to govern her?"⁵

Of course, Joseph himself did not know his nephew, not having seen him since he was a small child, and certainly it was an open question as to whether France would have been improved by another eighteen years of Napoleonic rule. But Joseph was a fiercely devoted brother, Corsican clan loyalty an integral part of his being, and he was faithful to the pledge he had made Napoleon to restore his son to the throne of France when the time came. No doubt Joseph would have been a benevolent ruler as regent of France. He had proved himself in his governance of Naples and his attempt at governing Spain, where he had been thrust into an impossible situation that checkmated all his good intentions. But in the present instance, he steadfastly refused to face the facts of the situation: that his nephew, whose health was poor, was under the control of his grandfather, the emperor Francis I of Austria, and that the faction that had proclaimed the Duke of Orléans king of France was firmly in control. As he learned to his dismay, the "Hero of Two Worlds" himself supported Louis-Philippe as the "citizen king."

Joseph's brother Lucien was angry when he heard of his older sibling's intention to reestablish the empire. Lucien had high hopes of returning to France, had commenced efforts to that effect, and was convinced that Joseph's actions would thwart his endeavor. He wrote to a friend, referring to Joseph's letter to the Chamber of Deputies with a reasonable argument that predicted the future: "Joseph's protest, which declares war on the king of the French from his camp in New York, where he is secure, is totally lost: when one has declared oneself the enemy, one has nothing to expect from the government."[6]

As the year wore on, the Count de Survilliers pondered seriously going to England to await the young Duke of Reichstadt, whom Napoleon had called the King of Rome. It was a painful decision because he loved his life in America, where he still had a few close friends, such as Joseph Hopkinson and Nathaniel Chapman, and a house and garden that were his pride and joy. England was his most obvious choice since he was forbidden to set foot in France, or Italy, but it was a choice with drawbacks. He had written the previous September to Count Charles de Flahaut (reputed son of Talleyrand and lover of Hortense, Napoleon's stepdaughter) that he would not have hesitated to go to England if the memories of St. Helena had not held him back. "Could you give me your opinion, Monsieur," he said, "you who have lived there a long time, on the welcome I could expect either from the government, or from the people?"[7] In March, he heard from Flahaut that he would be perfectly safe in England, but unwelcome, since the nation overwhelmingly sided with Louis-Philippe as king of the French.[8]

As Joseph was debating all this, news arrived of tragedy in his immediate family. Charlotte's husband, Napoleon-Louis, had died at Forli, Italy, on 15 March. The young man, with his brother Louis Napoleon, had been engaged in revolutionary activities to drive the invading Austrians out of Italy and to establish a republican government in Rome, much to the dismay of Charlotte, her uncles Louis and Jérôme Bonaparte, and Cardinal Fesch. But in the midst of his guerrilla involvement, Napoleon-Louis had come down with measles and died within a few days. There has always been speculation that, before he became ill, members of an opposing faction had wounded him in an attempted assassination. This would explain the rapidity of his death from measles, a result of his weakened condition.[9]

Charlotte's husband had been full of promise. He was an inventor with a great interest in aeronautics. Although men had been flying balloons for fifty years, Napoleon-Louis was experimenting with projects for mechanical flight by means of revolving propellers. He had invented a new method for producing steel and had opened a paper factory near Spezia, Italy, designing all the machines himself.[10] His death was a terrible blow to the entire Bonaparte family. In addition to the loss, it was particularly disappointing for Joseph, and perhaps for Charlotte, because now she would never be empress of France. Napoleon-Louis had been third in the line of succession after Napoleon's son and Joseph himself. For Joseph, so far away from all his family, the news urged on his plans to cross the ocean.

Early that summer of 1831, he notified Baron de Méneval, Napoleon's former secretary living in Paris, that "Monsieur Poinsett," a firm friend (*un ami sûr*), would be the bearer of the letter he was writing to Méneval. He assured Méneval that Poinsett was a man involved in the most important affairs of the United States—he was America's first ambassador to Mexico—and that he was totally trustworthy. "Treat everything you hear from him as though it came from my own mouth," he said.[11]

When the following fall, Joel Roberts Poinsett returned from Europe convinced that the Duke of Reichstadt should be called to the French throne, his opinion reinforced Joseph's determination to depart. A letter from Victor Hugo, brought by Poinsett, further confirmed his decision. This sign of respect from the young poet—whose father, Léopold, had been one of Napoleon's generals and whose brother, Abel, had been a page in Joseph's Spanish court and his godson—no doubt moved him with nostalgia. Joseph wrote to Méneval in September concerning his possible return to France, "It will make me very happy to breathe again the air of my country, with friends who, from the beginning of my life, have thought and felt as I have, and those younger ones who have not ceased to love me even though I have been in exile and far from them."[12]

There was certainly a cult of Napoleon at the time. Hugo's defense of freedom and promotion of this cult had caused him to write such poems as "*À la Colonne* [the Austerlitz column]," and "*Lui* [Him]." He had been further liberalized by Charles X's restrictions on freedom of the press. Emilie Lacoste's friend Béranger, also immensely popular in the nineteenth century, had glorified the era of Napoleon and had ridiculed the Bourbon monarchy and the reactionary clergy. During the 1820s collections of Béranger's works had landed him in prison, which only increased his popularity. Even more important than poetry for the legend of Napoleon were the accounts published one after the other by the generals and others who had accompanied Napoleon to St. Helena: Las Cases, Montholon, Gourgaud, and his Irish physician Barry O'Meara.

Baron de Méneval told Joseph that the name of Napoleon's son was "more than ever magic," but that a profound obscurity enveloped the young duke and was harmful to his cause. However, he said, "intimations of success exist incontestably."[13] Joseph's nephew, Louis-Napoleon, the future Napoleon III, advised him that the party of Napoleon II was without doubt the most numerous in France, although it was not well funded, and that the emperor's name was still held in veneration by the lower classes.[14] Joseph also heard from his former mistress, the Countess Saint-Jean d'Angély, in Paris, urging him to return. They all thought he should position himself in either England or Switzerland to be ready to lead a movement to overthrow Louis-Philippe and restore the Bonapartes. The republicans were said to be prepared to join the Bonapartists, and four deputies were reputed favorable to Napoleon II.

But along with the encouragement of Poinsett, Hugo, Méneval, Louis-Napoleon, and the countess was the presentiment of his nephew's illness. Joseph told Poinsett in early February that he acknowledged the foreboding (*augure*) in Poinsett's recent letter, and in order to discuss things further he hoped to see his friend shortly at Point Breeze, if the river was navigable (not frozen). "I still have here the person of whom I spoke to you who wishes to undertake a voyage to Vienna," in order to see the Duke of Reichstadt, he says. "His name is Goubaud and he is an artist of renown. . . . He has been the director of many art academies and his paintings have figured in expositions at the Louvre among those of David, Gros, and Gérard!" Joseph asks Poinsett for a letter of introduction to "votre belle Comtesse" at Vienna for Goubaud and concludes by saying he has had no direct news from Paris about his petition to the Chamber of Deputies by the last packet boat, but he awaits each one that leaves from Le Havre.[15]

Joachim Goubaud, accompanied by the young Count Joseph Orsi of Florence (twenty-three at the time), had arrived in Philadelphia at the end of December 1831 with letters of introduction to Joseph Bonaparte from Hortense and her son Louis-Napoleon, a friend of Orsi. Goubaud wished to see the downfall of Louis-Philippe and agreed to undertake a mission to the Duke of Reichstadt on Joseph's behalf. Count Orsi had taken part in the revolutionary activities of Napoleon-Louis and his brother, but after the death of the former he had escaped under threat of arrest for his subversive involvement. Orsi had met Goubaud in London, where they had decided on a trip to America to see Joseph and further plans for a Bonapartist revival in France. They stayed several months at Point Breeze, and while there, Goubaud painted a portrait of the Count de Survilliers, which also included the images of three other men.

The portrait (see plate 11), dated 2 February 1832, depicts the ex-king seated somewhat tensely in a French armchair, his right hand in his pocket and his youthful, feminine-looking left hand resting on a chair arm. His elegant jacket and white silk vest have a European look. On his left side is a table piled high with handsomely bound books and surmounted by Canova's life-size bust of Napoleon, his head crowned with laurel leaves like a Roman emperor, and his name carved below in the Italian, *Napoleone*. The emperor appears to be looking down on the small framed picture of his son, the Duke of Reichstadt. With curly blond hair and the shadowed eyes that denote his tuberculosis, the youth looks decidedly frail and haunted. Also on the table is a partially unfurled drawing of another young man, with a small mustache, perhaps the dashing revolutionary Count Orsi, Goubaud's companion. Joseph's dark hair is combed forward in the same style Napoleon favored, and his large blue eyes are intelligent, pensive, even a bit wary, as they look directly at the viewer. He has a prominent Roman nose and a small, somewhat pursed mouth. The impression is that of a man deeply involved in a serious situation who has now made up his mind how to deal with it.

The solemn, resolute expression in the Goubaud portrait is not evident in that of Joseph by Charles Willson Peale (see frontispiece), painted eight years earlier, between 21 February and 7 March 1824. The Peale painting shows a considerably younger-looking man, relaxed, content with his life, undisturbed by conflict, yet with the same alert intelligent expression. In both portraits there is the suggestion of a sensuous nature: heavy-lidded eyes, full lips, and a slight double chin. Peale wrote, commenting on an observation by Charles, "that a hundred pictures had been taken of his uncle and not one of them was so like as mine."[16]

Goubaud also made a sketch of the high-ceilinged salon at Point Breeze (fig. 33). In the center of the picture Joseph stands before a blazing fire braced by his right foot on the grate and right arm on the mantel, talking with Joseph Hopkinson, who stands to his left. Also on the left are seated Orsi and Sari conversing. To the right are three armchairs with Emma Sari seated in the middle one and the Duke of Montebello, a career diplomat and son of Marshal Lannes, talking with her. There is apparently a large painting over the fireplace, but it is indistinct. However, to the right of the mantle, Gérard's portrait of Julie with Zénaïde and Charlotte is vaguely outlined. A wide-patterned carpet covers the floor. This is the only known picture of the interior of Point Breeze.[17]

At Joseph's behest, Goubaud would undertake a mission to Vienna that winter

33. **Interior of Point Breeze** *by Innocent J. L. Goubaud, 1833. Pencil drawing, photograph at the Historical Society of Pennsylvania.*

in order to see the Duke of Reichstadt and further his uncle's plans for a Bonaparte restoration. In the letter Joseph sent with Goubaud to his nephew, he said: "I was born eighteen months before your father, we were raised together, nothing ever lessened the intimate friendship that united us; at his death he left you in my care to realize his last wishes. . . . When you were born in Paris, 20 March 1811, your father had become, through the love of the French people . . . the most powerful prince of Europe. Even at this hour, I think that you have been called upon to continue the work with which a divine genius inspired your father." He ended the letter, "From Point Breeze, State of Jersey, United States of America, where I have been as happy as I could be far from my homeland, in the most prosperous country on earth, under the name I have adopted, the Count de Survilliers."[18]

Another man Joseph had sent earlier on a mission to Vienna was Baron Hippolyte Colins de Ham, the brother-in-law of the count's secretary and assistant, Mathieu Sari. The two men were married to the Saint-Georges sisters from Cuba. Colins, a fervent Bonapartist, had been in the United States in 1818, fired with a plan to deliver Napoleon from St. Helena, and for this purpose Generals Bernard and Lallemand had introduced him to Joseph. Colins had also thought to join the settlement at the

Champ d'Asile, but the colony by then had already dispersed. As nothing developed from either plan, Colins had gone to Cuba to engage in agriculture. It was there he met his future wife, Aspasie, Emma Sari's sister. When news of the fall of the Bourbon dynasty reached Havana, there was much rejoicing, and shortly after Colins saw the tricolor flag of the Revolution flying on the first French ships to arrive in Cuba, he set off for Paris. From there he proceeded to Vienna, where he had access to the Austrian court through a relative, charged with Joseph Bonaparte's plea to his nephew to assert himself as Napoleon II.[19]

Colins returned to Point Breeze on 7 July, having passed through Paris on his way. He reported to Joseph that his nephew was well brought up, educated, religious, and resembled Napoleon in feature, with blue eyes, although he was tall and blond (fig. 34). The young duke was devoted to the memory of his father and took delight in surprising his grandfather, the emperor of Austria, with stories his tutor had withheld from him. In Edmond Rostand's play *L'Aiglon* (*The Eaglet*), Franz—the duke's name was Napoleon Francis Joseph Charles—says at one point: "Metternich, the fool, Thought to scrawl 'Duke of Reichstadt' o'er my name, But hold the paper up before the sun: You'll see 'Napoleon' in the watermark!"[20] Apparently the Austrian emperor Francis, who loved his grandson, had said he would not oppose the national will of France, or his grandson's plans when he came of age. Colins was full of enthusiasm for the Count de Survilliers to set sail for England as soon as possible.[21]

The day before Christmas, 1831, in a last-ditch attempt to raise the large sums Joseph felt he would need for his enterprise, he went to see his old friend Stephen Girard (fig. 35) to ask him again if he would buy his Black River lands. But as fate would have it, Girard was very ill with influenza and would die only forty-eight hours later.[22] Aside from the money he would have to raise in other ways, Joseph was sorely grieved by the death of his oldest French friend in America, his loyal banker, and provider of so many services, from materials and plants for his house and garden to ships for transporting his children and his possessions from Europe. And there had been Joseph's paternal relationship with Girard's orphaned nieces who lived with him and were the merchant's only family. Since he had no children of his own, Girard's nieces were very precious to him.[23]

In the early years of Joseph's stay in America, he had often joined Marshal Grouchy, the Lallemand brothers, and General Lefebvre-Desnouettes at Girard's house on Water Street in Philadelphia for convivial Sunday afternoon dinners.[24] There had been a certain irony in these get-togethers because Philadelphia society fastidiously shunned Girard—perhaps because he was a merchant, not a profession thought suitable for a gentleman—and yet the wealthy businessman was on familiar

The Duke de Reichstadt

Francesco Duca Reichstadt

34. **The Duke de Reichstadt, François-Charles-Joseph, Herzog von Reichstadt (1811–1832), Napoleon's son.** *Engraving after painting by Michaël Morris Daffinger (1790–1849). Engraved in Paris by Pourvoyeur. Historical Society of Pennsylvania.*

35. **Portrait of Stephen Girard** *by Bass Otis, 1823. Oil. Girard College Collection.*

terms with all the distinguished French refugees, especially the ex-king of Spain and Naples, all of whom were sought after by the city's prominent hostesses.

None of these friends were around any longer. Grouchy had gone back to France; Lefebvre-Desnouettes, tragically, drowned when the *Albion* sank off the coast of Ireland in 1822; a year later, Henri Lallemand, married to Girard's niece Henriette, died of fever. After Louis-Philippe gained the throne of France, little by little most of the ex-patriate Bonapartists, granted amnesty by the new king, had left the United States. As Joseph saw the exiles around him disappear, he wondered if the sacrifices he was making for Napoleonic propaganda in America were now pointless. Still, he was aware that his fellow Frenchmen who were left were eager for news from France and still read Félix Lacoste's journal, *Le Courrier des États-Unis,* subvented by Joseph. "I have just returned from Philadelphia where I have seen many of your subscribers," he wrote Lacoste in April. "In general they think you have too many articles on science and even literature at a time when they are avid for political news. They like your Parisian correspondent . . . [his dispatches] excite more interest than your articles on *Blood Transfusion* which scares your readers. I am not speaking for myself because I am interested in those articles."[25]

By then Joseph was determined to embark for England, thinking it safer than Switzerland, surrounded, as it was, by countries unfriendly to him (with the possible exception of Germany). Before leaving, he gave Nicholas Biddle a gift. His accompanying note read: "I beg you to accept as a remembrance from a man who has learned to appreciate you throughout many years, a painting by Snyders, which will go well in your parlor or in your dining room."[26] Joseph's interest in interior decoration, that he had demonstrated with such taste at Point Breeze, would even surface in this note, for he cannot resist suggesting where in Biddle's house the painting should be hung.

In addition to Biddle, Joseph gave other friends exceptional works of art from his collection as farewell presents. To Joseph Hopkinson he also gave a painting by Snyders as well as a *Virgin and Child* by Guido Reni, and to his personal physician and dear friend, Dr. Nathaniel Chapman, he presented Andrea del Sarto's *Charity.* Some years later he would give General Thomas Cadwalader, who would accompany him on the voyage to England, *The Rape of Europa* by Nicolas Coypel—the large picture that may have hung in his bedroom and scandalized his Quaker-lady visitors. (fig. 36).[27]

One last visit was a trip to Washington to bid farewell to President Andrew Jackson. How very different his reception was this time, seventeen years after he had arrived in the United States and was warned off by Richard Rush from paying his respects to President Madison. The "Corsican adventurer" had proved himself a loyal and enthusiastic citizen of the country, with no ulterior motives for rescuing his brother from St. Helena, or stirring up revolution in Alabama, Texas, or Mexico.

The Count de Survilliers set sail for England from Philadelphia on 20 July 1832 aboard the *Alexander,* on a favorable tide down the meandering Delaware River to the Delaware Bay and out into the open sea. Accompanying him were Louis Mailliard, Mathieu Sari, his wife, and three children, Colonel Colins—leaving his wife and five children in Cuba to whom he would never return, preferring to stay with his former mistress in Paris—and François Parrot, the chef who had originally come

36. **The Rape of Europa** *by Noël-Nicolas Coypel, 1726–1727. Oil on canvas. Philadelphia Museum of Art.*

with Joseph to America, three manservants and a maid. General Cadwalader, on business for the Bank of the United States, his son, and a servant were also aboard. Sixty-three others made up the passenger list. A Philadelphia paper reported, "[The count's] public works will speak for him to posterity for they are enduring as they are generous. . . . A more fervent and sincere 'God bless you' never was uttered than that which came from the heart and lips of the rich and the poor of the village of Bordentown to their neighbor and friend on his departure from them."[28] Joseph had been accepted entirely for himself and could look back with pleasure to his years at Point Breeze.

After a voyage of twenty-eight days, when the ship docked at Liverpool on 24 July, he learned to his dismay that there was no longer any reason for him to have left the United States.[29] His nephew, the Duke of Reichstadt, was dead.

Chapter 14 A BONAPARTE IN
ENGLAND

It's true that I love the United States as much as you do, but I am near France and I don't wish to see it flee from my sight like a new Ithaca.

—Joseph Bonaparte to Lafayette, London,
10 November 1832

Joseph set foot on English soil for the first time in his life in July 1832, an occasion that may well have brought forth conflicting emotions. England had been France's traditional enemy ever since he could remember, even from his youth in Corsica, and it was Napoleon's nemesis during his entire career as general, first consul, and emperor. The expedition to Egypt in 1798 had been an attempt to cut off England's most direct route to its richest colony, India; the continental blockade was designed to halt British trade with European countries; even the sale of Louisiana was motivated in part by Napoleon's determination to keep the English out of North America. Worst of all for Joseph, the English had been the jailers of his beloved brother. Bonaparte sympathizers used the myth of Prometheus chained to a rock where an eagle daily ate his liver, as a metaphor for Napoleon on St. Helena suffering from the cancer (or arsenic) that ate away his stomach. For Joseph, the final irony was the fact that England was the only country near France where he would be entirely safe from arrest.

All these feelings were no doubt crowding about him when he learned that his nephew, upon whom he had pinned all his hopes for a Bonaparte restoration, was dead. The whole point of his journey and the agonizing he had gone through at leaving Point Breeze now seemed for nothing. He had been warned that his nephew was seriously ill. Charles Ingersoll had even thought at one point to tell him he should cancel his trip because it would be pointless, but Ingersoll had found Joseph so set on his mission that he had decided not to broach the subject. Joseph had been encouraged by the enactment of the English Reform Bill to believe that the establishment of popular sovereignty in England would help overthrow divine right royalty in France. In England, as the senior member of the Bonaparte family, he would be at hand for any Bonapartist movement in France.

Joseph would hear from Innocent-Joachim-Louis Goubaud that when he eventually reached Schoenbrunn Palace, Napoleon's son had only just succumbed to the tuberculosis from which he had been suffering for some time. Being a well-known artist, Goubaud was permitted to make a drawing of the young man on his deathbed. At the Paris salon of 1838, he would exhibit a painting he made of this drawing, *La Mort du Duc de Reichstadt à Schoenbrunn (22 juillet 1832)*, a poignant picture that Joseph would never see.

In October, Joseph received a warm letter from Lafayette offering his condolences. "My dear count, I am very touched by the honorable marks of confidence and friendship you have given me, and I deserve them from all the sentiments that attach me to you. It is with profound sympathy that I feel your sorrow from two cruel losses [referring also to Napoleon Louis]; and I hurry to write you at London, since it is said you are proscribed from going to Rome [to visit his mother], by base and barbarous politics, to fulfill your filial piety." Lafayette continues that he understands Joseph's natural desire to see again their mutual country and he has been "particularly sensible to the national and disinterested sentiments" Joseph has expressed to him. "You remember, my dear count, that in the first burst of patriotic hopes [when they met in 1824 at Point Breeze], in part destroyed or rather delayed; I had agreed to your immediate return. . . . I like to think that you will not be more sorry than I am of this declaration of our mutual sentiments." He says that for a long time the American papers have spoken of Joseph's ideas relative to the French government. At the moment he, Lafayette, is only a deputy and the chamber will not meet for another month, implying that in any case, nothing could be accomplished until then. "Some things that you judge should be done will find a willing accomplice in me," he concludes, "as persevering as my devotion to liberty and to the country that I know you speak of with a love touching mine. Believe me, my dear count, that I also render you complete justice and accept the expression of wishes and unswerving sentiments of respect and attachment that I have avowed to you with all my heart."[1]

Joseph's reply to Lafayette was equally warm. "It's true that I love the United States as much as you do," he said, "but I am near France and I don't wish to see it flee from my sight like a new Ithaca; I still prefer it to the United States in which to end my days and I count on your powerful cooperation for that." He assured Lafayette that he would always wish to see France as happy as the country he had just left. "A day will come, without doubt, when France will not have to envy the happiness of America. Will we not live to witness this! And will I not have the joy to renew my old friendship with you in our common country and sometime tell you of the admiration and respect I held for you in the new world!"[2]

All that fall Joseph was as uncertain of his future course as the day he landed in England. He was always waiting for answers that never came. At least his reception at Liverpool and at London had been a pleasant surprise. Negative attitudes of the English about his family seem to have changed, so that he almost felt as if he were in the United States. In fact, he found "the public mind in Europe much Americanized."[3] But the enormous wealth and display of the English upper-class world in which he moved and to which he had been so accustomed in Europe, stood out in sharp contrast to what he had experienced in America for so many years. There, he and his grand house filled with elegant works of art had been unique and fascinating to many of his friends and acquaintances, but in England there were many such great collections. Some years earlier, Richard Rush, then ambassador to England, had reflected on the wealth of the English to Charles Ingersoll: "I was at the house of a nobleman last week where stood eight massive vases of gold as the mere ornaments of a single sideboard, and where hung four pictures, among a suite of apartments containing for aught I know four hundred, that were lately purchased (the four) for twenty thousand pounds. I shall dine tomorrow at the house of another where I shall probably see to the value of fifty thousand pounds sterling in plate. Pause upon these things. They may supply new topics of political reflection, or for a book." Rush goes on to point out the huge discrepancy between the rich and the poor and says that "if we but start in this race, our Republick will be toppled down long before we reach anything like such a goal."[4]

With all Joseph's professed republicanism, there is no evidence that he saw the social situation in England in the same manner as Rush did. Even after seventeen years in the United States, he did not appear to have been "Americanized" in such a way as to relate his own situation to the larger picture; his thinking about political and social realities seems to have been somewhat abstract. He was always concerned with the dignity of his position, a position to be maintained at whatever cost. He would gradually sell off his possessions in order to raise the funds necessary to sustain his status as the ex-king of Naples and Spain and brother of Napoleon. Each of these sales must have been degrading for someone who, as king, had lived in the magnificent palace at Naples overlooking the famous bay, and in Caserta, the summer palace of the Neapolitan kings, its walls hung with gorgeous silks, as well as the equally enormous royal palace in Madrid with ceilings painted by Anton-Raphael Mengs, among others. It was a reversal of fortune to live in rented houses and be obliged to sell off belongings in order to meet one's daily expenses. But most disheartening of all for the Count de Survilliers was his proscription from going home to France.

Joseph was not lonely in England, since many family members came to see him. His brother Lucien, whom he had not seen since 1815, arrived for a reunion in August, although the meeting somehow proved controversial for he and Joseph were soon at odds. Mailliard, who clearly found Lucien difficult, described him as "a man who speaks well, but doesn't feel anything."[5] Joseph's prodigal youngest brother, Jérôme, with his son Prince Napoleon, known familiarly as Plon Plon, also arrived. Best of all, however, was the arrival in mid-November of his beloved Charlotte, now a widow, who came for a year. The house the count rented at 23 Park Crescent, in a fashionable section of London on the south side of Regent's Park, was by then quite full with these assorted relations in addition to his faithful Mailliard, as well as the Saris.

Louis-Napoleon, the son of their brother Louis, came from Arenenberg, Switzerland, to see him in November, shortly before Charlotte arrived. Joseph received him coldly, for he disapproved of the young man's revolutionary activities. "[He] received me as a stranger and not as a nephew," Louis Napoleon would later write of his uncle.[6] As a true Bonapartist, Louis-Napoleon now saw Joseph as emperor of the French being next in the line of succession, after Napoleon's son, a decree laid down in the Act of the Senate and approved by the French people in an 1804 referendum. The Bonapartists considered this act still viable, as it had been repealed by an illegal government and imposed by foreign armies of occupation. Louis-Napoleon—young, vigorous, and headstrong—was impatient with Joseph for not planning a strategy to reclaim the throne of France. But at Joseph's age, being emperor was a different proposition from serving as regent, or mentor for the Duke of Reichstadt. He had never wanted to be a king in the first place, and now it was certainly too late to agitate for such a role.

It was gratifying, however, as far as kingship went, to receive a visit from his old enemy in Spain, the fierce guerrilla leader, Francisco Espoz y Mina, uncle of the General Mina who had offered him the crown of Mexico. Ironically, Espoz regretted that José Primo was no longer king of Spain, the restored monarch, Ferdinand VII, being such a tyrant. Espoz told Joseph he would have accepted him as king if he had dismissed his generals and French troops, and one in particular. Marshal Soult, who had stolen pictures from the Alcazar and made a fortune from the mines of Almaden, was now being overwhelmed with honors by Louis-Philippe and was no doubt behind the continued exile of the Bonapartes.[7] Joseph probably agreed with Espoz about dismissing his generals (who had disobeyed his every command), and about the cruelty and rapacity of the troops to his Spanish subjects, although he may not have said so.

In December the count had a surprising visit from Emilie Lacoste's lover, Prosper Mérimée, whose works he had read in America and whom he was most eager to meet. *Le Vase étrusque* had appeared for the first time in the *Revue de Paris* of 14 February 1830 and Joseph may have read it at Point Breeze. More than likely he did not suspect that he was the unwitting inspiration of the work. Mérimée, who had been wildly jealous of Emilie's first lover after he found out that Joseph was not the old man she had pictured him, was determined to see Joseph for himself. No doubt he was provoked to find that the *vieillard* of Emilie's description was a handsome, middle-aged man of much distinction. He therefore cut their interview short and refused the count any opportunity of meeting with him again, declining all Joseph's subsequent invitations for dinner. He would have nothing more to do with his attractive competitor.[8]

Coincidentally, Félix Lacoste arrived from New York shortly after this encounter, perhaps brought over by Joseph for reconciliation with Emilie in Paris. But when Emilie, who was four months pregnant, learned that her husband was en route to France, she panicked and abruptly left the city. Mérimée was not the father, as many of her acquaintances suspected; instead, he was Félix's first cousin, Louis-Edmond Antoine Duranty, a journalist and great friend of the painter Edgar Degas, who would paint Duranty's portrait many years later. The child, a boy born on 5 June 1833, was registered in Paris as Louis-Emile Duranty, son of Emilie Duranty, father unknown.[9]

In August, Emilie wrote to thank Joseph for the money he had given her by way of his banker, Presle, in Paris. She was sorry to hear that her husband had left him and gone back to New York, implying that Joseph and Félix had some disagreement. (Apparently there had been a dispute over Félix's journal in New York—Joseph seems to have thought his handling of it was too lax.) "He was very attached to you," she says in defense of her husband,

> and trustworthy, not a flatterer, a true [*juste*] person according to Béranger, who had seen him often while he was in Paris, and of all those around you he was certainly the most capable. . . . His

future is not brilliant, nor is that of his children, as for me it is even more frightening, and I know that I will be unhappy for the rest of my life. I am sorry for him that he has left you, but this makes it possible for me to see you sooner or later . . . which would make me happy because I have not stopped thinking of you. . . . I have written you sometimes of the bitterness I felt at offending you. . . . No one has loved you more for yourself alone. I feared to compromise the happiness that you still had on earth. If I could hope to express to you all my gratitude, to thank you for your kindness, it would make a beautiful moment in my life, and I would have nothing more to complain of.[10]

She mentions the reinstallation of Napoleon's statue on top of the Vendôme column, an attempt to appease the Bonapartist faction, and describes Louis-Philippe as "a man without eminence, who possesses common shrewdness hidden beneath the exterior of a simple good-natured man." In conclusion, she says she has heard from Charlotte and is so happy not to have been entirely forgotten by one to whom she will always be the *"respectueuse et attachée servante."*[11] The disagreement between Joseph and Félix seems to have evaporated by September, since the count wrote to him that he had learned with much pleasure of his arrival in New York and only wished he could have been with him.[12]

Joseph had not seen his aged mother since 1815, as Italy was forbidden territory. Therefore he decided in the winter of 1833 to send Sari to visit her as he was not able to himself. He knew of no one better, he told her, than a man who had lived with him for fifteen years and knew his least thoughts. Thus, Sari could respond to everything she would wish to know about her son's past, present, and future. He himself will stay in England (rather than the United States) because he thinks it multiplies his chances for coming to see her eventually, "the dearest wish" of his heart. English laws and the people's good will give him total security until he can find the same thing elsewhere. Charlotte will remain with him until Sari returns, and when the weather improves she will go back to her mother in Florence and her grandmother and sister in Rome. He adds that Charlotte is very sensitive to the dignity she must maintain toward her name and her social position. "We have often had discussions about this in which we agree that one cannot always do what one wants but what one must."[13] Charlotte's husband had once remarked on her near-obsession with the importance of her Bonaparte name. No doubt this had been drilled into her from childhood, since her father and Uncle Napoleon had wanted her to marry only a Bonaparte, so that her children would bear the name. Both she and Zénaïde had complied by marrying cousins.

However depressed Joseph might have felt by his continuing exile and deflated by the collapse of his mission, it was heartwarming to hear with much respect from Victor Hugo, now famous as the author of *Notre-Dame de Paris*. Hugo, with fond memories of his childhood at Joseph's court in Madrid, addressed him as "Your Majesty." "Permit me, Sire, to always treat you royally," the author wrote in February 1833.

> According to me, nothing can unmake [*défaire*] the kings made by Napoleon. There is not a human hand that could efface the august mark that that great man put on a person's forehead. I have been profoundly touched by the sympathy Your Majesty has shown me for the legal proceedings [*procès*] concerning *Le Roi s'amuse*. You love liberty, Sire; and liberty loves you. . . . I would be happy, Sire, to go to London, and to press the royal hand that so many times pressed the hand of my father. M[onsieur] Presle will tell Your Majesty of the obstacles that prevent me at the moment from realizing this dear wish. . . . I would have had so many things of all kinds to tell you. . . . You carry the greatest of historic names. The truth is we march rather towards a republic than toward a monarchy; but to a sage like you the exterior form of the government is not important. You have proved, Sire, that you know how to be worthily the citizen of a republic. Adieu, Sire, the day when I will be able to take your hand in mine will be one of the most beautiful of my life. In waiting, your letters make me proud and happy.[14]

Le Roi s'amuse had premiered on 22 November 1832, to such an uproar from the aristocrats in the audience for the play's ridicule of the monarchy that the next day all further performances were banned. The Court could not endure such derision on the public stage, even if the king depicted was François I from a different century.

When Hugo had appeared before the bar, he had indicted the July monarchy of Louis-Philippe, accusing it of taking away, one after the other, the rights of the citizens. He had had to agree that in the days of Napoleon, censorship had been heavy, with advertisements announcing plays often torn down. Still, he had proclaimed, "there was one unfailing answer to our grievances: Marengo! Jena! Austerlitz!"[15] Nearly twenty years later, Verdi would use *Le Roi s'amuse* as his text for *Rigoletto* (1851) and also be subject to censorship because the story contained the attempted assassination of a king, a subject that remained politically taboo. In this case the "king" was the repressive Austrian emperor.

There is no doubt that Joseph was on the side of freedom from undue censorship by the government. He had lived with this freedom for seventeen years in the United States and had seen how well it worked in a republic. It must have been frustrating to think that had he been the regent for his nephew, he would never have permitted the censorship of such free thinkers as Victor Hugo and those like him. He was therefore pleased when Barry O'Meara, Napoleon's benevolent physician on St. Helena, introduced him to a great liberal, Daniel O'Connell, the Irish political leader known as the Liberator for, among other things, his efforts to abolish anti-Catholic laws in Ireland. O'Connell spoke French, having been schooled in France, which made for easy communication. At O'Connell's invitation, Joseph visited Ireland and was gratified by his welcome.[16] The two men were both lawyers, Catholics, devoted to equal human rights, and had a mutual friend in O'Meara. Joseph would later describe O'Meara as his only true friend in England.

To his astonishment, Joseph was visited that spring by "le haute noblesse," as Mailliard described the Duke of Wellington and the dukes of Hamilton and Gordon.[17] Having been driven out of Spain by Wellington, who two years later had defeated Napoleon at Waterloo and was thus ultimately responsible for the collapse of the empire, Joseph must have summoned all his dignity and *savoir-faire* to shake hands amicably with Arthur Wellesley, the "Iron Duke."

Several days later, according to protocol, he, along with Lucien and Lucien's son-in-law, Lord Dudley Stuart, repaid the visit at Apsley House, the duke's magnificent mansion in Hyde Park. How astonished the two Bonaparte brothers must have been to behold, at the foot of the staircase, Antonio Canova's almost twice life-sized marble statue of their brother as a naked, idealized figure. When the emperor had first seen the finished work in 1811, he had ordered it into storage, concerned that it would expose him to ridicule if exhibited. At the time the public no longer cared to see their leaders depicted as Greek gods, but rather as ordinary citizens in contemporary clothes. After the restoration of the Bourbon monarchy, Wellington had the statue, which ironically bore the title of *Napoleon as Mars the Peacemaker* (fig. 37), shipped to him from Paris.[18]

During the same visit to Apsley House, Joseph must have seen the Spanish paintings Wellington had captured from his carriages at the battle of Vitoria. If so, neither he nor Lucien could have had regrets, since they both had Spanish pictures on the walls of their dwellings; Lucien having found his tour of duty as ambassador to Spain from 1800 to 1801 extremely lucrative, particularly in the form of diamonds and works of art.

In early April 1833, the count moved his entire entourage for the spring and summer to a country house, Marden Park, a mile from the village of Godstone, south of London. Lucien took a house nearby. Sari returned from Rome on 15 April, and several weeks later Mailliard noted in his journal that there was dissatisfaction with the Saris, who were sullen with everyone (*boudent tout le monde*). "This family is in a false position," he observed, "and she [Emma] is very extravagant." The count wanted Sari to go back to the United States and attempt to sell his Black River lands, but Emma was not interested in settling down in the remote village of Carthage, New York, when there was a chance she could live in Paris. "I doubt if this will happen," observed Mailliard, in reference to the Black River idea. "A stranger would be better [to deal with the land]—Mr. Sari sulks. I hunt with bassets and kill two rabbits."[19]

As the months went on, Joseph increasingly found his expenses in England higher than they had been in America. He also had the cost of keeping up Point Breeze. In an attempt to raise funds he decided to sell some of his diamonds and a few paintings that he had had sent over from the United States, since he could not sell them there. On 27 June the diamonds were offered at a public sale in London but they remained unsold, as the count's minimum price was not realized. Two days later, however, a group of paintings offered at Christie and Manson's auction house in St. James Square did sell. They were all different from the ones Charles had brought to London in 1827, all of which had presumably been bought by this time. According to the catalog they included *The Boar at Bay*, "a grand picture, very powerfully painted and brilliantly coloured," with its companion, *The Creation*, by Franz Snyders; "an upright landscape, with a wind-mill, and figures on a road," and "a fair at a village in Holland, with a post-waggon and numerous figures," both by Breughel; "a man's head seen in profile, circular" by Van Dyck; "A hunting party returning from the chase, with a dead boar and stag on a mule, with a village and extensive distant view" by Esaias Van de Velde; "Dead partridges and other birds" by Jan Fyt; "*The Holy Family*" by Andrea del Sarto; and "The Virgin presenting an apple to the infant Christ, who is seated on a pedestal, with landscape distance—a small upright

37. **Napoleon as Mars the Peacemaker** *by Antonio Canova, 1806. Marble. Victoria & Albert Museum, from Apsley House, London. Art Resource, NY.*

with arched top, on panel" by "Raffaelle."[20] Mailliard says in his memoirs that these pictures were sold for "nothing" and that Sari came back from the sale *"tout furieux."*[21]

It is not surprising that the subjects of many of these works of art had to do with hunting since Joseph had been an enthusiast of the sport for years. The fact that a majority of Dutch and Flemish artists are represented would suggest that these pictures had come from Spain. Many paintings from the lowlands were in the Spanish royal collections because Spain had occupied the Netherlands for an extended time. These works either escaped capture from the battlefield of Vitoria, or had been taken previously to France.

Various associates of Joseph sold other paintings for him at different times. James Carret, who had originally accompanied him to America as his interpreter, sold diverse paintings by way of Batard Stanley and Company in London; and Dr. Stockoë, the physician who had attended both Charlotte and Zénaïde on their voyages to the New World, also sold works of art on Joseph's behalf. Félix Lacoste sold paintings for him in France, including "a Venus," while a Mr. Binda sold others and sent some on to Julie. And, according to Mailliard, in place of a pension, Stockoë received "a great Rubens" from the count.[22]

It had been heartening for Joseph, who held stock in several American concerns, mostly canals, to hear from Hopkinson that spring that his Schuylkill Navigation stock was still rising and would probably continue to rise "as the trade [bringing anthracite coal from the Lehigh Valley] which passes through that canal [on the Schuylkill River] is immense and constantly increasing." Not welcoming was the news that his nephew Pierre, Lucien's black-sheep son, was still in Bordentown and living with Lucien Murat. Hopkinson says he does not know what Pierre's intentions are about returning to his father, as he has not seen him since he returned from South America. "Lucien [Murat] once asked me to advance Pierre some money, on your account," he adds, "but I had no authority to do so—this may have offended him, and be the reason he has not called upon me."[23]

On 12 October Charlotte departed for Italy, much to Joseph's sorrow, but he hoped she might return in the spring and perhaps accompany him back to Point Breeze. In order to lift his spirits, he, Mailliard, and Barry O'Meara toured Windsor Castle, admiring the round tower, the Chapel of St. George, the gallery, the grand apartments, and the magnificent view. Joseph was a sightseer, for Mailliard records that earlier they had visited Blenheim Castle and Woburn Abbey. But he was not feeling well, perhaps a recurrence of "the gravel" from which, as he had told Girard in 1830 he had been suffering for ten years. Girard had recommended mixing gin with oil and water, and drinking it every morning and evening.[24] Either this remedy was unsuccessful, as he no longer felt well enough to hunt, or the expense of Marden Park was too much, for in July 1834 the count moved again, this time to Denham Place in Buckinghamshire, only twenty-five kilometers from London.

He was deeply saddened to learn of Lafayette's death in May 1834. Another strong link to his past and a possible connection to his future return to France were now gone. At one time he had pinned his hopes on Lafayette's influence with the Chamber of Deputies, but the deputies had ruled against the Bonaparte family ever returning to France, making an exception of Madame Mère, who promptly refused to separate herself from her children and grandchildren. Joseph and Lucien had together written a long document of appeal to the Chamber, but it was all to no avail. It seemed the Bonapartes would be exiles forever. Discouraged, Joseph told Ingersoll in July that he would be with him as soon as his letter, if not detained by purely domestic responsibilities. He had assured his sick wife and octogenarian mother that he would wait in England for another year, hoping there might be "a moment of light in politics" to allow him to bid them a last farewell. "I am more than ever disgusted with Europe, and if I could hope to snatch from it my mother and wife, without fearing to lose them both on the way, you would not be delayed in seeing us all on your happy shores. But, apprehending the fate of the Trojan [Ulysses], I give one more year to filial piety and conjugal love."[25] It often seems as though Joseph, when in the United States, wrote to his family and friends in Europe of his strong desire to return to that side of the Atlantic, but when in England he would write to his friends in America that he was disgusted with Europe and wanted to come back to Point Breeze.

Joseph was also more and more dismayed by his domestic predicament since the difficulties with the Saris were increasing. There seems to have been much jealousy of Mailliard on their part, aside from other problems. Joseph's financial advisors had for sometime been cautioning him that he was living beyond his means and he would need to cut down on expenses. Maintaining the Saris was costly, and it was clear they would have to live on their own. He offered Mathieu Sari 100,000 francs in land at the Black River if he would go to America and take charge of his affairs in northern New York State. Since Emma wanted no part of this arrangement, things appeared to be at a standstill, until a letter arrived from Cardinal Fesch in Rome that set events in motion. The cardinal asserted that gossip in the Eternal City had it that Emma Sari was Joseph's mistress. Then it was said that Lucien was having an affair with

Emma. Mathieu, enraged and true Corsican that he was, challenged Lucien to a duel. But the whole business was settled by Joseph's intervention before things went too far. There was now no doubt the Saris must leave.

In November, Mailliard noted that "The Prince of Canino [Lucien] is not content with us, he has left to spend some days in London!!" Lucien soon returned to Denham Place, but left abruptly once again. "The patron is angry with his brother who leaves us and returns to London," Mailliard recorded. "The Prince of Canino is as he always has been: an enemy of the Emperor. Madame Sari is the cause of this argument between the two brothers. Ah! Women!"²⁶ Lucien did not return to Denham Place.

Much to everyone's relief, the Saris departed for Paris the first of May 1835. "I think we will not miss them," Mailliard noted ironically in his journal, "but they will regret not having accepted the 100,000 francs they had been offered in the United States where they could have been comfortable and rendered service to their patron. This woman will be the downfall [*la perte*] of her family!"²⁷ Joseph and Mailliard accompanied the Saris to London to see them off. That evening the two men went to O'Meara's house to meet with Count Léon, who had just arrived from Paris. Léon, a rascal and a deadbeat, was Napoleon's natural son by a mistress, Eleanora Denuelle. Mailliard notes that Count Léon, "as always," laid out "extravagant plans." "All these people are crazy [*fou*]!" the faithful secretary exclaimed to his journal. "The best would be for us to go back to Point Breeze."²⁸

The next day, Joseph and Mailliard went to see Lucien, who was soon to leave for Italy because his wife was ill. He complained about the gossip against him in Rome and said he was delighted the Saris had left. Perhaps it was just as well that Lucien also was leaving because of the terrible quarrels the two brothers so often had, particularly over politics. Once Joseph had been so worked up that Sari had had to take him by the hand and pull him from the room, fearing he would have a stroke.²⁹

After the Saris' departure, William Thibaud and his lovely seventeen-year-old daughter, Josephine, took their place, the latter replacing Emma Sari as Joseph's hostess. Thibaud's father had served as the Joseph's crown treasurer in Naples and again in Spain. He was killed in the massacre at Vitoria. Subsequently his son joined Joseph's entourage at Point Breeze to assist in managing his financial affairs.

By that spring of 1835, Joseph had finally decided to give up all hope of entering France and to return to the United States, where he could live more economically. "Here we would be ruined," Mailliard noted in his journal. Joseph had sold many of his possessions and had even appealed to Cardinal Fesch to leave his famous collection of paintings to the family, rather than to churches in Corsica as he had planned.

Joseph's financial situation would be somewhat relieved that summer, however, when he sold his entire Black River holdings, exclusive of land parcels previously given away, to John Lafarge for $80,000. On 8 September Joseph and Mailliard, accompanied by William Thibaud and his daughter, set out for America aboard one of Girard's ships, the *Monongahela*, having been away for three years.[30]

Chapter 15 # RETURN TO POINT BREEZE

I want to be in America before the end of next year because I don't find here the tranquillity of spirit I left on the banks of the Delaware.
—Joseph Bonaparte to Joseph Hopkinson,
London, 12 December 1836

*J*oseph sailed up the Delaware to Philadelphia on 18 October 1835. There was a certain relief in being back in America where he still had friends and his handsome house and park to enjoy. After the turbulent life he had led in London, Point Breeze would be a tranquil haven. Yet the opportunity to have seen his brothers again, his daughter especially, and other members of his family had meant a great deal to him. He always enjoyed the camaraderie and gaiety of a full house of guests, and French-speaking guests at that. The count was hospitable to a fault; certainly that had been the case with the Saris who eventually wore out their welcome.

There had been a major change at Point Breeze since he left, for now a railroad crossed part of his land. He had opposed it from the beginning, even bringing an injunction against the company that planned to build it, but without much success. At least he was not alone in his negative attitude. Deborah Logan wrote in her diary for 1830, "I have said nothing about the Rail Road whose ugly unfinished sections we passed in several places—people through whose land it comes, dislike it exceedingly, and I do not wonder at it."[1] Nevertheless it was a boon for travelers. By the beginning of 1833 the first railroad in the country had been finished with a single track between Bordentown and Amboy (now Perth Amboy), New Jersey, pulled by a steam-driven locomotive imported from England, dubbed the "John Bull." Passengers boarded a steamboat in Philadelphia for Bordentown, where they transferred to the train for Amboy and a ferry for New York. By 1834, this journey of ninety-four miles would be accomplished in four and a half hours.[2] By horse-drawn coach it had taken overnight.

Perhaps it was the effect of seeing his beautiful property defaced by the railroad, or else age was beginning to dictate a new lifestyle; in any case, Joseph thought to move into Philadelphia for good. In February he told Joseph Hopkinson he had learned that a Mr. Powel planned to sell his large house on Locust Street before leaving for Europe. Joseph had asked the architect William Strickland to look it over.[3] Winter was now too much for him in Bordentown, so he was seriously considering this acquisition, with or without the furniture, if the price and terms of payment were right. He was hoping to sell a house he had bought a while back in Union Street (today Delancey Street, which then ran from Front Street to Fourth) for twelve thousand dollars and would expect to pay about that for the Powel house. If it were more, he would pay the remainder in personal property or real estate. Joseph reminded Hopkinson that "Mr. Sully" said his paintings were the best of his things and he, or any other artist selected by Powel, could choose from them. However, if the price of the house were more than that of Union Street and cash was required, he would not be able to afford it. He could sacrifice the paintings because he could easily replace them, thanks to the benevolence of his uncle, Cardinal Fesch, who would send him any paintings he wanted. Hopkinson knew as well as he did, Joseph went on, that his properties in Bordentown would one day be very valuable in the eyes of speculators, but he does not have time to wait. It is the same with the farms, but they require more supervision than his health permits. He would sacrifice them for a large house in Philadelphia, regardless of what street it was on.[4] Apparently, he did not intend to sell Point Breeze.

Joseph may not have been particularly concerned over which paintings Sully might select for Powel, because he had already sold in London what he believed to be the best. One treasure remained, however. In early January he wrote Hopkinson, still president of the Pennsylvania Academy of the Fine Arts, to have "the hunt of Diana" by Rubens put in a lighter frame, as the one it was in was too heavy for transport. The picture was to be sent to Barry O'Meara in London to arrange for repairs.[5] While in England he had asked Hopkinson a year earlier to send him "la chasse de Diane" if it could arrive by the end of the year; clearly it had not been sent.[6] This large painting, *Diana and Her Nymphs Hunting Deer*, which Joseph Bonaparte took from Spain, is considered from the studio of Rubens and was painted for the Torre della Parada, King Philip IV's hunting lodge outside Madrid, sometime between 1701 and 1703. It has not been traced since the 1950s.

One wonders how much Joseph really cared about the quality of paintings, as opposed to the quantity, from his statement about an arbitrary selection from Cardinal Fesch. And yet he does seem to have been knowledgeable about great works of art, in that he knew which of his paintings were the most valuable and would do best at auction when he needed money. But more important to him seems to have been the need to surround himself with objects of a certain elegance. Then again, he may not have been impressed with the quality of his uncle's pictures. Portraits of family members were the paintings Joseph especially treasured, not surprising for an expatriate.

Aside from his friends and neighbors in Bordentown, Joseph's large country house was too isolated for someone who had always surrounded himself with lively company. He was feeling the pain of exile more than ever as he grew older. Julie was contentedly ensconced in the Villa Serristori in Florence with her beloved Charlotte and her half-sister, Honorine de Villeneuve. She would never come to America, and there was little probability that even Charlotte would cross the Atlantic again. Zénaïde and Charles were fixed in Rome at the Villa Paulina with their ever-increasing family, now numbering six children, the second child born in America having died. Charles, an accomplished and highly regarded ornithologist, was deeply involved with writing and publishing a history of the fauna of Italy, *Icongrafia della Fauna Italica*, including sections that dealt with the mammals, birds, amphibians, and fish found in Italy. He was also beginning what would become almost total immersion in politics and founding scientific congresses with political undertones. The Italian cause of independence and freedom from Austrian domination was paramount in his life. He was the true republican in his actions that Joseph only professed to be. Charles would never be persuaded to bring his family to live in the United States.

For sometime there had been disturbing reports about Charles's personality and lifestyle. Madame Mère had said to his mother-in-law, Julie, in 1833, "I am very displeased with Charles, but since you know this it will not astonish you. He talks too much and she [Zénaïde] permits truly inexcusable faults [*écarts*]."[7] It seems he had taken up gambling and was running through Zénaïde's money. This he constantly excused, perhaps with justification, by saying he needed funds to purchase books and the endless supply of natural history specimens for his work, to say nothing of the expenses of his constant traveling for science as well as politics.

Two of Joseph's brothers, Jérôme and Louis, also lived in Florence, and Lucien was not far away on his estate at Canino near Viterbo. Madame Mère—old, blind, and nearly paralyzed—lived on in the immense Villa Bonaparte on the Piazza Venetia with Cardinal Fesch nearby. All Joseph's loved ones were close to each other; only he was thousands of miles away. His only relations in America, aside from Jérôme Patterson-Bonaparte in Baltimore, were his two Murat nephews, Achille and Lucien, both of whom were more of an annoyance to him than anything else. Both had tried to extract as much money from their uncle as possible, particularly Lucien, who squandered it in drinking and carousing until his poor wife, whose fortune he had run through, had to open a boarding school in Bordentown in order to keep her family solvent. Achille, the older and more intelligent of the two, though less physically attractive, lived and farmed in Tallahassee, Florida, with his wife, a great-niece of George Washington. Achille had become an American citizen shortly after his arrival and was devoted to his adopted country, perhaps the only thing he shared with his uncle.

America had become a true refuge for Joseph after the more than seventeen years he had spent there. If he could find a handsome house in Philadelphia, perhaps the stimulation of his friends at the American Philosophical Society and the Pennsylvania Academy of the Fine Arts would ease the isolation of his exile. He was now sixty-eight and beginning to feel it. The past was the past and he cared more to see again his ever-faithful wife after so many years of separation than to have anything to do with former mistresses. He did not yearn for past loves, certainly not for Anna now living with her husband, Delafolie, daughter Caroline Charlotte, and several children by Delafolie, at Ox Bow, near the Black River, nor even for Emilie and little Félix-Joseph in Paris. Both women had lost their charms for him, and he preferred not to acknowledge his children by them so as to shield his legitimate family.

Emilie was only too painfully aware of this. At the end of February 1833, after months of frustration at receiving no answer from Joseph to her letters, she wrote to Louis Mailliard. She had learned that the count had gone back to America and was afraid he might never return to Europe. In that case she would lose all hope of ever seeing him again and of speaking to him of his son. Since Mailliard had always shown attachment and affection for her children, she asked him what she should do. Because the count is so fond of Mailliard, anything coming from him would be more effective than what she might say, her argument ran; he could not let the count forget what he promised to do for his child. The poor little one was delicate and might not be able to earn his living. "It is a mother who requests this of you, my dear Mailliard," she says, "for it would be great peace and tranquillity for me to be sure that the count would make provisions for his child. Since he does not write a single word to me on the most serious subject of my life, I put all my hopes in your hands. Great men [*les grands Seigneurs*] easily forget how little it takes to bring satisfaction and tranquillity. Be my intermediary, dear Mailliard, I know your excellent heart, so just and fine, and the generosity of all your sentiments. You are the only person in the world who could intervene on behalf of my child."[8]

She mentions that she and her husband are on good terms again and that she often receives news of him. Her son Léon is definitely going to be a sailor, much to her chagrin, since it is a career with continual privations. "Alas," she says, "if I had a little money I would be able to object more overtly to this project. Write to your son who comes to see us sometimes—he is the most charming young man." (Adolphe was attending the elite Collège Henri IV in Paris.) Several times she has seen "Madame Sari, who says the stupidest nonsense possible [*les plus grosses bêtises possibles*]." She concludes, "Adieu, dear Mailliard, speak sometimes of the mother and the child to your *seigneur*."[9]

Joseph was not entirely insensitive to Emilie's request, and he would provide for Félix-Joseph, but at the time he was distracted by the death of his revered mother. When she breathed her last on 2 February 1836, Madame Mère was eighty-six, a strong and viable presence for her children and grandchildren until the end (fig. 38). Like her eldest son, Joseph, she had not approved of Napoleon declaring himself emperor of the French. She had even refused to attend his coronation, remaining in Rome. Even so, Napoleon had directed Jacques-Louis David, in his famous painting of the event, *Le Sacré de Napoleon*, to include his mother in the picture. A strong, courageous woman of great dignity, Letizia Ramolino Buonaparte was a true daughter of Corsica, where her rough but noble family had been established for generations. Once Joseph had told Nicholas Biddle that although it was not a thing to boast of, his family was one of the oldest in Europe, dating back eight hundred years to the Galfonière of Florence.[10]

Baron de Méneval told Joseph that his mother's death had produced a marked impression on the French people. Many wreaths had been placed at the base of Napoleon's Austerlitz column in the Place Vendôme, and one of the most distinguished French poets (perhaps Victor Hugo) had written heartfelt articles about her in several newspapers and in the *Revue de Paris*. Méneval added that, perhaps in reaction to Bonapartist sentiment generated by her death, a certain citizen had presented a petition to the Chamber of Paris asking that the emperor's mortal remains be returned to France from St. Helena. The baron had heard that Lord Palmerson's deputy was willing to put forth a motion from the English in this regard, but the response of the French minister had been silence. Nevertheless, Méneval was quite sanguine that at long last the hostility against the Bonapartes was, at the least, beginning to dissipate.[11]

His mother's death may have stirred thoughts of Joseph's own mortality; possibly exacerbated by an illness he had had that winter. Together with the old burning desire

38. **Portrait of Madame Mère** *by Charlotte Bonaparte, 1835. Watercolor. Collection of Giuseppe Primoli, Museo Napoleonico, Rome.*

to go home, these factors convinced him by spring to return to Europe. Also, in a statement to Méneval that would have dismayed his American friends, he said that for some months a rupture had been feared between France and the United States and he "did not care to stay in an enemy country."[12] This sentiment shows how tired he was of exile and how much he still identified with France. He told his brother-in-law Félix Bacciochi, his sister Elisa's widower, that he had resolved not to spend another winter in the United States. Losses of every kind determined his departure from a country that had become for him a second homeland (*patrie*). The news of his mother's decease made up his mind.[13] But there was little joy in the decision; he had earlier told Hopkinson that England, the only country open to him in Europe, was a place where he had "no possessions, no friends, and no memories."[14]

At his house in Bordentown, however, as well as friends and memories of events and people, there were possessions filled with memories, *souvenirs*, as the French say. A visitor to Point Breeze in the summer of 1836, perhaps shortly before Joseph left the second time for England, described her tour of the count's inner sanctum. With several others he had conducted her to his private library on the second floor where bookcases filled with "handsomely bound" books reached from floor to ceiling. After his guests had admired the collection, the count touched a secret spring causing a line of skillfully imitated book covers to fly open and reveal a set of drawers. From these he had drawn out a number of caskets containing splendid jewels. "Several clusters looked like the jewel-encrusted handles of swords and daggers," recorded his awe-struck guest, "others like portions of crowns broken off." Even more dazzling were the crown and rings Joseph had worn as king of Spain and Napoleon's crown, robes, and jewels from his coronation. In other drawers were many of Napoleon's valuable papers: treaties, and letters carefully bound with ribbons and fastened with jeweled clasps, all of which the count handled with a kind of reverence. Earlier, when he had shown them "costly engravings" of Napoleon's life and career, his visitor noted that he had said in broken English, "I sigh for the death of my poor brother!"[15]

Nevertheless, leaving behind him, locked in secret drawers, these valuable *souvenirs* from an incredible life of war, death, plunder, passion, and royal splendor, Joseph set sail in the summer of 1836 with Mailliard, Thibaud and his daughter, and his usual retinue of servants, leaving the overall management of Point Breeze, the farms, the woods, and the houses with Edmund DuBarry, a young doctor in Bordentown who was also Joseph's manager. Two of his retainers, Maury and Thorn, were left in charge of the main house, while the garden was under the special care of Benjamin Higgins. The cultivable part of the park Joseph turned over to Alexander Wood, and a Mr. W. Lippincott rented the Lake House. He told DuBarry he did not intend to sell any portion of the land and, in a display of unusual firmness, said that he had nothing more to say on the subject.[16]

Before he left he had been incredibly generous, showering beautiful gifts on his friends and retainers. To his close friend, lawyer, and confidant Joseph Hopkinson, he gave a green carriage, a gray horse, and thirty bottles of Madeira wine; for Hopkinson's wife, a lovely vase and a barometer; and for their son James, a pair of pistols that had belonged to Ali Pasha, the cruel Turkish "Lion of Janina," who at times had sided with Napoleon, at other times with the English. Charles Ingersoll received a large green caleche (a two-wheeled horse-drawn vehicle), and Dr. Nathaniel Chapman, a *couvert en vermeil* (a set of knives and forks in gilded silver) that had belonged to Napoleon. To Nicholas Biddle he gave a Greek chalice excavated by Lucien at Canino, together with Lucien's handsome book on his discoveries of Greek and Etruscan artifacts. Also included in his gift to Biddle were all the pheasants at Point Breeze, presumably in cages ready to be released for hunting. Pierre Du Ponceau received a valuable codex of Virgil, and the American Philosophical Society, of which Du Ponceau was president, another of Lucien's antique chalices and a copy of Charles's massive study of the fauna of Italy, *Fauna Italica*. Usually gearing his gifts to the person, Joseph gave his hard-living nephew, Lucien Murat, two horses with harnesses and twelve dozen bottles of red wine. To Félix Lacoste he presented a magnificent religious book (*volume sacré*) that had belonged to Louis XV. And finally, to his local physician and property manager, DuBarry, he gave a sulky with harnesses, and to Alphonse Lejambre of Bordentown, from whom he had bought furniture and china, his billiard table from Point Breeze along with a set of ivory billiard balls.[17]

In late August 1833 Joseph arrived back in London, where he rented a house at 24 Park Crescent. It seems that every time he crossed the ocean he was greeted with the death of someone he sincerely cared for. This time it was his close friend Barry O'Meara and also the Duke of Gordon. "Thus Fortune or Fate appears to rebuke your return to Europe," wrote Hopkinson, "and to remind you that it is more fit for you to close your excellent life in the quiet and philosophical repose of the new world, rather than with the turbulent, unsettled and corrupt intrigues of the old." He remembers Mailliard saying that O'Meara was the only man in England Joseph could truly call his friend; the rest were polite acquaintances, but not really friends of his or his family. Hopkinson anticipates that these deaths will not be the only changes he will find in his situation in England.

The English are famous for running after novelties, violently excited by what they call Lions; but they are equally famous for changing the object of their attentions, and devoting themselves to some new idol—They will shout at the heels of a general one day— and of an elephant the next—As for yourself it is impossible for you to go among any people however fickle or rude, that your character will not command the respect and kindness of the wise and good. A man whose life and fortune are so constantly employed in acts of benevolence and generosity must be respected and beloved unless mankind should become universally selfish and depraved.[18]

No wonder Joseph missed the warmth of his American friends. He replied that Lucien was there with him but no longer O'Meara or Gordon, "the two best friends that I had here, like you and Chapman in Philadelphia." He says he expects to return to the United States in the second half of 1837.[19] England was suddenly less appealing without these two men.

It was therefore also immensely gratifying to hear from Hopkinson that September that he had recently met William Short and another Philadelphia friend, George Harrison, and that "we spoke much of you, and Mr. Short showed a feeling for you that you would hardly believe him capable of—the Good Harrisons also strongly expressed their kindness and affection for you. Indeed," continued the faithful Hopkinson, "I firmly believe that not one individual can be found in this country who does not entertain for you the same sentiments; and how could it be otherwise?"[20]

It was definitely otherwise in Europe. By the time he reached England, there was a great dispute raging among Joseph's brothers, and especially his sister Caroline, over their mother's will. Madame Mère had definitely favored Joseph and Louis. For one thing, she left to Joseph her palace on the Piazza Venetia, which Zénaïde and Charles soon occupied. Caroline was the most vehement of the siblings, as her mother had deducted a previous loan from her portion. In response Caroline brought suit in Paris, where the government had permitted her to visit. "If she succeeds in improving the lot of her children," Joseph wrote Félix Lacoste in thinly veiled disgust, "one might pardon a mother's heart, but it is a sojourn less excusable for the sister of the emperor."[21] In order to keep harmony in the family and especially to keep the Bonaparte disputes out of the newspapers, but perhaps as much to assuage his conscience at having been unduly favored, Joseph turned his share over to Caroline. He told Cardinal Fesch to give Louis all the vermeil he wanted and the silver to Jérôme. Even so, the papers in England got wind of the story and made much of it.

For years, a great deal of Joseph's time had been spent in defending his family, and principally Napoleon, against libels in the French press. He had written voluminously on the subject for Lacoste's paper, the New York-based *Courrier des États-Unis,* which he financed. On his arrival in England he found to his dismay that the *Courrier Français* in Paris had lately written that, in all his enterprises, Napoleon had consulted only his overwhelming arrogance and the convenience of his family. Joseph responded at once to the article: "Napoleon put his brothers on the vacant thrones of Europe. What Frenchmen could give him better guarantees? But was it really for their personal benefit, or in the interests of France? When he judged the politics of France more important than his family's friendship, did he hesitate an instant? Was not Holland occupied by French troops? [Napoleon took over Holland from his brother Louis.] Were not military governments established in Spain?" And, he added with a note of bitterness, "Were not his brothers surrounded every day with adversity?"[22]

Worse was to happen to denigrate the name of Bonaparte in the public mind. On 30 October 1836, Joseph's nephew, Louis Napoleon, with a handful of fellow conspirators, attempted a coup d'état by seizing the town of Strasburg, France, on the Swiss border, proclaiming the empire, and calling on the army and the people of France to overthrow the government of Louis-Philippe. The coup was a complete failure; Louis Napoleon was declared an impostor, and two and a half hours after it began he was in French custody. Louis-Philippe, not wishing to make a hero of him, dropped all charges, put the renegade aboard a French warship, and deported him to the United States. His followers were tried for high treason, but they were eventually acquitted.

In mid-ocean, the captain of Louis Napoleon's prison ship found that his sealed instructions were for Rio de Janeiro instead of New York, so the vessel spent a month in that Brazilian harbor with the prisoner confined to the ship. Two months later, he was put ashore at Norfolk, Virginia, where he took a steamboat to Baltimore and Philadelphia then another to Bordentown. His uncle Joseph being in London at the time, Louis Napoleon did not stop at Point Breeze, but transferred to the railroad for the trip to New York. There he was a great social success entertained by many of the leading families, including Washington Irving, who invited him to his country estate in Tarrytown.[23]

Joseph was furious at the attempted coup. His nephew had not only usurped his (Joseph's) dynastic rights, but had closed the door for the foreseeable future on any possibility of the Bonaparte family's return to France. "This alleged Bonapartist plot is a foolhardy attempt aimed as much against us [Joseph and his brothers] as against the government," he told Lacoste. His disgust with Louis Napoleon was complete. "You recall my complaints to him about his ambition; they were only too-well founded. His dissimulation has been extreme; he has regarded his father and his uncles as already dead. I have decided not to receive him on my return to America."[24] Joseph was unswervingly opposed to all conspiracy, insurrection, and violence of any kind; he was convinced that only a spontaneous popular movement could restore the Bonapartes. His young ambitious nephew was not willing to wait for such an unlikely event and considered his Uncle Joseph too old to launch any meaningful activity in that direction.

Jérôme wrote Joseph from Florence, "All that you say about the folly of our nephew Louis, is so true. We only know here what the papers say and it is enough to groan [*gémir*] over such a ridiculous enterprise. You know the state of his unhappy father."[25] Louis had told him that every time he received a letter from his "wretched son," he burned it unread.[26]

Sometime later, Joseph, still angry, would say that Louis Napoleon did not have a drop of Napoleonic blood in his veins.[27] This was not entirely a figure of speech. Louis Napoleon's parents, Hortense and Joseph's brother, Louis, despised each other and it had been suspected for years that Louis Napoleon had been fathered by one of Hortense's lovers. The fact that he did not resemble the Bonapartes in the least only added to this conjecture. But, like most Bonapartes, he was quick-witted. Once after Louis Napoleon had refused to give Lucien Murat, always in debt, more money to squander, Lucien had snapped, "You have nothing of your uncle [Napoleon] about you." "Pardon," Louis Napoleon replied, "I have his relatives."[28]

In early December, Joseph wrote Hopkinson: "I want to be in America before the end of next year because I don't find here the tranquillity of spirit that I left on the banks of the Delaware." He says he does not want any of his nephews near him: "They don't listen to me, therefore I don't want to give or sell land to any of them, nor to encourage them to establish themselves near me. I am convinced it would not be good for them, or for me."[29] Joseph's nephews had all been a thorn in his side at one time or other, including his own son-in-law Charles, with whom he had not gotten along when they lived together at Point Breeze.

A few weeks later he told Hopkinson how overcome (*accablée*) his family was, especially his brother Lucien, who was with him, by the "events of Strasbourg and of Rome." This last refers to Lucien's son Pierre, a black sheep from the beginning, who, back in Italy, had committed murder. An irresponsible would-be revolutionary,

Pierre had conspired against the pope, and when tracked down at his father's home in Canino, had fatally shot the papal policeman sent to arrest him. He had been taken into custody and imprisoned in Rome's Castel St. Angelo. The pope would eventually commute Pierre's sentence to exile, but because of his choleric temperament, his life would be chaotic. In later years Pierre would be popularly known as "the Corsican wild boar."[30]

In the same letter to Hopkinson, Joseph says that everyone in his household has influenza, "and in this state of things, can you doubt that I regret my active, independent, tranquil life at Point Breeze? However, I don't think I can leave here in May as I had hoped, unless the scene changes by the intervention of a God who can lower the curtain, as Horace says, and permit us to depart with full sails toward you. Thank you so much for the cranberries and apples you have sent in such abundance."[31] Point Breeze in Joseph's mind is once again wrapped in the aura of a heavenly retreat.

In spite of all his difficulties, Joseph maintained his sense of humor. He says that he has had the honor to meet Hopkinson's friend, a Mr. Robinson, who speaks better French than Joseph speaks English, so they have decided to speak French between them. "He does not agree that I speak passable English and prefers that I reserve my English for you and Dr. Chapman when I return to Bordentown and Philadelphia."[32]

Hopkinson had also introduced him to another friend, a distinguished visitor from Philadelphia: Professor Alexander Dallas Bache, a great-grandson of Benjamin Franklin who, Hopkinson wrote, had inherited more of "the talents and genius of the celebrated man than any other of his descendants." Bache had lately been appointed president of Girard College, a school for poor and orphaned boys, the legacy of Joseph's friend Stephen Girard, and he was going to Europe to obtain information on the best possible course of education for that institution. Hopkinson asked Joseph to give him whatever aid he can. "You are particularly acquainted with the scientific persons in France and Italy from whom he will be able to get the knowledge he is seeking."[33] Joseph eagerly welcomed such persons as Bache, who drew him out of the world of politics and intrigue and into the intellectual sphere that he most enjoyed.

It was reassuring to hear from Edmund Du Barry, left in charge of Point Breeze, that people in Bordentown spoke of the Strasbourg affair only as the folly of a young man. "I repudiate any idea that you had the least part in it. I cite the opinion of respected individuals who say that if you come to live again on your beautiful property it is because you love this country and that your opinions '*toutes républicaines*' accord better with our ideas than with those of the highly aristocratic English."[34]

In April, Louis Napoleon wrote to Joseph from New York in an attempt to justify himself. On arriving in the United States he had hoped to find a letter from his uncle and had been hurt, even astonished, to learn that Joseph was angry with him. He accused Joseph of being wrong in spurning as enemies men who had devoted themselves to the cause of the empire. He had risked his life and thought that even his death would be useful to the cause in an enterprise to reestablish what twenty years of peace had forgotten. And what did he find on the part of his family but contempt and disdain. "Public opinion will only see a schism between you and me. No one will understand that you disavowed your nephew because he exposed himself for your cause." He says that he has been given proof that he has done the right thing and—what must have made Joseph wince—he was persuaded that if the emperor looked down from heaven, he would be pleased with him. His enterprise was aborted, true, but it announced to France that Napoleon's family was not yet dead and that it still counted devoted friends among its followers. "This is what I have done. Is it for you to resent me?" He then concludes, "Never doubt my unalterable attachment to you, your affectionate and respectful nephew."[35] Summoned to Switzerland where his mother, Hortense, was dying of cancer, he shortly left the country.

Joseph responded in July: "You have broken the ties that attach me to you in thinking yourself capable of taking my place and that of your father. From now on I want you to leave me in peace in my retreat."[36]

There had been nothing but trouble since Joseph returned to England. He now longed to be back at Point Breeze. The letter that Hopkinson had written to Mailliard in early January, which Joseph had no doubt read, had summed up his situation in America and had been immensely pleasing in its sentiments. Such a letter made him nostalgic for the gilded exile he had so enjoyed. Hopkinson wrote that he had often reflected on the splendid position of the count at Point Breeze. He had had a sufficient fortune for "bountiful hospitality" and enough to live better than any other gentlemen of the countryside. With a pure conscience, untroubled by his past life (one wonders if this were true), he had been able to help others and receive the gratitude of those about him. At Point Breeze he had been able to withdrawn from the "whirlwind" of the world. "What dethroned monarch has been more fortunate than he to fall in such a way?" Hopkinson asks, "Generally they have become beggars for aid, or pensioners or prisoners. This is a change rather than a fall."

He continues, that in the United States there have been no fawning nobles ready to betray and abandon him at the first shift of his fortunes, nor treacherous counselors working to deceive him, but instead, American friends who are honest and sincere in their attachment with no agenda for personal reward. Not one of us expects or desires anything but the count's friendship, he says, and we are proud of that, not because of what he was but of what we know he is.[37] This sentiment is exactly what

Joseph did not find in England. The English had a persistent and underlying resentment of who he was: the brother of Napoleon.

Hopkinson wrote to Joseph himself in mid-April 1837 to ask the cause of the bitter animosity against him and his family in the leading London journals. "On your former visit you were treated at least with personal decency, indeed with some degree of complement and respect, but now every epithet which hatred and contempt can supply is poured with unsparing wrath upon every member of your family—they always have hated and always will hate every drop of Bonaparte Blood—they remember how once they feared it, and this now rankles in their hearts." He says that Mailliard is right that the count has no friends in that country.[38]

There may not have been fawning nobles or treacherous counselors to trouble Joseph in England, but there was always his family and their disputes. Lucien came in the summer and in September his son, Charles, arrived to stay for three months along with Joseph's grandson Lucien, or Luciano, the nine-year-old "Loulou" who one day would be a cardinal. Zénaïde's dowry, still not paid to the young couple, was a continuing source of serious contention between Charles and his father. Once in London, Charles sued Lucien. A statement signed by Joseph, perhaps in connection with the lawsuit, expresses his deep dismay at this unhappy development: "The Count de Survilliers is profoundly tormented by the proceedings against all the laws of nature and of civilized society that exist between his brother Lucien and his son-in-law and nephew, because of the dowry of his daughter Zénaïde, which was by the contract of marriage put on the mortgage of the principality of Canino at 4%."[39]

Since there is no further mention of the lawsuit in Charles's subsequent letters, it may have been settled, and Charles must also have been getting along with Joseph for the time being, since he took Loulou hunting on his father-in-law's rented estate in Suffolk. The little boy wrote Zénaïde proudly that while out with his grandfather he had not held his ears when the guns went off.[40]

At Point Breeze itself there were issues to be dealt with. Edmund DuBarry wrote that he was not making enough money to support his family and that he would have to leave Bordentown and join the navy. Bordentown was becoming worse every day, no one paid for his services and everything cost double what it used to. His principal aim was to ensure the future of his wife and children: if he should die, as things are she would have nothing, but if he were in the navy his widow would receive seven hundred dollars. "If you should sell Point Breeze, which is very possible," he says, "or if by some misfortune I should learn of your death, because we are all mortal, what would become of my family, what would become of me, I am certain Bordentown could not sustain me with all my efforts."[41] He asks the count for an advance of five hundred dollars, to which Joseph readily agreed. It would have been to the count's advantage to have offered DuBarry more salary to stay on, as it turns out. Hopkinson wrote at the end of the year that a road would be put through one of Joseph's farms, an unwanted development "that could have been prevented if your agent Dubarry had acted on it, but he did not."[42]

By the summer of 1838 Joseph's relatives had all gone back to Italy. It was time to return to Bordentown, so he departed England yet again, embarking on 20 August aboard a packet boat appropriately named the *Philadelphia*.

Chapter 16 DEATH IN THE
FAMILY

Bad news has wings! . . . and you will have known for sometime that
which has thrown us into the most terrible depression.
                    —Charles-Lucien Bonaparte to Joseph
                    Bonaparte, Florence, Italy, 30 March 1839

Joseph and party arrived back in the United States on 30 September 1838. Samuel Breck met him on the street in Philadelphia and thought his appearance was that of a "very plain country gentleman." Breck wondered why none of the nine servants the count had brought with him from England had brushed his hat, which looked shabby. At an evening gala it was reported that Joseph was "taciturn and grave." Word had it that he had returned to America to seek the sun, as he was tired of living in the midst of rain and fog.[1]

It was more than that. He was tired of living where he was not loved and respected as he was in America. He was getting old and, at seventy, definitely feeling his age. And it was still difficult to decide where to live, considering all the countries that were forbidden to him, but the time had come to settle his affairs one way or the other.

He spent the winter in Philadelphia but kept a strict eye on the maintenance of Point Breeze. Mailliard wrote, in his somewhat uncertain English, to the caretaker, Langhorn Thorn, to have both levels of the count's house painted on the inside. "You must also have all the pedestals painted, after they'll be repaired because some of them are in bad order, take care that the marbles busts should not be injury—have the big Wood Box painted too." He wants the job done as soon as possible "as much for the goodness of the work than for the smell." The curtains in the dining room are to be washed, as they are very dirty. "Write me often what is going there[;] the Count like to know every thing as you well know."[2]

Then in April, a letter from Joseph's brother Jérôme dealt the count the severest blow of his life, one that would age and depress him more than anything else could have done: His beloved Charlotte was dead. He was told she died of an aneurysm, but the truth, that her father would apparently never know, was that she died in childbirth.

Charlotte had seemed marked for tragedy. She had become a childless widow at twenty-eight, after which she had lived quietly with her mother and aunt at the Villa Serristori on the left bank of the Arno, near the Pitti Palace in Florence. She had acted as secretary for her mother and aunt, had embroidered and painted, and enjoyed a certain social life with other artists. One of these friends, whose companionship she had shared with her husband, was a homely, melancholy, somewhat unbalanced, but talented man named Léopold Robert, who fell in love with Charlotte. But as much as she admired Robert and valued his friendship, she did not return his affection.

In 1831, after he had been away for a short time, Robert wrote a friend that during his absence the Princess Charlotte had preferred other occupations than those they had pursued together, presumably painting; that she was absorbed with litera-ture and searched for those men who were distinguished in one literary genre or another. Perhaps he had this assessment of Charlotte in mind when he painted her portrait (fig. 39). Seated with beringed hands in her lap, her ankles demurely crossed, wearing an elegant fur-trimmed coat, a tiara in her carefully coifed black hair, she has just put down a book to turn toward the viewer, the gaze in her large dark eyes direct and her expression calm, even perhaps patient.

Petite, frail, and rather plain looking, Charlotte nevertheless had a mysterious, irresistible attraction. But for a woman so proud of her name, Robert, with his mod-est background, was not to be taken seriously as a lover, in spite of what she may have felt for him. In March 1835 Robert, in the throes of despair exacerbated by his depressive personality and a family history of suicide, slit his throat with a razor in Venice. Charlotte, deeply upset by his death, though apparently unaware that his unrequited love for her was the cause, as his friends believed, wrote to his brother, Aurèle, "If there really is another existence he must be very happy, he who was so good and whose sentiments were so elevated and beautiful . . . it is with tears that I write to you."[3]

Several years after this tragic event, Charlotte met a dashing Polish officer, Count Potocki, who, with a group of other exiled Polish aristocrats, frequented her family's soirees. This time it was Charlotte who gave her heart. The count was married, but

39. **Portrait of Charlotte Bonaparte** *by Léopold Robert. Oil on canvas. Collection of Giuseppe Primoli, courtesy of the Museo Napoleonico, Rome.*

his wife, described as a "disagreeable hunchback [*méchante et bossue*]," was in Po-
land.[4] Finding herself pregnant and not wishing to be seen in Florence—she had
no wish to besmirch her name by having it known she was carrying an illegitimate
child—Charlotte went to Rome to stay with Zénaïde and Charles. But as her term
drew near she sought total seclusion, and although Zénaïde pleaded with her to return to Florence and confide in their mother, she refused and left Rome in mid-
February for Genoa, traveling by sea with her private physician, Dr. Allertz. Soon
after leaving port a violent storm forced the captain to put in at Leghorn, and Charlotte and the doctor proceeded overland. But the rough roads brought on a dangerous hemorrhage and they had to stop for a time at Lucca to allow Charlotte to
recover. After resuming their journey at the end of February, they reached Sarzana,
where she was too ill to continue. Another doctor was called in for consultation.
Believing himself inadequate for the situation, this second physician sent to Pisa for
a famous gynecologist who delivered the baby by cesarean section. The child died a
few hours later, and Charlotte, who had lost such a quantity of blood, succumbed
shortly after her baby on 3 March 1839.

Charles, who had sincerely loved his gentle sister-in-law, wrote to Joseph from
Florence where he and Zénaïde had gone at once to be with her mother: "Bad news
has wings! . . . and you will have known for some time of that which has plunged us
into the most terrible depression." From then on their family reunions would lack
the person who was the "soul" of them. The grief of Zénaïde and their children was
only equaled by Joseph's and his own, but surpassed by the total prostration of "the
most sensitive of mothers." Julie took to her room for a month and would speak to
no one. In an effort to assuage Joseph's torment, Charles added that he felt sure
nothing had been neglected that might have prevented the fatal catastrophe.[5]

Charlotte was buried in the beautiful church of Santa Croce in Florence where
her tombstone reads simply: "Here lies Charlotte-Napoleon-Bonaparte, worthy of
her name, 3 March 1839." Her mother wrote a friend that in losing "the adorable
angel" for whom the monument was raised, she had lost all the charm and happiness
of her life.[6] She told Baron de Méneval that she did not know how she could go on
without her "adorable Charlotte." Just hearing from him had recalled to her memories of a happy time when, surrounded by her children, she and Joseph had many
times witnessed Méneval's affection for them. She confided further that she dreaded
the effect on her husband of this fatal blow. Joseph, alone and distraught with the
terrible news, at once sent money for the celebration of twelve masses and for a lamp
to burn day and night in the chapel.[7]

As all too often occurs when there is a death in the family, haggling soon begins over the deceased one's will. In Charles's letter at the end of March, after expressing his sorrow, he launched into a discussion of the meaning of Charlotte's last testament. According to him, her obvious intention had been to favor his children, but it seems that those who had drawn up the document had made a major mistake and most of her money had been left to her father. Charles asks that Joseph only take a third of the estate. Julie apparently had not been mentioned in the will and could have protested this omission. But, Charles says, she means to submit to the wishes of her daughter and to renounce any rights she has in favor of other heirs. He intends to show this letter to his mother-in-law, and if she approves it, which he has no doubt she will, he will send it off in the hope of having an answer from "Papa" as soon as possible. He concludes on a warm filial note, not impolitic under the circumstances: "Think how nine children (I do not aspire to count myself among them) wait to cherish you, and how their great pleasure will be to light up your declining years with their love. Yes, my dear Papa, take care of yourself for us, for your wife, for your friends, and permit me to embrace you for them all, with affection and respect."[8]

Zénaïde followed up this letter in the middle of August, having just received Joseph's letter dated 17 June. She begins by saying how much she regrets the circumstances that against her wishes keep her so far from her father and deprive her of the joy of seeing him surrounded by her children. She goes on to say how difficult it is to raise eight offspring on the little money they have, and that it is only by the strictest privations they have succeeded. Her poor sister had been very close to her children and had wanted to do as much as possible for them. "Do not be astonished therefore," she says, "if I, who have never asked you for anything, entreat you to interpret my sister's will in a manner more favorable for them. I know very well that what you inherit will, unhappily, one day be theirs, but above all it is now that we need the income from the capital. Charles has submitted to you the articles of the law asking you to apply them, and I confess that I have been unhappily affected in seeing Maman give all rights to you in the largest possible sense." She asks him to take only 33,000 francs in lieu of 100,000 francs, adding that she is not sure the law of Tuscany allows him this last sum. She is sure her arguments will weigh with her father's sense of justice, but it is above all to his generosity and goodness that she addresses him, and not with a demand but a request. He must know that her mother has already given her share to the children, including part of Charlotte's jewelry and furniture.[9]

There is also the question of the valuable diamond necklace that Napoleon gave Madame Mère and that she, in turn, gave Joseph. According to Mailliard's notes, Joseph sold the necklace to Charlotte in 1833 for 100,000 francs.[10] The count was then living in England and much in need of cash. But Zénaïde complains that the necklace, which her mother inherited from Charlotte, has been estimated at an extremely low value. The implication is clear that Joseph had charged Charlotte too much for it.

Two more deaths soon followed Charlotte's: Joseph's contentious sister Caroline Murat died on 18 May 1839, preceded only five days by Cardinal Fesch. Joseph Fesch, whose personality was unstable, had amassed a fortune under the empire by toadying to Napoleon. When Lucien defied his imperial brother by refusing to divorce the woman he loved and the mother of his son, Charles-Lucien, in order to make a dynastic marriage to suit the emperor, Cardinal Fesch urged him to accede to Napoleon's wishes. Lucien wrote him an angry letter that succinctly sums up the cardinal's character: "Have you forgotten all honor, all religion? I wish you would at least have sufficient common sense not to think I am like Jérôme [who deserted his pregnant American wife to please his brother] and to spare me the useless insult of your cowardly advice. In a word, don't write me again until religion and honor that you are trampling under foot have dissipated your blindness. At least hide your base sentiments under your purple robes, and follow in silence your own path along the highway of ambition."[11]

The cardinal left his huge gallery of paintings to Joseph, but in many ways the bequest was more of a burden than anything else. A niece of Julie's wrote a friend that the cardinal's will was a masterpiece of confusion (*un chef-d'oeuvre d'imbroglio*) and would give her Uncle Joseph more trouble than profit. She also said the value of the pictures had been much exaggerated.[12] Only a few months earlier, Cardinal Fesch had written Joseph that he had secreted (*enfoui*) most of the money he had in his lifetime in his immense art collection, which he estimated at three thousand paintings, and that Joseph was to sell a number of them and procure the highest price possible. Since Joseph is so far away, and not knowing what his plans are, he suggests substituting Joseph's brothers to take over the sales because he does not want Charles involved.[13]

Charles had been the cardinal's *bête noire* for years, and vice-versa, but Joseph, perhaps wishing to keep a closer hold on things than he might have had with his brothers, ignored the cardinal's wishes and turned the job of selling the pictures over to his nephew and son-in-law. This was particularly burdensome for Charles, who was deeply involved with the politics of the Resorgimento and his scientific writing and cared nothing for art. He sold a few of the best pictures as specified in the will. The rest would be left for Joseph's secretary, Thibaud, to deal with after the count's death, including a superb collection of drawings that were turned over to the French government for a museum in Fesch's native Corsica. Eventually, the collection was transferred to the island and a public gallery established at Ajaccio in Cardinal Fesch's name.[14]

Before turning the job over to Charles, Joseph had broached the idea to Charles Ingersoll of offering the cardinal's collection to the United States government for the nucleus of a national gallery in exchange for government lands. It was a clever thought because it would have given his estate valuable holdings in America while providing his beloved adopted country with a museum of fine European art. But Ingersoll, who was running for Congress, did not wish to jeopardize his position with an unpopular cause.[15] Even such a collector as Thomas Jefferson, who brought sixty paintings and seven Houdon masterpieces back from France when he was Secretary of State in the late eighteenth century, could warn that painting and sculpture were "too expensive for the state of wealth of our country. It would be useless, therefore, and preposterous for us to make ourselves connoisseurs of those arts."[16] This attitude prevailed for the majority of Americans as far as the government was concerned.

When Joseph had left the United States before, in 1836, he seems to have thought he would not return because he gave away his horses and carriages and dozens of bottles of red wine from his cellar. Now, clearly, he was even more convinced that he would never come back and he set about giving important valuable works of art to his favorite friends. He gave Joseph Hopkinson *Virgin and Child* by Guido Reni and a painting on wood by Franz Snyders. To Dr. Nathaniel Chapman he presented a seascape and a view of Rome. To Nicholas Biddle he gave a large painting of animals by Rubens and Snyders, and to Thomas Cadwalader the controversial *Rape of Europa* by Noël-Nicolas Coypel, knowing the sophisticated Cadwalader would not object to the subject matter, an ancient myth. He wrote to Cadwalader on 25 October: "My dear General, I am obliged to leave for England on the first of November, with the anticipation but not the certainty of returning; I hope you will be pleased to accept the souvenir that I send, united with the affection I have had for you and your family throughout the long sojourn I have had among you. Please accept my best wishes from the new world and the old." He added a postscript that the *Rape of Europa* was one of the best paintings by Coypel, a member of the French school from the last century.[17] Since William Short had much admired Joseph's sister Pauline, he presented Short with a small marble bust of her. And for his nephew, "Jérôme of Baltimore," there was a portrait of Jérôme's beautiful half-sister, Mathilde, daughter of his father's second wife, Catherine of Württemberg, in addition to another painting of animals by Rubens and Snyders.[18]

Captain Morgan of the packet ship *Philadelphia* came to see the Count de Survilliers at Point Breeze to assure him of a short pleasant voyage from New York to Liverpool. Joseph was feeling more confident at this point about his possible return to France, as the French and English journals reported that the French statesman and historian Louis Adolphe Thiers was bringing Louis-Philippe's government nearer to Bonapartist viewpoints than ever before. He agreed to leave on the first of November.

As Joseph traveled to New York to embark for Europe, his luggage may have contained Napoleon's chair from his Council Chamber at Malmaison that Joseph presented to Félix Lacoste as a parting gift. Lacoste had been loyal and devoted to Joseph, who may have felt some remorse that he had been less than genuine with Lacoste. As far as Joseph knew, Félix had never suspected that his second son was not his, and Joseph hoped the boy's true paternity would remain a secret. As far as we know, it did.

A terrible tragedy had struck the Lacostes the previous year when their beloved son, Léon, died on 22 September 1838, still a student at the Naval Academy in Brest. At his tomb the long-separated couple met once again, both devastated by the untimely death of their child.

Emilie, still suffering deeply from her loss, wrote to Joseph with concern over his journey. She said she knew of his departure from the papers, but since the moment of his embarking the weather has been so bad she worries the strong winds will cause him to suffer unduly during the crossing because he is so apt to be seasick. "Write to me," she says, "I beg you not to forget a poor woman who has kept up such an attachment to you." In referring to his arrival at Bordentown the previous year, she says, "You will have seen your beautiful Point Breeze again with pleasure, with paternal interest, and with that melancholy which one finds on seeing again places left for a long time. I think that my husband would have been the first to receive you when you landed and would have been so happy at your return to America." She says she wants to be reconciled with Félix and that the ice is already broken since they have been in regular correspondence. If only the count would take her part, his eloquence would prove irresistible for her husband. "I have already put aside all useless pride in telling him my sincere desire to obtain a complete pardon from him. It seems to me that it is almost ridiculous in novels when there is no forgiveness, after age, time, and the generosity of characters has weakened the offense. . . . Since our separation my conduct has been composed [*calme*] and strong [*courageuse*] which gives me the right to ask him for a reconciliation. . . . I hope that time, my conduct, your intercession, and his justice will have a happy result." She believes that Félix will have more confidence in Joseph's words than in hers. "Adieu," she concludes, "pardon my importuning you, if I count on your interest and your friendship it is not without having been encouraged by you."[19] She leaves the letter unsigned, with only a slash where her signature should be.

Perhaps Joseph had told her he hoped her mutual tragedy with her husband would bring them back together. But perhaps he had forgotten that little Pauline's death long ago had had no impact on his failing relationship with Anna Savage. At the top of Emilie's letter there is a large R for *répondu,* which means he replied, no doubt agreeing to do whatever he could.

Chapter 17 FAREWELL TO
AMERICA

By leaving the United States . . . he sacrificed himself to his relations.
—Louis Mailliard to Charles Ingersoll,
London, 1840

Captain Morgan made good his promise, as the voyage to England was relatively short and pleasant, apparently without the high winds predicted by
Emilie. Joseph was gratified to learn upon landing that the government had given
orders that his belongings should pass customs without examination, a concession
usually granted only to princes and foreign ministers. He rented a comfortable house
in Cavendish Square and settled down with a sanguine feeling about the possible
change of attitude in France. His nephew Louis Napoleon was in London at the time
and managed to be reconciled with him. The ambitious young man wisely treated
his uncle with great respect.

Much to Joseph's gratification and sense of justice, he heard in the spring that
the French Chamber of Deputies had agreed, with the approval of the English government, to bring Napoleon's remains from St. Helena for burial at Les Invalides in
Paris. Louis-Philippe had thought that in allowing this he would ally himself with the
Bonapartists and would lessen their opposition to him. Mailliard wrote, "All the
young and generous want to go to St. Helena. The affair must bring about great
changes. If the ministry expect to do things by halves and only popularize Louis-
Philippe, they may mistake; for the masses in France clearly pronounce themselves
in favor of the great man and his family."[1]

Joseph thus deemed it the right time for a magnanimous gesture: He would give
Napoleon's sword, used at the great battle of Austerlitz, to the nation. All these years

since the death of Napoleon's son, who had inherited it, the sword had been entrusted to the care of General Bertrand. Joseph wrote Bertrand that he was to place this great relic on Napoleon's tomb when the emperor's remains were brought back to Paris. He then wrote Marshal Moncey, governor of Les Invalides, that he had thought since 1832, after the death of his nephew, that the emperor's sword should be "given to the care of his old companions in glory and that it should be a part of France's heritage." He now believed the state of affairs that had opposed this until the present had at last given way before the power of public opinion. At the ceremony, Napoleon's grand marshal, Bertrand, would present the sword to Moncey as governor of Les Invalides. He asks Moncey to plan with Bertrand the necessary measures to give this commission all the solemnity appertaining to "*souvenirs de tant de grandeurs, de tant de gloire française!*"[2]

Moncey replied that his emotion had been profound on receiving Joseph's letter. He had been so proud to have such an honor in his old age as to receive the arms of the Emperor Napoleon. But that very day General Bertrand had delivered the sword to King Louis-Philippe. "I must express to you, Prince, all my regrets at not being able to conform to your wishes," he apologized, "but your intentions will not be the less adhered to as the arms of your immortal brother will be deposited on his tomb the day of the funeral ceremony destined to glorify his memory in the eyes of the nation. Please accept, Prince, my humble thanks for the sacred relic you have kept, and the homage of my profound respect."[3]

Joseph was furious. How could Bertrand have betrayed him by turning the sword over to Louis-Philippe to be placed on the tomb? The king, for obvious reasons, had said he could not receive the sword at the ceremony from the hands of the Bonapartes, Bertrand of course acting as their representative. He, the king, must be the one to hand it to Moncey. Joseph thought that Bertrand should have refused to surrender it under such circumstances. But it was too late. He wrote Bertrand a dignified letter protesting the general's subservience.

The situation with the sword was bad enough, but worse was soon to follow. Long before, on July 1815, at Rochefort, when Napoleon was about to embark for America, he had made a will covering bonds secured on the national forests of France amounting to six million francs. This money was partly in lieu of pension funds granted the emperor for his support and that of his family after his escape from Elba and which had never been collected. After Waterloo, the money was needed to pay his soldiers, so Napoleon had had bonds issued instead of taking cash. He gave them to Joseph at their last meeting with the caveat that if they never met again, Joseph should dispose of the bonds, as his brother would have done, that is, divided among his relatives. Only four days after Waterloo, the restored monarch, Louis XVIII, canceled the bonds. Napoleon had warned he would do just that.

Although the Chamber of Deputies voted a million francs to bring the emperor's remains from St. Helena, it was found that another million was needed. But the Chamber rejected the second amount. On learning of this, Joseph, disregarding his brother's admonition and the king's action, wrote the Chamber offering to subscribe the extra million, and another million to be distributed among Napoleon's old guard, both sums payable out of the six million from the canceled bonds. These his nephew François Clary had buried in a strong box and restored to him in 1832 when he first visited London. The French government not only acted predictably by repudiating Joseph's offer out-of-hand as worthless, but also charged him with a cunning contrivance to realize a long extinguished claim.[4]

The press universally censored this unfortunate attempt by Joseph to demonstrate against Louis-Philippe and his government. In his history of the period, Ingersoll wrote, "Accused of an unworthy attempt to realize what had no value, and make a show of patriotic munificence by a fictitious, if not fraudulent, donation, that was, I believe, the first time when Joseph was ever charged with the duplicity often imputed to Napoleon as one of his Italian characteristics. . . . Instead of any credit for the gift he tried to present, the French government press impeached him for a fraud, and the republican press, the French republican party, by which he sought restoration to France and to power, joined in the impeachment."[5]

All Joseph's disappointments, but especially the mortifying outcome of his misguided offer of financial assistance to bring Napoleon's remains to France, were to have a devastating effect: In mid-June, he suffered a serious stroke. Paralyzed on the right side, he was advised by his doctor to take treatment at the spa of Wildbad in Württemberg, Germany. Napoleon had once made their youngest brother, Jérôme, king of Württemberg; but that was long ago. Mailliard wrote Hopkinson: "If I lose Monsieur to whom I am devoted body and soul, you will see me at once in Jersey where my duty and my preferences are."[6] He wrote from Wildbad that the count was confused and his sight somewhat affected. It had been necessary to apply leeches and cupping-glasses (*sangsues et des ventouses*) to relieve the pressure in his head. Because of his condition, the doctors had forbidden Mailliard to tell Joseph of his brother Lucien's death from cancer on 29 June.[7] Charles had been at Lucien's side.

While Joseph, suffering badly, was being transported to Wildbad, events were taking place in his name of which he knew nothing. Louis Napoleon, thinking the time had come to attempt another Bonapartist coup, in early August chartered a ship, the *Edinburgh Castle*, and assembled a group of sixty men, among them General

Montholon (who had been with Napoleon on St. Helena) and Count Orsi (the avid Bonapartist who had visited Joseph at Point Breeze). They would sail to Boulogne, seize a garrison at the port entrance, and march to Paris accompanied by the troops. Once in the capital, Louis Napoleon would establish a provisional government and hold a referendum to let the people decide if they wanted their emperor, Joseph Bonaparte, to rule them.[8]

As with the coup at Strasbourg, this one at Boulogne was a complete failure. Louis Napoleon and the majority of his followers were arrested. At his trial before the Chamber of Peers, Louis Napoleon told the court that the French people had never voted to rescind the referendum result of 1804, and that his uncle, Joseph Bonaparte, was the only lawful ruler of France.[9] That did not matter to the Chamber; he was declared guilty and sentenced to ten years in the prison of Ham. Louis-Philippe took credit for not having had him executed.

In spite of Joseph's physical condition, the controversy over bonds on the French forests was not over, at least as far as his family was concerned. In November, Mailliard received a letter from Hopkinson detailing an unpleasant visit he had just had from Lucien Murat claiming that his uncle owed him and his brother Achille money from the forests in France. Lucien said he and Achille planned to file a suit against Joseph for their share of the six million francs Napoleon had given Joseph. In fact, they called it eight million because of interest over twenty years. They claimed they wanted to settle this claim privately so as not to bring scandal on the family. Achille, who appeared at Hopkinson's house the next day, stated that he had consulted lawyers in Charleston, Richmond, Washington, and New Jersey all of whom advised him that he had a successful suit. He complained that while he had been wasting his life and ruining his health for twenty years in Florida (he was apparently a heavy drinker), his uncle had been spending their money at Point Breeze. He also said his uncle owed him twenty-five thousand dollars from Cardinal Fesch. All Hopkinson agreed to do was to write Joseph about the issue.[10]

Mailliard replied that although their *cher malade* was better, he would not tell him the contents of Hopkinson's letter for the time being because it would upset him too much. The count's nephews knew perfectly well that the French government had never paid anything on the state forests. Mailliard says he thinks, as Hopkinson does, that the Murats need the money and are trying to trick their sick uncle, who does not owe them anything. This would be very easy to prove, not only on the forests but also on the cardinal's will. They would receive this money only after the sale of the gallery; until then they have no right to anything, which they know perfectly well. In any case, they were to get twenty-five thousand *francs*, not dollars—quite a difference. Mailliard concludes that Hopkinson knows how much trust his *cher Patron* has in him and he confides that Hopkinson has been named one of the executors of the count's will. (Mailliard was the other.)

Mailliard also thanks Hopkinson and his wife for the interest they have taken in him and says that he has had the honor to be the friend of an illustrious man and to be faithful to him for more than thirty years. For this he has sacrificed the future of his son, whom the count wished to have near him, and by this Adolphe had missed a profession. "Those who do not understand such devotion," he says, "lack *sentiments élevés* and are full of prejudices that one does not find in the United States."[11]

Hopkinson wrote Joseph that he was "entirely satisfied" that the claim brought by his nephews had no foundation "in law or equity." He was happy to find by Mailliard's letter that Joseph entirely understood "the absurdity of this demand and the probable circumstances that induced it."[12]

So many bad and even annoying things had happened to Joseph since he arrived back in England, that although he was still an invalid after his stroke, it must have been heartening when he had news that the French warship *La Belle Poule* had sailed for St. Helena to bring Napoleon's body back to France. There is a certain irony in the ship's name—a term of endearment for a woman or girl in French (beautiful hen)—because the fierce eagle was Napoleon's emblem. Louis-Philippe's son, the Prince de Joinville, headed the contingent that sailed, which included General Bertrand. The emperor's body, surprisingly almost perfectly preserved, was exhumed on 15 October 1840.

Napoleon was laid to rest in the crypt of Les Invalides two months later on 15 December, amidst great funeral pomp in the presence of Louis-Philippe and a huge throng. Charles's scientist friend Isadore Geoffroy St. Hilaire wrote to him in disgust that not a single Bonaparte was there: "We deplored the absence at the head of the cortège the French family who should have walked first. What a grand and beautiful occasion [at which] to see the execrable traces of civil decrees, that is, the exile from the country of the family who had given it such brilliance."[13] He recounted how French soldiers had stolen many mementos from St. Helena and sold them to various admirers—French, but especially English.

In late October Joseph sent his servants and baggage to a country house, Newnham Paddox, six miles from Rugby, that he rented from Lord Denbigh. Two days later he and Mailliard followed traveling by the new railway, then by carriage. Mailliard commented in his diary that the house was handsome but too large for them as they lived a retired life and would no longer be receiving "*le grand monde*."[14]

The beginning of the New Year saw the surfacing of an old nemesis of the count.

No sooner had his demanding nephew Achille left him, than Anna Delafolie's mother, old Mrs. Savage, came "to torment Monsieur le Comte, even in the country," Mailliard wrote Hopkinson. "I had much difficulty getting rid of her. Thanks to the aid of Dr. Stokoë I got her on the same ship that brought her over here. She had the audacity to tell Dr. Stokoë that you had advised her to come. I think these dreadful [*vilaines*] people will follow Monsieur le Comte to the end of the world. Now that you are in charge of his affairs, try, if you can, to put an end to their absurd pretensions, because, according to this woman, her daughter's voyage here is to be feared, in spite of the bad reception she received."[15] Anna Savage Delafolie was intent on blackmail. She had notified Joseph the previous June that if he did not pay her twenty thousand dollars she would publish her memoirs exposing their relationship. Joseph had Mailliard answer for him that such a revelation would cause her daughter, Caroline Charlotte, much embarrassment—after all, she had taken Delafolie's name—and she had best not do it. "She is a devil of a woman," Mailliard noted in his diary. "She threatens Hopkinson and Alphonse [Lejambre, who was in charge of the Point Breeze house]."[16] Apparently, Mailliard and the doctor were able to convince Anna to drop her threats.

At that time it was increasingly obvious that Joseph, whose health continued to be precarious, should repair to a warmer climate. He knew he would never see America and Point Breeze again; it was out of the question to cross the Atlantic once more and he yearned to see Julie, Zénaïde, and his grandchildren. Italy was the natural choice, and surely now that he was old and ill and no longer a political threat, he would be allowed into the country. He wrote Charles in Rome to request a passport from the king of Piedmont, Charles Albert, for permission to land at Genoa. The king consented and Charles, with his son Lucien and the boy's tutor, left for England in the middle of April to bring Joseph at last to the continent. Joseph's doctor advised chartering a steamboat as the safest and most comfortable way for his patient to travel. But when Charles arrived his father-in-law was too ill to leave, so it was necessary to wait three weeks for his health to stabilize. During this time the well-established ornithologist spent the days calling on his scientific friends at the Natural History Museum, the Zoological Society, and elsewhere.

At last the day of departure arrived and the chartered *Hibernia* weighed anchor. The ship took on coal in Falmouth then stopped briefly at Rotterdam and Gibraltar before reaching Genoa on 6 June. It had been forty-six years since Joseph had lived in Genoa as a young married man. But in order for him to go on to Florence it was necessary to obtain permission from the Grand Duke of Tuscany. In the meantime, leaving Joseph, Mailliard, Thibault, Josephine Thibault, and the servants, Charles took ship for Rome to bring Zénaïde and the children back to Genoa.

Disaster struck. Charles was shipwrecked en route and survived only because he was a strong swimmer. Upon finally reaching Rome after much red tape and difficulties, he gathered up his large family, now consisting of eight children, and chartered a ship at Civitavecchia to take them all to Genoa for a joyous reunion with Joseph. There were five granddaughters Joseph had never seen: Julie-Charlotte, Charlotte-Honorine, Marie-Désirée, Augusta-Amélie, and Bathilde-Elise, as well as his namesake, Joseph-Lucien-Charles-Napoleon born in America, now sixteen, whom he had said good-bye to as a four-year-old, and the baby, Napoleon-Charles-Grégoire. Lucien (or Luciano) was the only one he knew, since the boy had accompanied his father to England on a previous trip. After the passport for Tuscany was granted, King Charles Albert sent his handsome private steamboat to transport Joseph and his retinue to the port of Leghorn, while Zénaïde, Charles, and the children stayed on in Genoa to enjoy the Riviera. From Leghorn, Joseph traveled overland to Florence and the Villa Serristori (fig. 40) for the reunion with his wife, Julie, delayed for twenty-six years.

The last time Julie had seen her husband was at the Luxembourg Palace in Paris when they had said goodbye as he rode off to join Napoleon at the port of Rochefort. He had been in the prime of life at a vigorous, handsome forty-seven. Now he was crippled with paralysis, partially blind, and in constant pain, a bent old man. Julie herself must also have shown the ravages of time, but she had always been small and frail and probably looked somewhat the same, only older. Certainly her life had been less harried than his, though the sudden loss of Charlotte must have been hard to bear. At least since 1828 she had had Zénaïde relatively nearby in Rome and the many other Bonaparte relatives in Florence and Rome.

Although they had been so long apart they were united by the love they both had for their two daughters and their grandchildren. They had shared political and financial concerns all along and had been constantly in touch through correspondence. Joseph must also have been grateful for her seeming tolerance of his numerous extramarital affairs, never mentioned in her letters. Even Napoleon had once pointed out to Joseph his wife's amazing indulgence in this respect.

In the summer of 1841, according to Mailliard's diary, the count talked to him seriously about his past. Joseph had decided, by way of his agent, Presle, to give Emilie Lacoste 25,000 francs in order to end *"une affaire de conscience."* Several days later, he changed his mind completely. He said he had found out that Charles had enlightened Zénaïde about his love affair with Madame Lacoste and she, in turn, had

40. **Garden of the Palazzo Serristori** *by Napoleone. Watercolor. Collection of Giuseppe Primoli, courtesy of the Museo Napoleonico, Rome.*

told her mother about it. Actually, Julie had known about Emilie for some time. Charles had apologized to his mother-in-law for "putting her in the same sentence with Mme. Lacoste" in a letter thirteen years before.[17] Joseph told Mailliard that "Madame Félix" had betrayed them all, had acted badly, and he would therefore not do what he had intended. A few days later, Mailliard noted that "Monsieur le Comte" told Presle, presumably in Florence, that he would continue to give Madame Félix 1,500 francs annually—presumably as a pension—but no capital.[18]

In spite of what Joseph, and no doubt many others, had assumed about Julie's forbearance with his *amours*, it seems that in fact she had been smoldering under the knowledge of them for years. One evening in March 1842 these embers flared up. Mailliard noted in his diary that "Monsieur and the Queen" assailed each other on the subject of his past: the mistresses he had had in the United States, both of whom he admitted to. Mailliard says he tried to defend Monsieur the best he could by replying to errors in the conversation. All this was in the presence of their grandson, young Joseph.[19] Possibly witnessing disagreements between his parents for years, and now those of his grandparents, may have had an effect on young Joseph; he would never marry.

In the middle of July, Mailliard received a note from Emilie saying that she and her son were in Florence and wished to visit the count. Of course she was told he was too ill to see her. Joseph sent Mailliard to give her five hundred francs and to explain his position. Given Julie's feelings on the subject, there was no way he could have admitted his "other family" to the Villa Serristori.

Emilie had been living with her aunt in Nice. Having become a widow, Aunt Davillier, at sixty-four, had remarried a man sixteen years her junior, the Vicomte de Sirionne, a dashing lieutenant of lancers. This marriage boded ill for Emilie, as the vicomte would inherit all the money she had anticipated from her aunt. After Joseph's rebuff she ventured to approach him by letter the day after Christmas. She had heard that his health was reestablished and says, "Permit me to rejoice with you and to hope that my letter will be better received than my person. Can I no longer find in you a little of the interest, of the good wishes, to which I think I have inalienable rights?" She is very upset because her husband plans to come to Paris in the fall to take Félix-Joseph with him to America, and is terrified that her son might meet with an accident at sea. Emilie also worries about her husband's financial situation; as she has not received any money from him since July, would it be possible for Joseph to send her part of the pension he had promised her? She then gets quite personal by saying she has heard that the Prince of Canino (Charles) has returned to Rome and this must give Joseph a great sense of relief. But since there are many others still there she hopes he is successfully contending with "all the inconveniences of a family reunion." She concludes, "Be as happy as it is possible to be, is my dearest wish and think sometimes of those who love and embrace you, and who are less happy."[20]

Perhaps because of her letter, Joseph would reconsider cutting off Emilie completely from any capital and in his will would charge Mailliard with a special legacy of ten thousand dollars to be disposed of as the count specified. "He shall never render any account of it," the will directed.[21] This money was undoubtedly for her son Félix-Joseph.

Emilie and her husband would not be reunited, but she continued to see Mérimée in spite of all the turmoil between them. In October 1845 she would dine with him at the home of their mutual friend, Béranger, and they would see each other off and on in the following years.[22] But the affair by then was purely platonic, for Mérimée was in love with someone else: the elusive, very attractive Valentine Delessert, whom he had met in 1829 and finally conquered in the late 1830s.[23]

Joseph's family reunion referred to by Emilie consisted of Zénaïde and her tribe of children. Zénaïde (fig. 41) was again pregnant and her father hoped she would deliver the baby in Florence, so she stayed on. Albertine-Marie, named judiciously after the king and queen of Piedmont, was born in early March, but on the first of June, the child, who had been asthmatic from the start, died suddenly in a violent fit of coughing. She was buried with her Aunt Charlotte in a chapel of Santa Croce. It was not until fall that Charles, in the meantime traveling to scientific meetings across Italy, took his family back to Rome where another baby, Charles-Albert, again named after the king, was born to them in March 1843. Four years later, this seemingly healthy child would also die.

Joseph's health continued to fail, but he was cheered the following July when he received the first two volumes of Méneval's memoirs. "I see in them your unalterable devotion to the emperor and your kind sentiments for me," he wrote Napoleon's faithful secretary. "I only regret that you did not come to see me in England ten years ago, because I could have helped you a lot. Today my health no longer permits me to be occupied with a serious work. I can only encourage you to continue writing; you will be read by all people of good faith." He then asks Méneval to accept a Titian that he had left in London and he encloses a letter to Baring Brothers, his bankers, to deliver the painting to him.[24] The work was the great *Tarquin and Lucretia,* now in the Fitzwilliam Museum in Cambridge.

The last letter Joseph sent Méneval is dated 12 January 1844. He concludes a brief note of goodwill and asks the baron to remember him to his family and to all those who still speak well of him. Was he still smarting under the adverse reaction

41. **Princess Zénaïde Bonaparte** *by Charlotte Bonaparte, 1835. Watercolor. Collection of Giuseppe Primoli, courtesy of the Museo Napoleonico, Rome.*

over the bonds on the French forests? Joseph would leave this loyal friend his cross of the Légion d'honneur that he had worn for so many years.[25] He was very weak, having had another stroke the previous October. Julie wrote her nephew Joachim Clary that his uncle's state was continually alarming and did not leave her a moment's rest. She wrote again at the end of May, saying that Joseph suffered a great deal and was so weak he could not get up.[26]

On 28 July 1844, shortly after midday, having received the sacraments of confession and extreme unction, "His Majesty the King Joseph Napoleon Bonaparte, Count of Survilliers, seventy-seven years of age, son of the late Signor Charles Bonaparte and the late Signora Letitia Ramolino Bonaparte, and husband of Her Majesty the Queen Maria Julia Clary Bonaparte, passed to Eternal Rest" (fig. 42). So read the

42. **Joseph Bonaparte on His Death Bed,** *nineteenth-century engraving after Carlo Morelli.*
Château de Malmaison.

death certificate issued at Florence. Julie wrote her nephew that her beloved husband
(*"mon epoux bien-aimé"*) had expired in her arms. Joseph was interred in the Church
of Santa Croce in Florence on 3 August. Two companies of the grand duke of Tuscany's grenadiers accompanied his funeral carriage along a road lined with thousands
assembled to pay their last respects to the former king of Naples and of Spain and
the brother of Napoleon. Joseph's obituary in *Le Siècle,* a Parisian newspaper, described him benignly as "a friend of study, of repose, and of quiet pleasures."[27]

By 1855, Joseph's nephew, Louis Napoleon, had become Emperor of the French
as Napoleon III, after having escaped his imprisonment for the coup of 1840, eventually elected president in 1848, then emperor in November 1852. After all these years,
Charles Ingersoll read an obituary notice of Joseph at the American Philosophical
Society in Philadelphia. It begins in a strangely negative way, particularly in view of
the fact that so many of Joseph's American friends had been members of the organization. But the battle to live down his brother's reputation in America that began
when he landed in New York in 1815, apparently continued long after his death.
Ingersoll said: "In 1844, when Joseph Bonaparte died, obituary truth regarding him
would have been coldly received by probably many of this Society, and by an incredu-
lous number of our countrymen throughout the United States. His immense brother,
as another of our fellow members, La Fayette, designated the Emperor, whom,

though his debtor for liberty and life, he felt it his duty to dethrone, was then still deemed by all Englishmen, many Americans, and some Frenchmen, a monster, and Joseph one of his worst instruments."

But now the times are different, he says, because Joseph's nephew is on the throne of France. Ingersoll concludes: "To appreciate Joseph justly, we must, therefore, understand his intimate connection with a younger brother, whose prodigious conquests gilded the iron ascendancy, of which, while always submissive, the elder constantly strove to check its excesses and temper its violence. The eldest was the mildest of the Bonapartes; just and tenacious, but considerate and forbearing; living ever affectionately with a large, multiplied, and mixed family of Bonapartes and Beauharnais, Corsicans, French, Americans, and Austrians, Republicans and Royalists."[28]

In his two-volume history of the period, Ingersoll wrote of Joseph: "As deputy, diplomatist, soldier, king, and exile, he was uniformly liberal. Well informed, and disposed, respectable, benevolent, and just. From the principles of '89 he never swerved; he would have incorporated them with the institutions of every country; and, after long, calm, clear, practical comprehension of them in their American development, he was convinced that they might be carried further than they ever had been elsewhere."[29]

EPILOGUE

$\mathcal{I}$n his will, Joseph designated his personal property in America as "land consisting of ten farms on the Crosswicks Creek and the Delaware, a park containing about a thousand acres, a large dwelling house and its appurtenances in the State of New Jersey near the village of Bordentown." In France he still owned two farms, Survilliers and Parant, and "important claims against the French Government" that he was sure would someday be honored. In London he had household effects, pictures, and other things of value. His estate also comprised what remained to him of the liquidated effects of his uncle Joseph Fesch after all the cardinal's legacies had been authorized or rejected by the French government.

Joseph left Point Breeze, exclusive of his adjacent two-hundred-and-fifty-acre Grosville Farm that he gave Louis Mailliard, to his grandson Joseph, Prince of Musignano (a papal title inherited from his father). To his "dear and well beloved wife, Marie Julie," Joseph left the income for life from his entire estate, including Point Breeze. "In the course of our long and happy union," he states, "my confidence in her has been full and entire." She could hardly have said the same of him. "In leaving her mistress of all I possess, except the several legacies, I know well that I shall take nothing from my dear daughter Zénaïde."[1]

Julie survived him by only one year, dying quietly on 7 April 1845 with Zénaïde, Charles, and their children beside her. Zénaïde and Charles were finally legally separated in 1854 by an imperial decree from Louis Napoleon, after many years of marital vicissitudes. In the same year Zénaïde died of diphtheria in Naples. After being exiled from Italy for his subversive activities against the pope in the cause of Italian independence, Charles had been living for some time in Paris. He died there of congestive heart failure in 1857. Ironically, his son Luciano would become a cardinal, serving the very pope Charles once tried to strip of his temporal powers. Today, a direct descendant of Joseph and Lucien, through a mutual granddaughter, is a bishop connected to the Vatican.

Louis Mailliard, described by Joseph as "devoted to me in my exile," received $6,000 in stocks of the Union Canal of Pennsylvania in addition to Grosville Farm. His son, Adolphe, inherited an equivalent amount of stock, as did William Thibault and his daughter Josephine. Adolphe was also given the count's dressing case of sterling silver toilet articles. The surplus of Joseph's capital in America was to be divided equally among his eight grandchildren by Zénaïde. All his papers were given over to Mailliard, who was to make an inventory of them, then release them to "Prince Joseph" when he reached the age of twenty-five. Joseph would be steadfast in seeing that his grandfather's memoirs were eventually published in 1855.

Among the numerous legacies of personal items to various relatives were gold snuff boxes, miniature portraits in cameo on rings and pins, decorations of the Légion d'honneur that he had worn, a Chinese inkstand that he had used "ever since his arrival in Spain." Joseph left his friends in America even more treasures. Dr. Nathaniel Chapman was to receive a set of Voltaire in calf; William Short, a marble bas-relief of Joseph's sister Pauline; and Charles Ingersoll, "a little bronze statue representing my brother General Bonaparte when he was General-in-Chief of the Army in Italy."

To "the people of his house" he left ten thousand francs each to Madame Arsène, his housekeeper; Monsieur Chandelier, his chief cook "who was my brother's at St. Helene"; Leopold Stocker, his *valet de chambre*; Dikes, his *maître d'hôtel*; and Langhorn Thorn, "my manager and keeper of my house at Point Breeze."

The last item on the list was the "special legacy of ten thousand dollars" of which Mailliard has been instructed concerning its use and that "his honor be referred to without any question or claim ever being addressed to him on the subject." This was young Félix-Joseph's inheritance.

Prince Joseph went to America against his father's will shortly after his grandfather's death. Charles was furious at his son's willfulness and aghast to hear from an American naturalist friend, George Ord, that a strange story was making the rounds of the newspapers about young Joseph's departure from Europe. The gist was that because he was underage the boy's parents had taken legal steps to stop him, but with the help of Adolphe Mailliard he had been smuggled in female attire aboard a Swedish ship at Leghorn and had sailed for New York (fig. 43).[2]

The following year, in September 1845, after his grandmother Julie died and young Joseph had sole possession of his inheritance, he sold the contents of Point Breeze at a spectacular auction crowded with buyers. Collectors from all over the country, as well as from Europe, bought the large number of paintings still *in situ*. Everything else, including more pictures, statuary, furniture, lamps, china, bedding, and kitchen utensils was auctioned off in June 1847.

There are many households to this day in and around Philadelphia and Bordentown, and perhaps in other parts of the country as well, which contain relics of that

43. **Portrait of Young Joseph Bonaparte and Adolphe Mailliard in Rome Making Plans** *by Carlo Morelli, c. 1845. Private collection.*

sale, some authentic, some not, but nevertheless treasured by their owners as once having belonged to Joseph Bonaparte, ex-king of Naples and Spain and Napoleon's brother. Certain local museums, among them the New Jersey State Museum in Trenton and the Bordentown and Burlington County Historical Societies, have a number of mostly verifiable artifacts from Point Breeze. The Athenaeum of Philadelphia has an exhibition devoted to Joseph Bonaparte: furniture, pictures, statues, the silver toilet articles bequeathed to Adolphe Mailliard, china, and fabric samples, all from Point Breeze.

Louis Mailliard returned to America after his patron's death to perform his duties as executor. Joseph Hopkinson had died in the meantime, so Mailliard alone carried out the Count de Survilliers's final wishes. He returned to his native land when Louis Napoleon became emperor of the French and there accomplished his patron's last assignments: to publish Joseph's correspondence with Napoleon and to see Joseph's remains interred in Paris, which he accomplished with the aid of Joseph's granddaughter Julie. His son Adolphe, having married an American, stayed on in Bordentown for some years, and then moved to California where his descendants still live.

Anna Delafolie became a widow in 1840 amid much speculation that she had murdered Delafolie. He had been perfectly well in the afternoon, then dead at night. Anna refused to call a doctor, or anyone but the gravedigger, and had her husband buried immediately. Her contemporaries' aged grandchildren were known to say: "That de la Folie woman certainly upset Grandpa, Grandma was awful glad when she up and married someone else."[3] The someone else, two years after the mysterious death, was Henry Horr, the sheriff of Watertown, New York. Anna and her second husband moved to New York City, where she died in 1865.

Her daughter, Caroline Charlotte (fig. 44), had an unhappy marriage to Zebulon Howell Benton (fig. 45), who was so fascinated with becoming the son-in-law of a king that he pretended to be a man of great wealth and soon squandered in wild speculations the thirty thousand dollars Joseph had given his illegitimate daughter at the time of her marriage. "Colonel" Benton had insisted on a lavish wedding in Watertown with the couple riding in a carriage drawn by four horses in tandem and a footman in uniform. No more strangely costumed figure ever appeared in the Adirondack backwoods than Benton. Fancying himself a nephew of Napoleon, if only by marriage, he adopted a costume he wore the rest of his life: cocked hat, ruffled shirt and white stock, like Napoleon, and a long Prince Albert coat in a military cut. He usually had himself photographed "with hand in coat." The Bentons lived for a time in the house at Alpina that Joseph had built, but—tired of the wilderness and her husband's bombast—Caroline Charlotte, with her five children (two named Charlotte and Zénaïde after half-sisters she would never meet), left him and taught French in Philadelphia.[4] One of her sons attended the University of Pennsylvania. The story that Louis Napoleon subsequently received her at court, named her a maid-of-honor to his wife Eugénie, and gave her a pension for life, is entirely false. She did go to France in 1859 and wrote a book about her trip, but there is no mention of a meeting with the emperor. A Benton family collection still contains letters from Bonapartes who refused to meet her, as well as others from aged staff members at Point Breeze who stood behind her claims but were ignored.[5]

44. **Caroline Charlotte Delafolie Benton.** *Daguerreotype, Philadelphia, 1848. Private collection.*

Emilie Lacoste was not reconciled to her husband and never remarried after his death. She lived in Paris still seeing Mérimée, Béranger, and others of that literary circle. By 1878 she was living in Passy and died at an unknown date.[6] Félix stayed in New York and was named consul general of France in 1850 by Louis Napoleon, but he died not long afterward on 14 November 1853. At the sale of his possessions, the history-laden Napoleon armchair was acquired by Louis Borg, Félix's vice consul and his successor as consul general. When Borg returned to France some years later, he donated the chair to the New-York Historical Society.[7] Félix-Joseph served as tax

45. **Zebulon Howell
Benton.** *Daguerreotype.
Private collection.*

collector (*receveur des finances*) at Sisteron and later at Thionville and married the
Baron de Gerando's daughter, Isabelle. They named their son Maurice de Lacoste.[8]

Prince Joseph sold the estate of Point Breeze in the summer of 1847 to Thomas
Richards, who three years later conveyed the property to Henry Beckett, son of Sir
John Beckett, the British consul in Philadelphia. The younger Beckett had such an
extreme dislike of everything French that he moved into the gatehouse and sold,
removed, or destroyed everything on the estate that reminded him of Joseph Bonaparte before building his own mansion. The Vincentian Fathers of Philadelphia

bought the property in 1874 and the priests used it for a summer home until 1911, when Harris Hammond bought Point Breeze. Hammond spent a great deal on improvements to the house and grounds, but lost everything in the stock market crash of 1929. After being derelict for many years, Point Breeze was bought by the Society of the Divine Word in 1941. Hammond's grand house burned to the ground in 1983 and an institutional building was erected in its place. Yet even today, the beautifully kept grounds of nearly one hundred acres that surround the mission and the bluff overlooking the Delaware evoke a feeling of that long-ago landscape.

As much as Joseph had loved America and his gilded life of exile at Point Breeze, he was ever devoted to France. He wrote in his will: "The injustice of those who have had the power in France since 1815 has only increased in me a love for this country from which I have been absent. As soon as my family shall be free to reenter, by the will of the French Nation, I desire that my ashes repose there in free ground."[9]

In 1862, Joseph Bonaparte at last reentered Paris when his remains were entombed in the church of Les Invalides near those of his brother, whose body had only a year earlier been transferred to the sarcophagus under the dome from a nearby chapel. This historic seventeenth-century building designed by Jules Hardouin-Mansart, one of France's greatest architects, was such a visible and impressive site in the center of Paris for the burial of Napoleon that it had been hotly debated for its symbolism at the time the emperor's tomb was planned in the 1840s.

Joseph's granddaughter, the princess Julie Bonaparte, Marquise de Roccagiovine (fig. 46), recorded in her memoirs that, at her grandfather's internment in Les Invalides, which lasted only ten minutes, Louis Napoleon (then Emperor Napoleon III) did not bother to come, nor even to send a representative to pay final homage (*pieux-devoir*) to his uncle. Several of her aunts, Lucien's daughters, who happened to be in Paris, were the only Bonapartes present.[10] Of course, Julie his wife, Zénaïde, and Charles were long since dead. Even so, the lonely exile was all but forgotten by the time he finally got his wish of returning to France. A would-be republican entombed in an imperial mausoleum, was an irony inherent in Joseph Bonaparte's conflicting politics carried right out to the end.

In life as in death, because of their firm fraternal bond, despite opposite personalities and points of view, Joseph and Napoleon were never far apart. As Napoleon had once written Joseph long before: "We have lived together for so many years, so closely united, that our hearts have become one, and you know best how entirely mine belongs to you. While I write these lines I feel an emotion which I have seldom experienced. I fear that it will be long before we see each other again, and I can write no more."[11]

46. **Julie Bonaparte, Marquise del Gallo di Roccagiovine,** *by A. Balloté. Watercolor. Collection of Giuseppe Primoli, courtesy of the Museo Napoleonico, Rome.*

Napoleon at one time described his older brother pejoratively as an ornament to society[12] because he had not been the fierce warrior and commanding leader the emperor wanted, but in his gilded exile in America, Joseph was indeed an ornament to society in the best sense of the word. He loaned numerous masterpieces of art to academies in various cities to be seen by interested citizens, as well as to be copied by aspiring young artists. And according to many accounts, those who enjoyed the hospitality of Joseph Bonaparte at Point Breeze, and at the houses he rented in Philadelphia, came away inspired by great masters of world art and by a special glimpse into European glamour and elegance—even if it was a world the former king recreated to replace what he had lost forever.

CHRONOLOGY

1768	7 January: Joseph Bonaparte born at Corte, Corsica.
1769	15 August: Napoleon born at Ajaccio, Corsica.
1789	French Revolution begins.
1793	January: execution of Louis XVI. The Reign of Terror in France. Bonaparte family escapes from Corsica, lands at Toulon.
1794	Joseph marries Marie-Julie Clary, daughter of a rich merchant of Marseilles.
1797	Joseph elected to Council of Five Hundred in Paris. Joseph appointed Minister to Rome.
1798	Joseph buys the estate of Mortefontaine, 47 kilometers northeast of Paris.
1799	19 November: Napoleon's coup d'état establishes Consulate; he is soon First Consul.
1800	3 October: Joseph signs treaty with United States at Mortefontaine ending hostilities between the two countries.
1801	9 February: Signs Treaty of Lunéville with Austrian minister, Count Cobenzl, ending hostilities with Austria for the time being. 21 June: Signs Concordat with three cardinals representing Pope Pius VII restoring the Catholic religion in France. 8 July: Birth of daughter Zénaïde-Charlotte-Julie.
1802	27 March: Signs Treaty of Amiens with Lord Cornwallis, temporarily ending hostilities with England. 31 October: Birth of daughter Charlotte-Napoléone.
1803	24 May: Birth of Charles-Lucien Bonaparte, son of Joseph's brother Lucien and future husband of Zénaïde.
1804	4 December: Napoleon declares himself Emperor of the French.
1806	March: Joseph takes up duties as King of Naples.
1808	20 July: Enters Madrid as King of Spain and the Indies; disappointing reception, empty streets and shuttered windows.
1812	Retreat of French Army from Moscow.

1813   21 June: Defeat of French forces at Vitoria, Spain; Joseph returns to Mortefontaine. Defection of Prussia from French alliance precipitates war.

1814   June: Napoleon defeated by allied armies of Austria, Prussia, Great Britain, and Russia, abdicates, and is exiled to Elba.
        July: Joseph buys château of Prangins in Switzerland.
        At Blois, Joseph buys large tract of land in northern New York State from James Le Ray de Chaumont.

1815   1 March: Napoleon escapes from Elba, lands near Antibes and returns to Paris. Joseph joins him there.
        20 March: The Hundred Days begins.
        18 June: Napoleon defeated at the Battle of Waterloo.
        25 July: Joseph sails for America; Napoleon, a British prisoner, is taken to remote island of St. Helena off southwestern coast of Africa.
        20 August: Joseph lands in New York and calls himself the Count de Survilliers.

1815–16 Rents house on Ninth Street in Philadelphia.

1816   Leases Lansdowne on outskirts of Philadelphia.
        2 July: Buys estate of Point Breeze outside Bordentown, New Jersey; James Carret signs papers as Joseph is not a U.S. citizen and cannot own property.

1817   Charles and Henri Lallemande found ill-fated Champ d'Asile in Texas with Joseph's financial support.
        Late summer: Joseph first visits his Black River property in northern New York State.

1818   Winter: Leases Dunlop House in Philadelphia from Stephen Girard.
        Meets Anna Savage in Philadelphia; begins liaison.

1819   Rents Bow Hill near Trenton for Anna; birth of Joseph's natural daughter Pauline Josephe.

1820   4 January: Point Breeze house burns to the ground; Joseph starts at once to rebuild at a different site on the same property.

1821   5 May: Death of Napoleon on St. Helena.
        Fall: Arrival of Félix and Emilie Lacoste from France.
        21 December: Arrival of daughter Charlotte in Philadelphia.

1822   Birth of Joseph's natural daughter Caroline Charlotte.

           September: Zénaïde and Charles-Lucien arrive in New York.

           December: Accidental death of Anna's daughter Pauline Josephe.

1824   Emilie Lacoste takes up residence at Point Breeze while her husband is away in Saint Domingue on business.

           12 February: Birth of Zénaïde and Charles's first child, Joseph-Lucien-Charles-Napoleon.

           August: Charlotte returns to Europe aboard the *Crisis*.

1825   March: Birth of Emilie Lacoste's twin sons by Joseph. Only Félix will live past infancy.

           Death of Pauline Borghese; leaves Villa Paolina in Rome to Napoleon-Louis (son of Joseph's brother Louis).

           Anna Savage goes to Paris with daughter Caroline Charlotte.

1826   Anna marries Alexis de la Folie in Paris.

           Charlotte marries Napoleon-Louis in Italy.

1827   Emilie and Félix Lacoste return to France, taking young Félix but leaving son Léon at boarding school in New York under Joseph's oversight.

1828   Zénaïde and Charles-Lucien return to Italy.

1830   March: death of Napoleon-Louis at Forli, Italy.

           July Revolution in France; Louis-Philippe installed as king.

1832   July: Joseph sails for England in the hope of putting Napoleon's son on the throne of France with himself as regent.

           22 July: Death of the Duke of Reichstadt, Napoleon II, in Vienna.

1835   18 October: Joseph returns to America.

1836   February: Death of Madame Mère, Joseph's mother.

           August: Joseph sets sail for England.

1836   October: Louis Napoleon's failed coup d'état at Strasbourg.

1838   20 August: Joseph departs England for America, arrives 30 September.

1839   3 March: Charlotte dies in childbirth in Sarzana, Italy.

           April and May: Deaths of Joseph's sister Caroline Murat and his uncle Cardinal Fesch.

1840   June: Joseph suffers a serious stroke in rented house outside London.

           29 June: Joseph's brother Lucien dies of cancer in Viterbo, Italy.

August: At Boulogne, Louis Napoleon's second failed coup d'état.

15 December: Napoleon's remains interred in Les Invalides in Paris.

1841   6 June: Joseph arrives in Genoa, accompanied by Charles-Lucien and Louis Mailliard, via steamboat from London.

June: Reunited with Julie after twenty-six years.

1844   28 July: Joseph dies at Villa Serristori in Florence.

1845   7 April: Death of Julie at Villa Serristori in Florence.

1847   Sale of Point Breeze by Joseph's grandson Joseph, who had inherited it.

1862   Joseph Bonaparte's remains entombed at Les Invalides near Napoleon.

Dramatis Personae

ELISA BACCIOCCHI—Joseph's younger sister.

CHARLES-LUCIEN BONAPARTE—Zénaïde's husband, son of Joseph's brother Lucien.

CHARLOTTE BONAPARTE—Joseph and Julie's younger daughter.

JÉRÔME BONAPARTE—Joseph's youngest brother.

JOSEPH BONAPARTE—older brother of Napoleon and former king of Naples and Spain; known in America as the Count de Survilliers.

JOSEPH-LUCIEN-CHARLES-NAPOLEON BONAPARTE—Charles and Zénaïde's eldest son.

JULIE BONAPARTE—Charles and Zénaïde's eldest daughter who became the Marquise de Roccagiovine.

MARIE-JULIE CLARY BONAPARTE—Joseph's wife.

LETIZIA RAMOLINO BONAPARTE (MADAME MÈRE)—Joseph's mother.

LOUIS BONAPARTE—Joseph's younger brother.

LOUIS NAPOLEON BONAPARTE—second son of Joseph's brother Louis and the future emperor, Napoleon III.

LUCIEN BONAPARTE—Joseph's younger brother.

NAPOLEON-LOUIS BONAPARTE—Charlotte's husband, son of Joseph's brother Louis.

ZÉNAÏDE BONAPARTE—Joseph and Julie's eldest daughter.

PAULINE BONAPARTE LECLERC BORGHESE—Joseph's younger sister.

DÉSIRÉE CLARY—Julie's sister, married to Bernadotte, became queen of Sweden.

ACHILLE MURAT—Joseph's nephew, son of his sister Caroline; lived in Florida.

CAROLINE BONAPARTE MURAT—Napoleon's youngest sister, married to Napoleon's marshal, Joachim Murat, who took Joseph's place as king of Naples.

LUCIEN MURAT—Achille's brother; lived in Bordentown, N.J.

JÉRÔME NAPOLEON BONAPARTE-PATTERSON—Joseph's nephew, son of his brother Jérôme by Betsy Patterson

ANNA SAVAGE—Joseph's Philadelphia mistress.

PAULINE JOSEPHE—Joseph's natural daughter by Anna who died in a childhood accident.

CAROLINE CHARLOTTE—Joseph's second natural daughter by Anna.

FRANÇOIS ALEXIS DE LA FOLIE—Anna's first husband.

HENRY HORR—Anna's second husband.
ZEBULON HOWELL BENTON—Caroline Charlotte's husband.

EMILIE HÉMART LACOSTE—Married woman from Paris who became Joseph's mistress.

FÉLIX LACOSTE—Emilie's husband and Joseph's friend who edits *Courrier des États-Unis* in New York.

LÉON LACOSTE—Emilie and Félix's son.

FÉLIX JOSEPH LACOSTE—Emilie's son by Joseph.

NOTES

Chapter 1. A New Life

1. Alan Schom, *Napoleon Bonaparte* (New York: HarperCollins, 1997), 2.
2. Frank McLynn, *Napoleon: A Biography* (New York: Arcade, 2002), 6.
3. Ibid., 10.
4. Michael Ross, *The Reluctant King: Joseph Bonaparte, King of the Two Sicilies and Spain* (New York: Mason/Charter, 1977), 17.
5. Ibid., 12.
6. Joseph Bonaparte, *Mémoires et correspondance politique et militaire du roi Joseph*, ed. A. Du Casse, 10 vols. (Paris: Perrotin, 1855), vol. 1, 31–32.
7. Ibid., vol. 1, 46.
8. Owen Connelly, *The Gentle Bonaparte: A Biography of Joseph, Napoleon's Elder Brother* (New York: Macmillan, 1968), 17–18.
9. Schom, *Napoleon Bonaparte,* 17.
10. Mailliard Family Papers, Manuscripts and Archives, Yale University Library.
11. Roger G. Kennedy has written of America's shameful position on this issue: "A Napoleonic colony was to be preferred to a Negro republic in the West Indies, especially when France intended the re-imposition of slavery, and, thus, some alleviation of the fears of the slave owners" in America (*Orders from France: The Americans and the French in a Revolutionary World, 1780–1820* [Philadelphia: University of Pennsylvania Press, 1990], 154).
12. Ibid., 156.
13. Napoleon to Joseph, Presburg, 27 December 1805, quoted in Ross, *The Reluctant King,* 123.
14. Napoleon to Joseph, Stuttgart, 19 January 1806, quoted in ibid., 124.
15. Napoleon to Joseph, St. Cloud, 5 July 1806, in *The Confidential Correspondence of Napoleon Bonaparte with His Brother Joseph, Sometime King of Spain,* 2 vols. (New York: D. Appleton, 1856), vol. 1, 153.
16. Napoleon to Joseph, St. Cloud, 26 July 1806, *Confidential Correspondence,* vol. 1, 168.
17. Napoleon to Joseph, St. Cloud, 30 July 1806, *Confidential Correspondence,* vol. 1, 172.
18. General Jean Maximilien Lamarque to Joseph, Paris, 27 March 1824, quoted in "Biographical Sketch of Joseph Napoleon Bonaparte," by "A Young Patriot" (1834).
19. Joseph to the Duchess d'Atri, Bayonne, 7 July 1808, quoted in Ross, *The Reluctant King,* 144.
20. Georges Bertin, *Joseph Bonaparte en Amérique: 1815–1832* (Paris: Flammarion, [1893]), 70–72.
21. Hector Fleischmann, *Le roi Joseph Bonaparte: Lettres d'exil inédites (Amérique-Angleterre-Italie)* (Paris: Librairie Charpentier et Fasquelle, 1912), 31.
22. Charles J. Ingersoll to Alexander J. Dallas, Philadelphia, 30 April 1815, HSP.
23. Laure, Duchess d'Abrantes (Madame Junot), *Memoirs of Napoleon, His Court and Family,* 2 vols. (London, Richard Bentley: 1836), vol. 2, 165.
24. Bertin, *Joseph Bonaparte en Amérique,* 2.
25. Jean Orient, *Talleyrand ou le sphinx incompris* (Paris: Flammarion, 1970), 210–211.

26. Richard Rush to James Madison, Washington, 8 A.M., 13 September 1815, Rush Papers, HSP.

27. Richard Rush to James Madison, Washington, noon, 13 September 1815, Rush Papers, HSP.

28. Richard Rush to Commodore Jacob Lewis, Washington, 13 September 1815, Rush Papers, HSP.

29. The historical marker in front of Joseph's house on Ninth Street between Locust and Spruce reads: "Joseph Bonaparte (1768–1844). The elder brother of Napoleon and deposed king of Naples and Spain lived here, 1815–1816. The house was built about 1813. During Joseph's occupancy here, this was a gathering place for Bonapartist refugees & other French nationals."

30. John Francis Marion, *Bicentennial City* (Princeton: Princeton University Press, 1974), 77.

31. *Philadelphia: A 300-Year History*, ed. Russell F. Weigley, assoc. eds. Nicholas B. Wainwright and Edwin Wolf 2nd (New York: W. W. Norton, 1982), 178. For a full account of Lansdowne, see Roger W. Moss, *The American Country House* (New York: Henry Holt, 1990), 81–85. Moss states that Lansdowne was "the largest and most elegant pre-Revolutionary house in the Philadelphia area," and that, had it not burned in 1854, "it would be ranked among the most significant Palladian houses of the late colonial era in America."

32. Ingersoll to Dallas, Philadelphia, 27 April 1816, Ingersoll Papers, HSP.

33. Joseph Hopkinson to His Excellency Andrew Daschkoff, Philadelphia, 17 June 1814, Hopkinson Papers, HSP.

34. George Gordon, Lord Byron, "Ode to Napoleon Buonaparte," stanza XI, *Byron: Collected Works* (London: Oxford University Press, 1967), 74.

35. Richard Rush to Charles Ingersoll, Washington, 16 June 1814, Ingersoll Papers, HSP.

36. Richard Rush to Charles Ingersoll, Washington, 12 August 1815, Ingersoll Papers, HSP.

37. *Poulson's American Daily Advertiser*, 4 September 1815.

38. *United States Gazette*, 15 September 1815.

39. *Port Folio*, I (18 July 1901), 226. Chapman wrote under the pseudonym "Falkland."

40. Deborah Norris Logan's Diary, vol. II, p. 2 (1816), courtesy the Henry Francis Du Pont Winterthur Library, Joseph Downs Collection of Manuscripts and Printed Ephemera.

41. Nicholas B. Wainwright, "The Diary of Samuel Breck, 1814–1822," *PMHB*, 102, no. 4 (October 1978), 489.

42. Ibid., 504.

Chapter 2. A Man of Property

1. James Le Ray was the son of Jacques Le Ray, a slave-trading merchant from Nantes who had amassed a fortune in various enterprises and had supported the American Revolution with arms. Jacques Le Ray had rented a small portion of his large and elegant house in Passy, outside Paris, to Benjamin Franklin during his stay in France. In 1785, Jacques sent his son James to America to press his claims for money owed him by the American government for arms he had supplied. With this money, which had depreciated considerably, James was persuaded to buy land in the St. Lawrence valley of northern New York State, which was likely to be more hospitable to him than revolutionary France. Several friends in Paris bought shares

in the Company of New York, Le Ray's corporation, which owned thousands of acres around the projected city of Castorland (*castor* meaning beaver in Latin).A few years before going to Blois to see Joseph, he had returned to France to take over the chateau inherited from his father. At the time of Le Ray's return to Europe in 1810, the château de Chaumont was rented to Joseph Bonaparte's friend, Mme de Staël (also his neighbor at Prangins, Switzerland, in her father's château, Coppet). It was perhaps through her that Joseph had met James Le Ray. Roger G. Kennedy, *Orders from France: The Americans and the French in a Revolutionary World, 1780–1820* (Philadelphia: University of Pennsylvania Press, 1990), 40.

2. Ibid., 22.

3. Mahlon Dickerson to Joseph Bonaparte, Trenton, 28 January 1817, Mailliard Family Papers, Manuscripts and Archives, Yale University Library.

4. Georges Bertin, *Joseph Bonaparte en Amérique: 1815–1832* (Paris: Ernest Flammarion, [1893]), 114.

5. Stephen Girard to Joseph Bonaparte, Philadelphia, 5 December 1816, Stephen Girard Collection, Girard College, Letterbook 14, #388.

6. Girard to Joseph Bonaparte, Philadelphia, 7 August 1817, Girard Collection, Letterbook 15, #202.

7. Girard to Joseph Bonaparte, Philadelphia, 23 October 1816, Girard Collection, Letterbook 14, #330.

8. Charles J. Ingersoll, *History of the Second War Between the United States and Great Britain, second series,* 2 vols. (Philadelphia: Lippincott, Grambo, 1852), vol. 1, 413.

9. *Baltimore American,* 25 September 1816.

10. *Niles Weekly Register,* new series, 21, no. 15, 14 December 1822.

11. Owen Connelly, *The Gentle Bonaparte: A Biography of Napoleon's Elder Brother* (New York: Macmillan, 1968), 255

12. Quoted in A. Du Casse, *Mémoires et correspondence du roi Joseph* (Paris: Perrotin, 1854), vol. 10, 409–410.

13. Kennedy, *Orders from France,* 345.

14. *Niles Weekly Register,* 29 March 1817.

15. Ibid. Report from Geneva, 25 April 1817.

16. Fernand Beaucour, "Un fidèle de l'empereur en son époque: Jean-Mathieu-Alexandre Sari (1792–1862)," Ph.D. diss., University of Lille, 1972, 396–397.

17. Ibid., 398.

18. Kennedy, *Orders from France,* 369.

19. Ibid., 362–363.

20. Henri Lallemand to Stephen Girard, New Orleans, 10 April 1818 (translated from the French). Girard Collection, Letters Received Box 762, #389.

21. Ibid.

22. Ibid.

23. Barry O'Meara, *Napoleon à St. Hélène,* vol. 1, p. 317. Quoted in Bertin, *Joseph Bonaparte en Amérique,* 193.

24. Bertin, *Joseph Bonaparte en Amérique,* 141.

Chapter 3. Alone

1. Count de Las Cases to Joseph Bonaparte, Frankfurt, 21 February 1818. Quoted in Du Casse, *Mémoires,* vol. 10, 248–249.

2. Joseph to Julie Clary Bonaparte, Point Breeze, 27 June 1818, private archives of the Princess Napoleon.

3. Joseph to Julie, Point Breeze, 15 July 1817, private archives of the Princess Napoleon.

4. Joseph to Julie, Point Breeze, 15 July 1817, private archives of the Princess Napoleon.

5. Joseph to Julie, Philadelphia, 20 January 1818, private archives of the Princess Napoleon.

6. Joseph to Julie, Philadelphia, 28 February 1818, private archives of the Princess Napoleon.

7. Joseph to Zénaïde Bonaparte, New York, 30 January 1816, private archives of the Princess Napoleon.

8. Joseph to Zénaïde, Point Breeze, 14 September 1817, private archives of the Princess Napoleon.

9. Julie Bonaparte to Nicholas Clary, Frankfurt, 13 September 1816, quoted in Gabriel Girod de l'Ain, *Joseph Bonaparte: Le roi malgré lui* (Paris: Librairie Académique Perrin, 1970), 344.

10. Edward Biddle, "Joseph Bonaparte as Recorded in the Private Journal of Nicholas Biddle," *PMHB*, 55, no. 14 (1931), 215.

11. Girard to Bonaparte, Philadelphia, 19 July 1817, Girard Collection, Letterbook 15, #201.

12. Girard to Bonaparte, Philadelphia, 1 November 1817, Girard Collection, L15, #260. Edward George was Girard's officer in charge of commercial interests on the vessel.

13. Girard to Bonaparte, Philadelphia, 15 December 1817, Girard Collection, Letterbook 15, #307.

14. Girard to Bonaparte, Philadelphia, 21 December 1817, Girard Collection, Letterbook 15, #317.

15. Charles Ingersoll to Richard Rush, Philadelphia, 25 May 1817, Rush Papers, HSP.

16. Joseph to Julie, Point Breeze, 9 April 1819, private archives of the Princess Napoleon.

17. Joseph to Zénaïde, Point Breeze, 22 September 1819, private archives of the Princess Napoleon.

18. Joseph to Zénaïde, Point Breeze, 15 August 1820, private archives of the Princess Napoleon.

19. Quoted in Georges Bertin, *Joseph Bonaparte en Amérique* (Paris: Ernest Flammarion, [1893]), 57.

20. [Frances Wright], *Views of Society and Manners in America During the Years 1818, 1819 and 1820* (London: Longman, 1821), p. 101.

21. *Recollections of Samuel Breck with Passages from His Notebooks (1771–1862)*, ed. H. E. Scudder (Philadelphia: Porter & Coates, 1877), 249. Entry dated 1 September 1817.

22. Harry F. Landon, *The North Country: A History Embracing Jefferson, St. Lawrence, Oswego, Lewis and Franklin Counties, New York*, 3 vols. (Indianapolis: Historical Publishing Company, 1932), vol. 1, 101.

23. Quoted in Bertin, *Joseph Bonaparte en Amérique*, 42.

24. Ibid., 43.

25. *Poulson's Daily Advertiser*, 25 September 1817.

26. *Poulson's Daily Advertiser*, 3 August 1818.

27. *Biographical Sketch of Joseph Napoleon Bonaparte, Count de Survilliers*, 3rd ed., unsigned (London: J. Ridgway & Sons, 1834), 108–109.

28. *Poulson's Daily Advertiser*, 15 September 1817.

29. Franklin B. Hough, *History of Lewis County in the State of New York* (Albany, N.Y.: Munsell & Rowland, 1860), 96.

30. Claire Bonney, "French Émigré Houses in Jefferson County," Kunsthistorisches Seminar der Universitat Zurich, 31 May 1982.

31. Mabel A. Brown, "A King in Yankee Land," *National Historical Magazine*, 71, no. 12 (December 1937), pp.1090–1093, and T. Wood Clarke, *Émigrés in the Wilderness* (New York: Macmillan, 1941), 134.

32. Deborah Norris Logan, manuscript diary, vol. 4, p. 98. Courtesy the Henry Francis Du Pont Winterthur Library, Joseph Downs Collection of Manuscripts and Printed Ephemera.

Chapter 4: Friends, Family, and Anna

1. George Green Shackelford, *Jefferson's Adoptive Son: The Life of William Short, 1759–1848* (Lexington: University Press of Kentucky, 1993), 111–132.

2. Georges Bertin, *Joseph Bonaparte en Amérique: 1815–1832* (Paris: Flammarion, [1893]), 180.

3. *American National Biography* (New York: Oxford University Press, 1999), vol. 11, p. 647.

4. Richard Rush to Charles Ingersoll, Washington, 4 January 1817, HSP. Rush refers to *2 Henry IV*, III.i.31.

5. Susan Dillwyn Physick, *The Autobiography of S. Dillwyn, Daughter of Dr. Philip S. Physick and Wife to Commander Conner, USN, 1826* (Philadelphia: Independence Seaport Museum, 1996), 52–53.

6. Edward Biddle, "Joseph Bonaparte as Recorded in the Private Journal of Nicholas Biddle, with an Introduction and Notes," *PMHB*, 55, no. 14 (1931), 215–216.

7. Ibid., 218.

8. Ibid.

9. Helen Berkley, "A Sketch of Joseph Buonaparte," *Godey's Lady's Book*, April 1845, p.185.

10. Charles J. Ingersoll, *History of the Second War Between the United States and Great Britain*, second series, 2 vols. (Philadelphia: Lippincott, Grambo, 1852), vol. 1, 383.

11. Fernand Beaucour, "Un fidèle de l'empereur en son époque: Jean-Mathieu-Alexandre Sari (1792–1862)," Ph. D. diss., University of Lille, 1972, 461.

12. At Waterloo, Grouchy had been in charge of the entire right wing of the Grande Armée. His extraordinary slowness in joining the main army in the death throes with Wellington, or in cutting off the Prussians, led General Gourgaud to accuse him of treachery. Napoleon shared Gourgaud's opinion, but in the United States Grouchy was an intimate of Joseph, who did not regard him as a traitor to his brother.

13. Michael Ross, *The Reluctant King: Joseph Bonaparte, King of the Two Sicilies and Spain* (New York: Mason/Charter, 1977), 252.

14. James Grant Wilson, *Life and Letters of Fitz-Greene Halleck* (New York: D. Appleton, 1869), 519.

15. Ibid., 518.

16. Ingersoll, *History of the Second War,* vol. 1, 387.

17. Quoted in Bertin, *Joseph Bonaparte en Amérique,* 163

18. *Ibid.* 162–163.

19. There is a slight irony in this friendship, in that Biddle acted as editor of the Lewis and Clark journals which, primarily due to the suicide of Meriwether Lewis, were not published until 1814. The purpose of the expedition (1804–1806) had been to acquire knowledge of the Louisiana Purchase, which Joseph and his brother Lucien had bitterly opposed.

20. Biddle, "Joseph Bonaparte," 209.

21. Francis Lieber, "An account of Francis Lieber's visit to Joseph Bonaparte translated from a German letter, September 1829," Huntington Library.

22. Ibid. Charles James Fox (1749–1806) was an English statesman who favored the French Revolution and objected to wars with France.

23. Ibid.

24. Biddle, "Joseph Bonaparte," 219.

25. Ross, *The Reluctant King,* 117.

26. Joseph Bonaparte, *Le roi Joseph Bonaparte: Lettres d'exil inédites (Amérique—Angleterre—Italie) (1825–1844),* ed. Hector Fleischmann (Paris: Librairie Charpentier et Fasquelle, 1912), 68.

27. Charles J. Ingersoll to Richard Rush, Philadelphia, 25 May 1817, HSP.

28. Th. Iung, *Lucien Bonaparte et ses mémoires: 1775–1840* (Paris: G. Charpentier, 1882), 275.

29. Ross, *The Reluctant King,* 114.

30. Duchess d'Atri to Joseph, Naples, 29 April 1808, quoted in ibid., 134.

31. Albert Savine, *À la cour du roi Joseph: Souvenirs du Count de Girardin* (Paris: Louis-Michaud, 1911).

32. Ibid., 161.

33. Joseph to Julie Clary Bonaparte, Point Breeze, 2 June 1818, private archives of the Princess Napoleon. Julie moved to Frankfurt in 1816 and to Brussels in 1820 because of the better climate.

34. Joseph to Julie, New York, 7 July 1818, private archives of the Princess Napoleon.

35. Bryce Metcalf, *Original Members and Other Officers Eligible to the Society of the Cincinnati, 1783–1938* (Strasburg, Va., 1938), 276.

36. *Records of Christ Church Baptisms, 1794–1819,* p. 2033. Information kindly given to the author by Francis James Dallett, former director of the Athenaeum of Philadelphia and former archivist of the University of Pennsylvania.

37. M. de la Forest to Baron de Damas, Philadelphia, 25 January 1825, quoted in Gabriel Girod de l'Ain, *Joseph Bonaparte: Le roi malgré lui* (Paris: Librairie Académique Perrin, 1970), p. 372.

38. W. Jay Mills, *Historic Houses of New Jersey* (Philadelphia: J. P. Lippincott, 1903), 282.

Chapter 5. Point Breeze

1. Memorandum signed by Joseph Bonaparte, Philadelphia, 4 June 1818, Girard Collection, Letterbook 14, #331.

2. Stephen Girard to Daniel Crommelin & Sons, Philadelphia, 16 July 1817. Girard College Collection, Letters Sent Book 5, #199.

3. Georges Bertin, *Joseph Bonaparte en Amérique: 1815–1832* (Paris: Flammarion, [1893], 50–54.

4. Joseph to Girard, Point Breeze, 10 April 1818, Girard Collection, LB16, #135.

5. Charles J. Ingersoll, *History of the Second War Between the United States and Great Britain,* 2nd series, 2 vols. (Philadelphia: Lippincott, Grambo, 1852), 381.

6. Joseph to Julie Clary Bonaparte, Point Breeze, 17 April 1818, private archives of the Princess Napoleon.

7. Joseph to Julie, Point Breeze, 3 May 1818, private archives of the Princess Napoleon.

8. Joseph to Zénaïde, Point Breeze, New York, 7 July 1818, private archives of the Princess Napoleon.

9. Joseph to Zénaïde, Point Breeze, 19 August 1818, private archives of the Princess Napoleon.

10. Joseph to Lucien Bonaparte, Philadelphia, 20 March 1819, private archives of the Princess Napoleon.

11. John Curtis, "A Century of Grand Opera in Philadelphia," *PMHB* 44 (1920), 122–157.

12. Charles-Lucien Bonaparte to Charlotte and Napoleon Bonaparte, New York, 12 January 1826, Fondazioni Primoli, Rome.

13. Curtis, "A Century of Grand Opera," 133.

14. *Poulson's American Daily Advertiser,* 5 January 1820.

15. [Frances Wright], *Views of Society and Manners of America* (New York: E. Bliss & E. White, 1821), 349.

16. *Poulson's American Daily Advertiser,* 5 January 1820.

17. Bertin, *Joseph Bonaparte en Amérique,* 79–80.

18. Ibid., 76–77.

19. Stephen Girard to Joseph, 22 February 1820, Letterbook 17, p. 105, Stephen Girard Collection.

20. Scharf and Westcott, *History of Philadelphia, 1609–1884,* 3 vols. (Philadelphia, L. H. Everts: 1884), vol. 2, 873. Today the Woodlands is a cemetery containing the graves of many eminent Philadelphians. The house is in the process of being restored.

21. Nicholas B. Wainwright, "Diary of Samuel Breck," *PMHB,* 2, no. 4, October 1978, p. 408.

22. Bertin, *Joseph Bonaparte en Amérique,* 108.

23. Joseph to Julie, Point Breeze, 25 May 1820, private archives of the Princess Napoleon.

24. Joseph to Julie, Point Breeze, 11 August 1820, private archives of the Princess Napoleon.

25. Mary Vespa, "Bouvier epoque," *Colonial Homes,* 18, no. 5 (October 1992), 71.

26. A duplicate of the Snyders, *Two Young Lions Pursuing a Roebuck,* is now in the Bayerische Staatsgemaidesammlungen in Munich, Germany, but the one that had been at Point Breeze is unlocated. For a time it belonged to the Pennsylvania Academy of the Fine Arts, but it was sold in 1950 to the Academy of Music in Philadelphia for one dollar and its whereabouts are not known. The Natoire, *Toilette of Psyche,* is in the New Orleans Museum of Art. The name has been changed from *Toilette of Venus.*

27. *Central Jersey Monthly,* March 1982, 45.

28. Patricia Tyson Stroud, *The Emperor of Nature: Charles-Lucien Bonaparte and His World* (Philadelphia: University of Pennsylvania Press, 2000), 43.

29. [Wright], *Views of Society and Manners of America,* 100.

30. "A Sketch of Joseph Buonaparte," *Godey's Lady's Book,* April 1845, 187.

31. Bertin, *Joseph Bonaparte en Amérique,* 95–96.

32. James D. Magee, *Bordentown, 1632–1932: An Illustrated Story of a Colonial Town* (Bordentown, N.J., 1932), 78.

33. Wendy A. Cooper, *Classical Taste in America: 1800–1840* (New York: Abbeville Press, 1993), 71.

34. Bertin, *Joseph Bonaparte en Amérique,* 94–95.

35. Henry James, *The Ambassadors,* 2 vols. (New York: Charles Scribner's Sons, 1909), vol. 2, Book Ninth, p. 125.

36. "A Sketch of Joseph Buonaparte," 187.

37. The painting appeared six times at auction in London between 1845 and 1911 before entering the Fitzwilliam Museum in Cambridge, England. Information kindly given the author by David Scrase, Curator of Paintings, Fitzwilliam Museum, Cambridge, England.

38. Powell, *Curiosité,* 410.

39. John Trumbull to Thomas Sully, New York, 30 March 1819, PAFA Private archives.

Chapter 6. Bonaparte's Park

1. Constance A. Webster, "Bonaparte's Park: A French Picturesque Garden in America," *Journal of Garden History,* 6, no. 4 (October–December 1986), 330–347.

2. Dora Wiebenson, *The Picturesque Garden in France* (Princeton: Princeton University Press, 1978), 25.

3. [René-Louis de Girardin], *Promenade ou itinéraire des jardins d'Ermenonville* (Paris: Mérigot père, 1788), 10.

4. Ibid., 30.

5. *Memories of General Montholon,* vol. 1, p. 211, quoted in Gabriel Girod de l'Ain, *Joseph Bonaparte: Le roi malgré lui* (Paris: Librairie Académique Perrin, 1970), 343.

6. Previous accounts have all stated that Joseph Bonaparte dammed Crosswicks Creek, but according to the present mayor of Bordentown, William Collom, in October 2003, this would have been impossible, as the opening would have been entirely too large.

7. Girard to Joseph, Philadelphia, 18 March 1818, Girard Collection, Letterbook 16, #106.

8. Joseph to Girard, Point Breeze, 21 March 1818, Girard Collection, Letterbook 16, #300.

9. Girard to Joseph, Philadelphia, 23 May 1818, Girard Collection, Letterbook 16, #158.

10. *National Agricultural Catalog,* p. 24.

11. "History in Review," *Sentinel* (New Jersey), December 1972, 2.

12. E. M. Woodward, *Bonaparte's Park and the Murats* (Trenton, N.J.: MacCrellish & Quigley, 1879), 72.

13. Stephen Girard to Joseph, Philadelphia, 1 August 1818, Girard College Collection.

14. Woodward, *Bonaparte's Park,* 70.

15. *Catalogue of the Elegant Household Furniture, Choice Oil Paintings, Magnificent Carrara Marble Statuary, Many items of which are from the sale of Joseph Bonaparte's effects at Bordentown, New Jersey. Estate of the Late George W. Carpenter. June 6th, 7th, 8th, 1893.* Stan V. Henkels for Thos. Birch's Sons, auctioneers, Philadelphia.

16. Charles-Lucien Bonaparte to Alexandrine Bonaparte, Point Breeze, 1 November 1823 (Fondazioni Primoli).

17. Charles-Lucien Bonaparte's manuscript notebook (MS 2548, MNHN).

18. Bernardin de St. Pierre, *Paul and Virginia* (London: George Routledge and Sons, 1879), 188–189. Translator unknown. Originally published in French in 1788 appended to *Études de la Nature.*

19. Woodward, *Bonaparte's Park,* 43-44.

20. Webster, "Bonaparte's Park," 342, caption for figure 13.

21. John F. Watson, manuscript diary, "A Trip to Pennsbury & to Count Survilliers, 1826," Library of the Henry Francis Du Pont Winterthur Museum.

22. Richard Rush to Charles Ingersoll, Washington, 2 October 1816, Ingersoll Papers, HSP.

Chapter 7. The Last of Napoleon

1. The Count de Las Cases to Joseph Bonaparte, Frankfurt, 21 February 1818. Quoted in *Mémoires et correspondence politique et militaire du roi Joseph,* ed. A. Du Casse, 10 vols. (Paris: Perrotin, 1855), vol. 10, 248–249.

2. Count de Las Cases to Joseph Bonaparte, Frankfurt, 21 February 1818. Quoted in *Mémoires et correspondence politique et militaire du roi Joseph,* 250.

3. Joseph Bonaparte to Nicholas Biddle, Philadelphia, 10 July 1821, HSP.

4. The news of Napoleon's death first appeared in the *Boston Patriot* on 6 August 1821 and was published in Philadelphia in *Poulson's Daily Advertiser* on 10 August 1821.

5. Ben Weider. "The Assassination of Napoleon," lecture given at the International Military History Festival, "Borodino Day," Borodino, Russia, September 5–10, 1997.

6. Napoleon to Joseph, Paris, 25 June 1795. *The Confidential Correspondence of Napoleon Bonaparte with His Brother Joseph, Sometime King of Spain. Selected and translated, with explanatory notes, from the Mémoires du roi Joseph,* 2 vols. (New York: D. Appleton and Company, 1856), vol. 1, 14.

7. Joseph to Napoleon, Naples, 13 August 1806, ibid., 201.

8. Label on a tapestry portrait of Napoleon at the New-York Historical Society exhibit "Seat of Empire," 8 October 2002 to 12 January 2003.

9. Quoted in Edward Biddle, "Joseph Bonaparte as Recorded in the Private Journal of Nicholas Biddle," *PMHB,* 55, no. 14 (1931), 220.

10. Th. Iung, *Lucien Bonaparte et ses mémoires, 1775–1840,* 3 vols. (Paris: G. Charpentier, Editeur, 1882), vol. 2, p. 248.

11. Unjustly accused of attempting to assassinate Napoleon, these individuals were deported to a remote place in South America. It was later proved that Royalists were to blame.

12. Iung, *Lucien Bonaparte et ses mémoires,* vol. 3, 151–155.

13. Napoleon Bonaparte, *Confidential Correspondence,* vol. 2, 365–366.

14. George Gordon, Lord Byron, *Childe Harold's Pilgrimage,* Canto the third, XXXIX.

15. *Niles Weekly Register,* Baltimore, 22 January 1825.

16. Joseph to Zénaïde, Philadelphia, 20 January 1822, private archives of the Princess Napoleon.

Chapter 8. Charlotte

1. Georges Bertin, *Joseph Bonaparte en Amérique: 1815–1832* (Paris: Flammarion, [1893], 257–259.

2. E. M. Woodward, *Bonaparte's Park and the Murats* (Trenton, N.J.: MacCrellish & Quigley, 1879), 78. This breastpin was later broken up, and several Mickle-Hemphill brides had the diamonds set in engagement rings. Information kindly given to the author by Francis James Dallett, former Secretary and Librarian of the Athenaeum of Philadelphia and former Archivist for the University of Pennsylvania.

3. The original of David's painting of the two Bonaparte sisters is believed to be the one at the Getty Museum in Los Angeles; one copy is in the Museo Napoléonico in Rome while the other is in the Toulon Museum of Art and Archaeology.

4. Caroline-Eleanore Girard to Stephen Girard, Point Breeze, 3 April 1822, Girard Collection, Letterbook 17, #304.

5. Caroline-Eleanore Girard to Stephen Girard, Point Breeze, 4 April 1822, Girard Collection, Letterbook 17, #306.

6. Charlotte Bonaparte to Julie Bonaparte, Point Breeze, 14 December 1822, del Gallo family archives.

7. Catalog, "Fourteenth Annual Exhibition of the Pennsylvania Academy of the Fine Arts" (Philadelphia: John Bioren, 1825), 17 pages.

8. Catalog, "Eleventh Annual Exhibition of the Pennsylvania Academy of the Fine Arts" (Philadelphia: Hickman & Hazzard, 1822), 7 pages.

9. Véronique Gérard Powell, "Joseph Bonaparte et la collection des Bourbons d'Espagne," *Curiosité: Études d'histoire de l'art en l'honneur d'Antoine Schnapper*, compiled by Olivier Bonfait, Véronique Gérard Powell, and Philippe Sénéchal (Paris: Flammarion, 1998), 407–414. In this original version of David's painting Napoleon's mantle is yellow. It hangs at the château de Malmaison, a gift of Joseph Bonaparte's great-granddaughter, Eugenie Bonaparte, the Princess de la Moskowa. In a later version, painted for Napoleon himself, the emperor's mantle is red. This version, which is the one most often reproduced, hangs at Versailles.

10. Joseph Bonaparte to Joseph Hopkinson, Point Breeze, 18 May 1820. The Teniers painting of gypsies is listed in the catalog for 1822. PAFA archives.

11. "James Morrell's Trip in August 1813 to Ballston and Saratoga Springs," *PMHB*, 39, 1915.

12. Joseph to Julie Bonaparte, New York, 16 January 1819, private archives of the Princess Napoleon.

13. Joseph to Zénaïde, Philadelphia, 25 January 1819, private archives of the Princess Napoleon.

14. John F. Watson's manuscript diary, "A Trip to Pennsbury & to Count Survilliers—1826," Henry Francis Du Pont Winterthur Museum.

15. James Holmes, *"Dr. Bullie's" Notes: Reminiscences of Early Georgia and of Philadelphia and New Haven in the 1800s*, ed. Delma Eugene Presley (Atlanta: Cherokee, 1976), 25–26.

16. Theodore Justice, "Things I Learned at My Grandmother's Knee," unpublished manuscript at HSP.

17. Susan Dillwyn Physick, *The Autobiography of S. Dillwyn, Daughter of Dr. Philip S. Physick and Wife to Commander Conner, USN, 1826* (Philadelphia: Independence Seaport Museum, 1996), 64.

18. Joseph to Julie, Philadelphia, 8 January 1823, private archives of the Princess Napoleon.

19. Joseph to Julie, Philadelphia, 24 January 1823 and 4 February 1823, private archives of the Princess Napoleon.

20. Joseph to Julie, Philadelphia, 18 February 1823, private archives of the Princess Napoleon.

21. Joseph to Julie, Philadelphia, 5 March 1823; Point Breeze, 11 April 1823, private archives of the Princess Napoleon.

22. Ibid. Bow Hill is today owned by the Ukrainian-American Cultural Center.

23. From the Burlington County Index to Deeds: "Barnt D. Lalor of Lamberton, Co, Burlington, N.J., Farmer, & Ann Savage & Margaret Jewet Savage, of the city of Philadelphia for $6000 land in Lamberton, Nottingham Twp., Burlington Co., N.J. (1819)." The name Pine Grove was a later addition.

24. Bass Otis's notebook at the American Antiquarian Society ascribes "after June 1823" to the painting of "Mrs. Savage." Information about Anna's house given the author by Damon Tvaryanas, architectural historian in New Jersey.

Chapter 9. Zénaïde and Charles

1. Charles-Lucien Bonaparte to Conraad Jacob Temminck, Point Breeze, 1 October 1823 (MS 2612, Museum National d'Histoire Naturelle (MNHN).

2. Henriette Lallemand to Stephen Girard, Bordentown, 17 September 1823, Girard College Collection, Letters Recived Box 805, #749.

3. John F. Watson, manuscript diary, "Trip to Pennsbury & to Count Survilliers, 1826," Library of the Henry Francis Du Pont Winterthur Museum. Noël-Nicholas Coypel's *Rape of Europa* (1776–77) was once a gift of Joseph Bonaparte to his friend Thomas Cadwalader, whose descendant John Cadwalader gave it to the Philadelphia Museum of Art, its present home, with the assistance of several friends. The painting is more than four feet high by more than twelve feet wide.

4. Patricia Tyson Stroud, *The Emperor of Nature: Charles-Lucien Bonaparte and His World* (Philadelphia: University of Pennsylvania Press, 2000), 42.

5. Reuben Haines to Ann Haines, added to a letter from Jane Haines, Germantown, 3 July 1825 (Wyck Papers).

6. William S. Walsh, "The American St. Helena: A Reminiscent Sketch of Old Bordentown," *Frank Leslie's Popular Monthly*, 37, no. 2 (February 1894), 134.

7. *Records of St. Michael's Church*, Trenton, New Jersey, pp. 357–358.

8. The Newfoundland dog anecdote is in Francis James Dallett, "France and the Penn Country," *Pennsylvania Traveler*, 2, no. 2 (January–February 1960), 51.

9. Georges Bertin, *Joseph Bonaparte en Amérique: 1815–1832* (Paris: Flammarion, [1893]), 292.

10. Charles-Lucien Bonaparte to Alexandrine Bonaparte, Point Breeze, 1 November 1823 (MS 8299, Fondazione Primoli, Rome).

11. Quoted in Fernand Beaucour, "Un fidèle de l'empereur en son époque: Jean-Mathieu-Alexandre Sari (1792–1862)," Ph.D. diss., University of Lille, 1972, 670.

12. John James Audubon to Charles-Lucien Bonaparte, London, 14 July 1830 (MNHN; film 542, APS).

13. Donald MacDonald, *The Diaries of Donald MacDonald, 1824–1826* (Indianapolis, Indiana Historical Society, vol.14, no. 2, 1942), 302.

14. Deborah Norris Logan, diary, 7 August 1826, vol. 10, p. 34. Courtesy the Henry

Francis Du Pont Winterthur Library, Joseph Downs Collection of Manuscripts and Printed Ephemera.

15. Witmer Stone, "Some Philadelphia Collections and Collectors," *The Auk: A Quarterly Journal of Ornithology* 16 (April 1899).

16. William Swainson to Charles Lucien Bonaparte, St. Albans, 26 June 1830 (MS 2612, MNHN). At the time the name had to be changed to *Larus philadelphia* because the bird had already been named by George Ord, but the common name, Bonaparte's gull, has been retained.

17. Charles-Lucien to Zénaïde Bonaparte, scrap of a letter draft, Leiden? n.d. (probably early fall of 1849) (MS 2598, MNHN).

Chapter 10. Emilie

1. Joseph to Jacques-Louis David, New York, 1 August 1824, Fondazione Primoli, Rome.

2. Jacques-Louis David to Joseph, Brussels, 19 June 1823, quoted in *Mémoires et correspondance politique et militaire du roi Joseph*, ed. A. Du Casse, 10 vols. (Paris: Perrotin, 1854), vol. 10, 270–271.

3. Mary Bartlett Cowdrey, *The American Academy of Fine Arts and Art Union, 1816–1852*, 2 vols. (New York: New-York Historical Society, 1953), vol. 1, 45.

4. Joseph to Julie Bonaparte, Allaman, Switzerland, 21 June 1814, private archives of the Princess Napoleon.

5. Georges Bertin, *Joseph Bonaparte en Amérique* (Paris: Flammarion, [1893]), 388–389.

6. Zénaïde to Julie Bonaparte, Philadelphia, 1 January 1824, private archives of the Princess Napoleon.

7. Clarence Edward Macartney and Gordon Dorrance, *The Bonapartes in America* (Philadelphia: Dorrance & Company, 1939), 136–137.

8. Patricia Tyson Stroud, *The Emperor of Nature: Charles-Lucien Bonaparte and His World* (Philadelphia: University of Pennsylvania Press, 2000), 62.

9. Michael Ross, *The Reluctant King: Joseph Bonaparte, King of the Two Sicilies and Spain* (New York: Mason/Charter, 1977), 262–263.

10. John S. C. Abbott, *History of Joseph Bonaparte, King of Naples and of Italy* [*sic*] (New York: Harper Brothers, 1869), 335–336.

11. Gabriel Girod de l'Ain, *Joseph Bonaparte: Le roi malgré lui* (Paris: Librairie Académique Perrin, 1970), 381.

12. Information given the author by Francis James Dallett, who has done much research on Anna Savage and her descendants.

13. Fernand Beaucour, "Un fidèle de l'empereur en son époque: Jean-Mathieu-Alexandre Sari (1792–1862)," Ph.D. diss., University of Lille, 1972, 671.

14. Emilie Lacoste to Louis Mailliard, Paris, 27 February 1836, Mailliard Family Papers, Manuscripts and Archives, Yale University Library.

15. Joseph Bonaparte to Félix Lacoste, Point Breeze, 30 December 1825, Joseph Bonaparte Collection (HM 21551-22593), Huntingdon Library, San Marino, California.

16. Joseph to Zénaïde, New York, 3 January 1826, private archives of the Princess Napoleon.

17. Joseph to Zénaïde, Point Breeze, 18 January 1826, private archives of the Princess Napoleon.

18. Joseph to Emilie Lacoste, Point Breeze, 8 July 1826. Mailliard Family Papers, Yale.

19. Frank McLynn, *Napoleon: A Biography* (New York: Arcade, 2002), 584.

20. Girod de l'Ain, *Joseph Bonaparte,* 381. Pierre-Jean de Béranger (1780–1857) was a French songwriter of much wit who became immensely popular in the nineteenth century. Charles Dickens once described him as the most popular French songwriter with the British enlightened working class.

21. Joseph to Emilie Lacoste, Point Breeze, 29 June 1827. Quoted in Bertin, *Joseph Bonaparte en Amérique,* 319.

22. Bertin, *Joseph Bonaparte en Amérique,* 319.

23. Ibid., 325–326.

24. Beaucour, "Un fidèle de l'empereur en son époque," 368–369. Mérimée was future author of the novelette *Carmen* (1845), from which Bizet took the text of his opera.

25. Emilie Lacoste to Joseph Bonaparte, 12 April 1828, quoted in Beaucour, "Un fidèle de l'empereur en son époque," 369.

26. Ibid.

27. Ibid.

28. Girod de L'Ain, *Joseph Bonaparte,* 382.

29. Prosper Mérimée, *Carmen, Columba & Selected Stories,* trans. Walter J. Cobb (New York: New American Library of World Literature, a Signet Classic, 1963), 246–247.

Chapter 11. Connoisseur and Collector

1. Quoted in Wendy A. Cooper, *Classical Taste in America: 1800–1840* (New York: Abbeville Press, 1993), 96.

2. Thomas Sully, "Notes on Pictures and Painting," in William Dunlap, *A History of the Rise and Progress of the Arts of Design in the United States,* reprint of the original 1834 edition with a new introduction by James Thomas Flexner (New York: Dover, 1918), vol. 2, 137–138.

3. James McClelland, *George Robert Bonfield: Philadelphia Marine Painter, 1805–1898* (Philadelphia: Philadelphia Maritime Museum, 1978), 6–7.

4. Email to the author from the art historian Isadora Rose de Viejo of Madrid.

5. Michael Ross, *The Reluctant King, Joseph Bonaparte King of the Two Sicilies and Spain* (New York: Mason/Charter, 1977), 174, 176.

6. C. M. Kauffmann, *Catalog of Paintings in the Wellington Museum* (London: Her Majesty's Stationery Office, 1982), 5.

7. Ibid.

8. Cecil Gould, *Trophy of Conquest: The Musée Napoleon and the Creation of the Louvre* (London: Faber & Faber, 1965), 100. The Guido Reni was perhaps the "vierge et enfant" listed by Louis Mailliard as having been given by Joseph to Joseph Hopkinson in Philadelphia. Mailliard Family Papers, Manuscripts and Archives, Yale University Library.

9. The Bidauld is now at the Indianapolis Museum of Art.

10. Ibid., 79.

11. Gould, *Trophy of Conquest,* 99–100.

12. Harold E. Wethey, *The Paintings of Titian,* vol. 1, *The Religious Paintings* (London: Phaidon, 1969), p. 156, catalogue no. 135.

13. Louis Mailliard, "Memorandum—Objets donnés ou vendus," Mailliard Family Papers, Manuscripts and Archives, Yale University Library.

14. Georges Bertin, *Joseph Bonaparte en Amérique: 1815–1832* (Paris: Flammarion, [1893]), appendix B.

15. Harold E. Wethey, "Titian's Escorial-Asburton 'Magdalen,'" in Wethey, *Religious Paintings*.

16. Christie, Manson & Woods' Catalogue, "Important Old Master Pictures," 21 April 1989.

17. Fernand Beaucour, "Un fidèle de l'empereur en son époque: Jean-Mathieu-Alexandre Sari (1792–1862)," Ph.D. diss., University of Lille, 1972, 749.

18. Joel Roberts Poinsett to the Pennsylvania Academy of the Fine Arts, Charleston, 12 July 1823. Microfilm P63, the Henry Francis Du Pont Winterthur Museum Library.

19. Joseph Bonaparte to Joseph Hopkinson, Point Breeze, 12 April 1825. Microfilm P63, the Henry Francis Du Pont Winterthur Museum Library.

20. Joseph to Robert Gilmor, Point Breeze, 12 August 1831, Joseph Bonaparte Papers, HSP.

21. Joseph to Mr. and Mrs. Gilmor, Point Breeze, n.d., Joseph Bonaparte Papers, HSP.

22. The painting today belongs to the Art Gallery of South Australia at Adelaide (*Burlington Magazine*, 145, no. 1201 [(April 2003)], 327).

23. Mary Bartlett Cowdrey, *The American Academy of Fine Arts and Art Union, 1816–1852*, 2 vols. (New York: New-York Historical Society, 1953), vol. 1, 45.

24. Ibid., 47.

25. Dorothy Kent Hill, "A Handsome Greek Amphora," *Bulletin of the Walters Art Gallery*, 9, no. 1 (October 1956).

26. Charles Bonaparte to Lucien Bonaparte, Point Breeze, 19 November 1824, #8395, Fondazione Primoli.

27. Charles Bonaparte to Lucien Bonaparte, Point Breeze, 15 August 1825, #8396, Fondazione Primoli.

28. List in Charles-Lucien Bonaparte's handwriting, del Gallo family archives. The Murillo may be *The Virgin and Child with a Rosary* in the Wallace Collection, London.

29. Sampson Batard & Co. to Charles-Lucien Bonaparte, London, 29 December 1826, del Gallo family archives.

30. Charles-Lucien Bonaparte to Julie Bonaparte, Dublin, 30 June 1827, #8302, Fondazione Primoli.

31. Zénaïde to Julie Bonaparte, New York, 13 August 1826, private archives of the Princess Napoleon.

32. John Quincy Adams to Joseph Hopkinson, Washington, D.C., 6 November 1827, and Joseph Bonaparte to Joseph Hopkinson, Point Breeze, 2 December 1827. Quoted in Georges Bertin, *Joseph Bonaparte en Amérique* (Paris: Flammarion, 1893), 308–310.

33. Charles-Lucien Bonaparte to William Cooper, Leghorn from the Lazareth, 14 April 1828 (film 1514, APS).

34. Robert Hughes, *Goya* (New York: Alfred A. Knopf, 2003), 320.

35. Ibid., 301–302.

36. Christopher Benfey, "The Art of Disaster," a review of Hughes, *Goya*, in *New York Review of Books*, 50, no.19 (December 4, 2003).

37. This was the ill-fated project of Charles Willson Peale's son Rubens, quite unlike the prosperous Peale museums in Philadelphia.

38. Joseph to Zénaïde, Point Breeze, 13 July 1828, private archives of the Princess Napoleon.

39. Joseph to Zénaïde, Point Breeze, 8 July 1829, private archives of the Princess Napoleon.

40. Charles J. Ingersoll, *History of the Second War Between the United States and Great Britain*, second series, 2 vols. (Philadelphia: Lippincott, Grambo, 1852), 384.

41. Zénaïde to Julie Bonaparte, Point Breeze, 1 November 1824, #9079, Fondazione Primoli.

42. Roberta J. M. Olson and Margaret K. Hofer, *Seat of Empire*, exh. cat., 8 October 2002 to 12 January 2003, New-York Historical Society (New York: New-York Historical Society, 2002).

Chapter 12. Lafayette Changes His Position

1. John Fanning Watson, manuscript diary, library of the Henry Francis Du Pont Winterthur Museum.

2. Clarence Edward Macartney and Gordon Dorrance, *The Bonapartes in America* (Philadelphia: Dorrance & Company, 1939), 117.

3. Joseph to Stephen Girard, Point Breeze, 27 October 1829, Stephen Girard Collection, Girard College, Letters Received Box 861, #1060.

4. Stephen Girard to Joseph, Philadelphia, 31 October 1829, Stephen Girard Collection, Girard College, Letterbook 23, #356.

5. Stephen Girard to Joseph, Philadelphia, 16 January 1830, Stephen Girard Collection, Girard College, Letterbook 23, #445.

6. Information kindly given the author by the historian Francis James Dallett, former director of the Athenaeum of Philadelphia and former archivist of the University of Pennsylvania.

7. Gabriel Girod de l'Ain, *Joseph Bonaparte: Le roi malgré lui* (Paris: Librairie Académique Perrin, 1970), 374–375.

8. Information kindly given the author by the architectural historian Damon Tvaryanas.

9. Information kindly given the author by Francis James Dallett.

10. *Public Ledger*, Philadelphia, 13 August 1839.

11. Girod de l'Ain, *Joseph Bonaparte*, 383–384.

12. Ibid.

13. Georges Bertin, *Joseph Bonaparte en Amérique: 1815–1832* (Paris: Flammarion, [1893]), 335–336.

14. Charles J. Ingersoll, *History of the Second War Between the United States and Great Britain*, second series, 2 vols. (Philadelphia: Lippincott, Grambo, 1852), vol. 1, 378, 388.

15. John S. C. Abbott, *History of Joseph Bonaparte, King of Naples and of Italy* [sic] (New York: Harper & Brothers, 1869), 341

16. Ibid., 341–342.

17. Lloyd Kramer, *Lafayette in Two Worlds: Public Cultures and Personal Identities in an Age of Revolutions* (Chapel Hill: University of North Carolina Press, 1996), 244.

18. Lafayette to Joseph, Paris, 26 November 1830 in *Mémoires et correspondance politique et militaire du roi Joseph*, ed. A. Du Casse, 10 vols. (Paris: Perrotin, 1854), vol. 10, 370.

19. Edward Biddle, "Joseph Bonaparte as Recorded in the Private Journal of Nicholas Biddle," *PMHB*, 55, 14 (1931), 219.

20. Abbott, *History of Joseph Bonaparte*, 343–346.

21. Ingersoll, *History of the Second War,* vol. 1, 386.

22. Ibid., 353–355.

23. Ibid., 146.

24. Horace Fleischmann, *Le Roi Joseph Bonaparte: Lettres d'exil, inédites* (Paris: Librairie Charpentier et Fasquelle, 1912), 10.

25. Ingersoll, *History of the Second War,* vol. 1, 387.

Chapter 13. The Siren Call of Europe

1. Joseph to Charles J. Ingersoll, Point Breeze, 2 January 1831, Ingersoll Papers, HSP.

2. Joseph to General Jean Lamarque, Point Breeze, 26 September 1830, *Mémoires et correspondence politique et militaire du roi Joseph,* ed. A. Du Casse, 10 vols. (Paris: Perrotin, 1854), vol. 10, 358.

3. *Mémoires,* vol. 10, 359–360.

4. Joseph to Marshal Jean-Baptiste Jourdan, 27 September 1830, *Mémoires,* vol. 10, 362.

5. Joseph to Baron Bignon, Point Breeze, 19 September 1830, *Mémoires,* vol. 10, 354.

6. Lucien Bonaparte to M. Robaglia, Florence, 3 December 1830, quoted in Hector Fleischmann, *Le roi Joseph Bonaparte: Lettres d'exil, inédites (Amérique—Angleterre—Italie)* (Paris: Librairie Charpentier et Fasquelle, 1912), 157.

7. Joseph to Count Charles de Flahaut, Point Breeze, 24 September 1830, *Mémoires,* vol. 10, 356.

8. Charles J. Ingersoll, *History of the Second War Between the United States and Great Britain,* second series, 2 vols. (Philadelphia: Lippincott, Grambo, 1852), vol. 1, 390.

9. Gabriel Girod de l'Ain, *Joseph Bonaparte: Le roi malgré lui* (Paris: Librairie Académique Perrin, 1970), 398.

10. Jasper Ridley, *Napoleon III and Eugenie* (New York: Viking Press, 1980), 58.

11. Joseph to Baron Méneval, New York, 29 June 1831, quoted in Fleischmann, *Le roi Joseph Bonaparte,* 179–180.

12. Fleischmann, *Le roi Joseph Bonaparte,* 159.

13. Baron Menéval to Joseph, Hermitage de Gif, 16 September 1831, quoted in Fleischmann, *Le roi Joseph Bonaparte,* 182.

14. Louis Napoleon Bonaparte to Joseph, Arenenberg, 9 September 1831, quoted in Fleischmann, *Le roi Joseph Bonaparte,* 185.

15. Joseph to Joel Roberts Poinsett, Point Breeze, 6 February 1832, Poinsett Papers, HSP.

16. Quoted in Frank H. Sommers, "America's First King," *Winterthur Newsletter,* May 31, 1963.

17. This drawing was formerly in the collection of the Marquis de la Soudières in Nice, France, but is currently unlocated.

18. Joseph to Napoleon II, Point Breeze, 15 February 1832, *Mémoires,* vol. 10, 378–382.

19. Fernand Beaucour, "Un fidèle de l'empereur en son époque: Jean-Mathieu-Alexandre Sari (1792–1862)," Ph.D. diss., University of Lille, 1972, 177–178.

20. Edmond Rostand, *L'Aiglon,* trans. Louis N. Parker (New York: R. H. Russell, 1901), 74.

21. Beaucour, "Un fidèle de l'empereur," 179.

22. Ingersoll, *History of the Second War,* 398.

23. Girard, licensed as a ship captain at twenty-three, although blind since birth in one

eye, had married Mary Lum, the daughter of a local shipbuilder four years after he settled in Philadelphia. In 1791 Mary had a baby whom she named Mary Girard, despite the fact that her husband denied paternity. But Girard paid for the birth and the care of the child until she died five months later. A month after that he institutionalized his wife for life in the Pennsylvania Hospital for the insane.

24. "Barralet's 'The Dunlop House, 1807,' and Its Associations," *PMHB*, 99 (1975), 131–155.

25. Joseph to Félix Lacoste, 26 April 1831, quoted in Georges Bertin, *Joseph Bonaparte en Amérique: 1815–1832* (Paris: Flammarion, [1893]), 356.

26. Joseph to Nicholas Biddle, Point Breeze, 15 July 1832, Nicholas Biddle Papers, HSP.

27. Mailliard Family Papers, Manuscripts and Archives, Yale University Library.

28. *Poulson's Daily Advertiser*, 19 July 1832.

29. Joseph to Nicholas Biddle, London, 24 July 1832, Nicholas Biddle Papers, HSP.

Chapter 14. A Bonaparte in England

1. Lafayette to Joseph, La Grange, 13 October 1832, in Joseph Bonaparte, *Mémoires et correspondence politique et militaire du roi Joseph Bonaparte*, ed. A. Du Casse (Paris: Perrotin, 1854), vol. 10, 383–384.

2. Joseph to Lafayette, London, 10 November 1832, *Mémoires*, vol. 10, 384–385.

3. Joseph to Charles Ingersoll, London, 12 October 1832. Quoted in Charles J. Ingersoll, *History of the Second War Between the United States and Great Britain*, second series, 2 vols. (Philadelphia: Lippincott, Grambo, 1852), vol. 1, 401.

4. Richard Rush to Charles Ingersoll, London, 27 May 1819, Charles Ingersoll Papers, HSP.

5. Mailliard journal for 1833, Mailliard Family Papers, Manuscripts and Archives, Yale University Library.

6. Quoted in Gabriel Girod de l'Ain, *Joseph Bonaparte, Le roi malgré lui* (Paris: Librairie Académique Perrin, 1970), 401.

7. Michael Ross, *The Reluctant King: Joseph Bonaparte, King of the Two Sicilies and Spain* (New York: Mason/Charter, 1977), 269–270.

8. Girod de l'Ain, *Joseph Bonaparte*, 402.

9. Ibid., 402–403.

10. Emilie Lacoste to Joseph, Paris, 9 August 1833, Mailliard Family Papers, Manuscripts and Archives, Yale University Library.

11. Ibid.

12. Joseph to Félix Lacoste, Marden Park, 3 September 1833, Manuscript Department, Huntingdon Library.

13. Joseph to Madame Mère, London, 31 January 1833, *Mémoires*, vol. 10, 385–386.

14. Victor Hugo to Joseph, Paris, 27 February 1833, *Mémoires*, vol. 10, 386–387.

15. Quoted in André Maurois, *Victor Hugo* (London: Jonathan Cape, 1956), 187.

16. Mailliard journal for 1833, Mailliard Family Papers, Manuscripts and Archives Yale University Library.

17. Ibid.

18. David O'Brien, "Executive Authority: Images of Leadership in Post-Revolutionary

France and America," in *Jefferson's America and Napoleon's France: An Exhibition for the Louisiana Purchase Bicentennial* (New Orleans: New Orleans Museum of Art, 2003), 49–50.

19. Mailliard journal, Mailliard Family Papers, Manuscripts and Archives Yale University Library.

20. Auction catalog, Christie & Manson, 29 June 1833, London, 9–10. The painting by Raphael may be the one of that description in the Wallace Collection, London.

21. Fernand Beaucour, "Un fidèle de l'empereur en son époque: Jean-Mathieu-Alexandre Sari (1792–1862)," Ph.D. diss., University of Lille, 1972, 780.

22. "Memorandum—objets donnés ou vendus," Mailliard Family Papers, Manuscripts and Archives Yale University Library.

23. Joseph Hopkinson to Joseph, Philadelphia, 19 April 1833, Mailliard Family Papers, Manuscripts and Archives Yale University Library.

24. Stephen Girard to Joseph, Philadelphia, 25 March 1830, Stephen Girard Collection, Girard College, Letterbook 23, #511.

25. Joseph to Charles Ingersoll, London, 19 July 1834, quoted in Ingersoll, *History of the Second War*, vol. 1, 403.

26. Mailliard's journal, quoted in Beaucour, "Un fidèle de l'empereur en son époque," 801.

27. Ibid., 803.

28. Ibid.

29. Ibid.

30. Ingersoll, *History of the Second War*, vol. 1, 403.

Chapter 15. Return to Point Breeze

1. Deborah Norris Logan, Diary, vol. 13, p. 75 (1830), courtesy the Henry Francis Du Pont Winterthur Library: Joseph Downs Collection of Manuscripts and Printed Ephemera.

2. J. Thomas Scharf and Thompson Westcott, *History of Philadelphia, 1609–1884*, 3 vols. (Philadelphia: L. H. Everts, 1884), vol. 3, 2182.

3. Powel is no doubt "John Hare Powel, gent, Locust and Juniper," as listed in the *Philadelphia Directory* for 1836. The former Powel mansion is the present site of the Historical Society of Pennsylvania. According to Roger W. Moss, it is doubtful if Powel (1782–1856) ever occupied the house, although it was richly furnished in the latest style. The inventory shows items still in packing cases. The major source for information on the house is B. Keven Hawkins, "Historical Survey of the Property on the Southwest Corner of Locust and Thirteenth Streets: Once the Site of the Mansion of John Hare Powel," unpublished paper, University of Pennsylvania, 1985. A copy is on deposit at the Athenaeum of Philadelphia.

4. Joseph to Joseph Hopkinson, Point Breeze, 10 February 1836, Mailliard Family Papers, Manuscripts and Archives, Yale University Library.

5. Joseph to Joseph Hopkinson, Point Breeze, 4 January 1836, Society Collection, HSP.

6. Joseph to Joseph Hopkinson, London, 27 August 1834, Society Collection, HSP.

7. Fernand Beaucour, "Un fidèle de l'empereur en son époque: Jean-Mathieu-Alexandre Sari (1792–1862)," Ph.D. diss., University of Lille, 1972, 774.

8. Emilie Lacoste to Louis Mailliard, Paris, 27 February 1836, Mailliard Family Papers, Manuscripts and Archives, Yale University Library.

9. Ibid.

10. Quoted in Edward Biddle, "Joseph Bonaparte as Recorded in the Private Journal of Nicholas Biddle," *PMHB*, 55, no. 14 (1931), 220.

11. Baron de Méneval to Joseph, Paris, 1 March 1836, quoted in Hector Fleischmann, *Le Roi Joseph Bonaparte, Lettres d'exil inédites (Amérique—Angleterre—Italie, 1825–1844)* (Paris: Librairie Charpentier et Fasquelle, 1912), 206-207.

12. Joseph to Baron de Méneval, Point Breeze, 30 May 1836, quoted in *Lettres d'exil*, 210.

13. Ibid., 203.

14. Joseph to Joseph Hopkinson, London, 30 January 1835, Mailliard Family Papers, Manuscripts and Archives, Yale University Library.

15. Helen Berkley, "A Sketch of Joseph Buonaparte," *Godey's Lady's Book*, April 1845, 187.

16. Joseph to Edmund DuBarry, Point Breeze, 24 June 1836, Mailliard Family Papers, Manuscripts and Archives, Yale University Library.

17. "Memorandum—Objets donnés ou vendus," Mailliard Family Papers, Manuscripts and Archives, Yale University Library.

18. Joseph Hopkinson to Joseph, Bordentown, 21 July 1836, Mailliard Family Papers, Manuscripts and Archives, Yale University Library.

19. Joseph to Joseph Hopkinson, London, 2 August 1836, Mailliard Family Papers, Manuscripts and Archives, Yale University Library.

20. Joseph Hopkinson to Joseph, Bordentown, 18 September 1836, Mailliard Family Papers, Manuscripts and Archives, Yale University Library.

21. Joseph to Félix Lacoste, London, 20 September 1836, quoted in *Lettres d'exil*, 212.

22. Joseph to the *Courrier Français*, London, quoted in *Lettres d'exil*, 211.

23. Jasper Ridley, *Napoleon III and Eugenie* (New York: Viking Press, 1980), 110–111.

24. Joseph to Félix Lacoste, London, 16 November 1836, quoted in Gabriel Girod de L'Ain, *Joseph Bonaparte, Le roi malgré lui* (Paris: Librairie Académique Perrin, 1970), 418.

25. Quoted in *Lettres d'exil*, 223.

26. Quoted in Michael Ross, *The Reluctant King: Joseph Bonaparte King of the Two Sicilies and Spain* (New York: Mason/Charter, 1977), 272.

27. *Lettres d'exil*, 223.

28. "Reminiscences of Edward Shippen: Bordentown in the 1830s," *PMHB*, 78 (1954).

29. Joseph to Joseph Hopkinson, London, 12 December 1836, Mailliard Family Papers, Manuscripts and Archives, Yale University Library.

30. Patricia Tyson Stroud, *The Emperor of Nature: Charles-Lucien Bonaparte and His World* (Philadelphia: University of Pennsylvania Press, 2000), 135.

31. Joseph to Joseph Hopkinson, London, 9 January 1837, Mailliard Family Papers, Manuscripts and Archives, Yale University Library.

32. Ibid.

33. Joseph Hopkinson to Joseph, Bordentown, 17 September 1836, Mailliard Family Papers, Manuscripts and Archives, Yale University Library.

34. Edmund Du Barry to Joseph, Point Breeze, 30 January 1837, Mailliard Family Papers, Manuscripts and Archives, Yale University Library.

35. Louis Napoleon to Joseph, New York, 22 April 1837, *Mémoires et correspondance politique et militaire du roi Joseph*, ed. A. Du Casse, 10 vols. (Paris: Perrotin, 1854), vol.10, 400.

36. Joseph to Louis Napoleon, London, 10 July 1837, quoted in Girod de L'Ain, *Joseph Bonaparte*, 419.

37. Joseph Hopkinson to Louis Mailliard, Philadelphia, 4 January 1837, Hopkinson Papers, HSP.

38. Joseph Hopkinson to Joseph, Bordentown, 18 April 1837, Mailliard Family Papers, Manuscripts and Archives, Yale University Library.

39. A statement signed by Joseph, London, 16 October 1837, #8371, Fondazione Primoli, Rome.

40. Luciano Bonaparte to his mother Zénaïde, London, n.d., Museo Napoleonico, Rome.

41. Edmund DuBarry to Joseph, Point Breeze, 29 March 1837, Mailliard Family Papers, Yale University.

42. Joseph Hopkinson to Joseph, Bordentown, 19 December 1837, Mailliard Family Papers, Yale University.

Chapter 16. Death in the Family

1. Samuel Breck diary entry for 17 September 1838 in *Recollections of Samuel Breck with Passages from His Note-Books (1771–1862)*, ed. H. E. Scudder (Philadelphia: Porter and Coates, 1877), 251–252.

2. Louis Mailliard to Langhorn Thorn, Philadelphia, 10 January 1839, archives of the Divine Word Missionary, Bordentown, New Jersey. Courtesy of Dr. Andy Cosentino.

3. Quoted in Georges Bertin, *Joseph Bonaparte en Amérique: 1815–1832* (Paris: Flammarion, [1893]), 272–273.

4. Gabriel Girod de l'Ain, *Joseph Bonaparte, Le roi malgré lui* (Paris: Librairie Académique Perrin, 1970), 420.

5. Charles Bonaparte to Joseph, Florence, 30 March 1839, #8397, Fondazione Primoli, Rome.

6. Bertin, *Joseph Bonaparte en Amérique,* 279.

7. Joseph Bonaparte, *Lettres d'exil,* ed. Hector Fleischmann (Paris: Librairie Charpentier et Fasquelle, 1912), 241–242.

8. Charles Bonaparte to Joseph, Florence, 30 March 1839, #8397, Fondazione Primoli, Rome.

9. Zénaïde Bonaparte to Joseph, Ariccia, 19 August 1839, #10743, Fondazione Primoli, Rome.

10. Louis Mailliard, "Memorandum—Objets donnés ou vendus," Mailliard Family Papers, Manuscripts and Archives, Yale University Library.

11. A. Hilliard Atteridge, *Napoleon's Brothers* (London: Methuen, 1909), 175.

12. Juliette Clary to Mme. Thibaudeau, Florence, 12 June 1839, quoted in Girod de l'Ain, *Joseph Bonaparte,* 422.

13. Cardinal Joseph Fesch to Joseph, Rome, 19 January 1839, Mailliard Family Papers, Manuscripts and Archives, Yale University Library.

14. Charles-Lucien Bonaparte, "Autobiografici," quoted in Patricia Tyson Stroud, *The Emperor of Nature: Charles-Lucien Bonaparte and His World* (Philadelphia: University of Pennsylvania Press, 2000), 159.

15. Owen Connelly, *The Gentle Bonaparte: The Story of Napoleon's Elder Brother* (New York: Macmillan, 1968), 291.

16. William Howard Adams, ed., *The Eye of Thomas Jefferson* (Charlottesville: University Press of Virginia, 1981), xxxviii.

17. Joseph to General Thomas Cadwalader, Point Breeze, 25 October 1839, Society Collection, HSP. The painting was purchased by the Philadelphia Museum of Art in 1927 where it is attributed to Noël Coypel (1628–1707). Joseph apparently believed it was by another member of the family, perhaps the most famous, Antoine (1661–1722).

18. Mailliard, "Memorandum—Objets donnés ou vendus," Mailliard Family Papers, Manuscripts and Archives, Ylae University Library.

19. Emilie Lacoste to Joseph, [Paris], 12 November 1839, Mailliard Family Papers.

Chapter 17. Farewell to America

1. [Mailliard] to Charles Ingersoll, London, 1 June 1840, quoted in Charles J. Ingersoll, *History of the Second War Between the United States and Great Britain,* second series, 2 vols. (Philadelphia: Lippincott, Grambo, 1852), vol. 1, 407.

2. Joseph to Marshal Moncey, London, 26 May 1840, *Mémoires et correspondance politique et militaire du roi Joseph,* ed. A. Du Casse (Paris: Perrotin, 1854), vol. 10, 407.

3. Marshal Moncey to Joseph, Paris, 6 June 1840, in ibid.

4. Ingersoll, *History of the Second War,* vol. 1, 412.

5. Ibid., 412–413.

6. Louis Mailliard to Joseph Hopkinson, London, summer 1840, Mailliard Family Papers, Manuscripts and Archives, Yale University Library.

7. Louis Mailliard to Joseph Hopkinson, Wildbad, 8 August 1840, Mailliard Family Papers, Manuscripts and Archives, Yale University Library.

8. Jasper Ridley, *Napoleon III and Eugenie* (New York: Viking, 1979), 128.

9. Ibid., 133.

10. Joseph Hopkinson to Louis Mailliard, Philadelphia, 6 November 1840, Mailliard Family Papers, Manuscripts and Archives, Yale University Library.

11. Louis Mailliard to Joseph Hopkinson, London, 2 December 1840, Mailliard Family Papers, Manuscripts and Archives, Yale University Library.

12. Joseph Hopkinson to Joseph, Philadelphia, 27 December 1840, Mailliard Family Papers, Manuscripts and Archives, Yale University Library.

13. Isadore Geoffroy Saint-Hilaire to Charles-Lucien Bonaparte, Hyères, 6 January 1841 (MS2602, MNHN). Quoted in Patricia Tyson Stroud, *The Emperor of Nature: Charles-Lucien Bonaparte and His World* (Philadelphia: University of Pennsylvania Press, 2000), 166–167.

14. Louis Mailliard, diary, 24 and 26 October 1840, Mailliard Family Papers, Manuscripts and Archives, Yale University Library.

15. Louis Mailliard to Joseph Hopkinson, London, 17 January 1841, Mailliard Family Papers, Manuscripts and Archives, Yale University Library.

16. Louis Mailliard, diary, 13 June 1840, Mailliard Family Papers, Manuscripts and Archives, Yale University Library.

17. Charles-Lucien Bonaparte to Julie Bonaparte, Dublin, 30 June 1827, #8302, Fondazioni Primoli, Rome.

18. Louis Mailliard, diary, 22, 23, 27, and 28 July 1841, Mailliard Family Papers, Manuscripts and Archives, Yale University Library.

19. Ibid., 26 March 1842.

20. Emilie Lacoste to Joseph, Nice, 26 December 1842, quoted in Gabriel Girod de l'Ain, *Joseph Bonaparte, Le roi malgré lui* (Paris: Librairie Académique Perrin, 1970), 425–426.

21. An English translation of the last will and testament of Joseph Napoleon Bonaparte, Count of Survilliers, is in the Burlington County Historical Society.

22. Fernand Beaucour, "Un fidèle de l'empereur en son époque: Jean-Mathieu-Alexandre Sari (1792–1862)," Ph.D. diss., University of Lille, 1972, 373.

23. A. W. Raitt, *Prosper Mérimée* (New York: Charles Scribner's Sons, 170), 162.

24. Joseph to Baron de Méneval, Florence, 5 July 1843, Joseph Bonaparte, *Le roi Bonaparte: Lettres d'exil, inédites (Amérique—Angleterre—Italie)*, ed. Hector Fleischmann (Paris: Librairie Charpentier et Fasquelle, 1912), 267–268.

25. Ibid., 269–279.

26. Girod de l'Ain, *Joseph Bonaparte*, 427–428.

27. *Le Siècle* 216 (Paris), 7 August 1844, (MS2594, MNHN).

28. Obituary notice of Joseph Bonaparte read by Charles J. Ingersoll, from *Proceedings of the American Philosophical Society*, 5 January 1855.

29. Ingersoll, *History of the Second War*, vol. 1, 416.

Epilogue

1. English translation of the last will and testament of Joseph Napoleon Bonaparte, Count of Survilliers, Burlington County Historical Society.

2. George Ord to Charles Bonaparte, Philadelphia, 13 August 1845, MS2608, MNHN.

3. William Chapman White, *Adirondack Country*, ed. Erskine Caldwell (Boston: Little, Brown, 1954), 188.

4. Ibid., 187.

5. Information kindly given the author by Francis James Dallett, former archivist of the University of Pennsylvania.

6. Gabriel Girod de l'Ain, *Joseph Bonaparte, Le roi malgré lui* (Paris: Librairie Académique Perrin, 1970), 426–427.

7. Roberta J. M. Olson and Margaret K. Hofer, *Seat of Empire*, exh. cat., New-York Historical Society, 8 October 2002 to 12 January 2003, p. 8.

8. Fernand Beaucour, "Un fidèle de l'empereur en son époque: Jean-Mathieu-Sari (1792–1862)," Ph.D. diss., University of Lille, 1972, 373.

9. English copy of the last will and testament of Joseph Napoleon Bonaparte, Count of Survilliers.

10. Julie Bonaparte, *La Princesse Julie Bonaparte Marquise de Roccagiovine et son temps: Mémoires inédits*, ed. Isa Dardano Basso *(1853–1870)* (Rome: Edizioni de storia e letteratura, 1975), 207, n.22.

11. Napoleon to Joseph, Paris, 25 June 1795, *The Confidential Correspondence of Napoleon Bonaparte with His Brother Joseph, Sometime King of Spain*, 2 vols. (New York: D. Appleton, 1856), vol. 1, 14–15.

12. Quoted in Claude François, baron de Méneval, *Memoirs Illustrating the History of Napoleon I from 1802 to 1815*, ed. Baron Napoleon Joseph de Méneval (grandson), and trans. Robert H. Sherard, 3 vols. (New York: D. Appleton, 1894), vol. 3, p. 304.

BIBLIOGRAPHY

MANUSCRIPT COLLECTIONS

Academy of Natural Sciences of Philadelphia

American Philosophical Society Library

Bibliothèque Centrale du Museum National d'Histoire Naturelle, Paris, Charles-Lucien Bonaparte Papers.

Bonaparte Family Papers, Fondazione Primoli, Rome

Stephen Girard Papers and Collection, Girard College, Philadelphia

Historical Society of Pennsylvania

Huntington Library Collection

Library Company Manuscripts housed at the Historical Society of Pennsylvania

Mailliard Family Papers, Manuscripts and Archives, Yale University Library

Museo Napoleonico, Rome

Del Gallo family archives, Rome

Princess Napoleon private archives, Paris and Switzerland

Henry Francis Du Pont Winterthur Museum Library

Wyck Papers, American Philosophical Society Library

BOOKS AND ARTICLES

Abbott, John S. C. History of *Joseph Bonaparte, King of Naples and of Italy* [sic]. New York: Harper and Brothers, 1869.

Abrantes, Laure Junot, duchesse d'. *Memoirs of Napoleon, His Court and Family*. 2 vols. London: Richard Bentley, 1836.

Adams, Arthur G. *The Hudson Through the Years*. New York: Fordham University Press, 2000.

Adams, William Howard, ed. *The Eye of Thomas Jefferson*. Charlottesville: University Press of Virginia, 1981.

Aronson, Theodore. *The Golden Bees: the Story of the Bonapartes*. Greenwich, Conn.: New York Graphic Society, 1964.

Asprey, Robert. *The Rise of Napoleon Bonaparte*. New York: Basic Books, 2000.

————. *The Reign of Napoleon Bonaparte.* New York: Basic Books, 2001.

Atteridge, A. Hilliard. *Napoleon's Brothers.* London: Methuen, 1909.

Baridon, Michel. "The Garden of the Perfectibilists: Méréville and the Désert de Retz." In *Tradition and Innovation in French Garden Art: Chapters of a New History,* ed. John Dixon Hunt and Michel Conan with the assistance of Claire Goldstein. Philadelphia: University of Pennsylvania Press, 2002.

Beaucour, Fernand. "Un fidèle de l'empereur en son époque: Jean-Mathieu-Alexandre Sari (1792–1862)." 5 vols. Ph.D. diss., University of Lille, 1972.

Berkley, Helen. "A Sketch of Joseph Buonaparte." *Godey's Lady's Book,* April 1845.

Bertin, Georges. *Joseph Bonaparte en Amérique.* Paris: Flammarion, [1893].

Biddle, Edward. "Joseph Bonaparte as Recorded in the Private Journal of Nicholas Biddle." *Pennsylvania Magazine of History and Biography* 55, no. 14 (1931): 208-24.

Bierman, John. *Napoleon III and His Carnival Empire.* New York: St. Martin's Press, 1988.

Blanc, Olivier. *L'éminence grise de Napoléon: Reynaud de Saint-Jean d'Angély.* Paris: Pygmalion, 2002.

Blumenthal, Henry. *American and French Culture, 1800–1900: Interchanges in Art, Science, Literature, and Society.* Baton Rouge: Louisiana State University Press, 1975.

Bonaparte, Joseph. *Mémoires et correspondance politique et militaire du roi Joseph.* Ed. A. Du Casse. 10 vols. Paris: Perrotin, 1855.

————. *Le roi Joseph Bonaparte: Lettres d'éxil, inédites (Amérique—Angleterre—Italie) (1825–1844).* Introduction, notes and commentary by Hector Fleischmann. Paris: Librairie Charpentier et Fasquelle, 1912.

Bonaparte, Julie. *La princesse Julie Bonaparte, marquise de Roccagiovine et son temps: Mémoires inédits, 1853–1870.* Ed. Isa Dardano Basso. Rome: Edizioni de Storia e Letteratura, 1975.

Bonaparte, Lucien. *Memoirs of the Private and Political Life of Lucien Bonaparte, Prince of Canino.* Translated from the French. 2 vols. London: H. Colburn, 1818.

Bonaparte, Napoleon. *The Confidential Correspondence of Napoleon Bonaparte with His Brother Joseph, Sometime King of Spain.* 2 vols. New York: D. Appleton and Company, 1856.

Boorse, Henry A. "Barralet's 'The Dunlop House, 1807' and Its Associations." *Pennsylvania Magazine of History and Biography*, 99 (1975): 131–155.

Bourrienne, Louis Antoine Fauvelet de. *Memoirs of Napoleon Bonaparte*. Ed. R. W. Phipps. 4 vols. New York: Charles Scribner's Sons, 1890.

Breck, Samuel. *Recollections of Samuel Breck with Passages from His Notebooks (1771–1862)*. Ed. H. E. Scudder. Philadelphia: Porter & Coates, 1877.

Byron, George Gordon, Lord Byron. "Childe Harold's Pilgrimage." *Byron: Poetical Works*. London: Oxford University Press, 1967.

Castelot, André. *Au fil de l'histoire*. Paris: Librairie Académique Perrin, 1981.

Chevallier, Bernard. *Malmaison*. Paris: Artlys, 2001.

Clarke, T.Wood. *Émigrés in the Wilderness*. New York: Macmillan, 1941.

Connelly, Owen. *The Gentle Bonaparte: The Story of Napoleon's Elder Brother*. New York: Macmillan, 1968.

Cooper, Wendy A. *Classical Taste in America, 1800–1840*. Baltimore Museum of Art. New York: Abbeville Press, 1993.

Cowdry, Mary Bartlett. *The American Academy of Fine Arts and Art Union, 1816–1852*. New York: New-York Historical Society, 1953.

Cronin, Vincent. *Napoleon Bonaparte: An Intimate Biography*. New York: William Morrow, 1972.

Curtis, John. "A Century of Grand Opera in Philadelphia." *Pennsylvania Magazine of History and Biography*, 44 (1920): 122-157.

DeLorme, Eleanor P. *Joséphine, Napoléon's Incomparable Empress*. New York: Harry N. Abrams, 2002.

Driskel, Michael Paul. *As Befits a Legend: Building a Tomb for Napoleon, 1840–1861*. Kent, Ohio: Kent State University Press, 1993.

Dunlap, William. *The History of the Rise and Progress of the Arts of Design in the United States*. 3 vols. Boston: C. E. Goodspeed, 1918.

Gengembre, Gérard, in collaboration with Pierre Jean Chalençon and David Chanteranne. *Napoleon, The Immortal Emperor*. New York: Vendome Press, 2003.

Girardin, Louis-Stanislas-Xavier de. *Promenade ou itinéraire des jardins d'Ermenonville*. Paris: Merigot & Gattey & Guyot, 1788.

Girod de l'Ain, Gabriel. *Joseph Bonaparte: Le roi malgré lui*. Paris: Librairie Académique Perrin, 1970.

Glover, Michael. *Legacy of Glory: The Bonaparte Kingdom of Spain, 1808–1813.* New York: Charles Scribner's Sons, 1971.

Gould, Cecil. *Trophy of Conquest, the Musée Napoléon and the Creation of the Louvre.* London: Faber & Faber, 1965.

Eugénie de Grèce. *Pierre-Napoleon Bonaparte, 1815–1881.* Paris: Hachette, 1963.

Herold, J. Christopher. *The Age of Napoleon.* New York: American Heritage, 1963, reprint, New York: Mariner Books, Houghton Mifflin, 2002.

———. *Mistress to an Age: A Life of Madame de Staël.* New York: Grove Press, 1958.

Hobson, Anthony. "The Escorial." *Great Palaces,* intro. Sacheverell Sitwell. New York: Spring Books, 1964.

Hughes, Robert. *Goya.* New York: Alfred A. Knopf, 2003.

Ingersoll, Charles J. *History of the Second War Between the United States and Great Britain,* Second Series. 2 vols. Philadelphia: Lippincott, Grambo, 1852.

———. "Obituary Notice of Joseph Bonaparte." *Proceedings of the American Philosophical Society,* 5 January 1855.

Iung, Th. *Lucien Bonaparte et ses mémoires, 1775–1840, d'après les papiers déposés aux archives étrangères et d'autres documents inédits.* 3 vols. Paris: G. Charpentier, 1882.

Jefferson's America and Napoleon's France: An Exhibition for the Louisiana Purchase Bicentennial. New Orleans: New Orleans Museum of Art in association with the University of Washington Press in Seattle, 2003.

Kennedy, Roger G. *Orders from France: The Americans and the French in a Revolutionary World, 1780–1820.* Philadelphia: University of Pennsylvania Press, 1990.

Knoles, Thomas. *The Notebook of Bass Otis, Philadelphia Portrait Painter.* Worcester: American Antiquarian Society, 1993.

Kramer, Lloyd. *Lafayette in Two Worlds: Public Cultures and Personal Identities in an Age of Revolutions.* Chapel Hill: University of North Carolina Press, 1996.

Landon, Harry F. *The North Country: A History Embracing Jefferson, St. Lawrence, Oswego, Lewis and Franklin Counties, New York.* 3 vols. Indianapolis: Historical Publishing Company, 1932.

Lang, Paul, Anna Stoll and Thomas Becker. *Joseph Bonaparte et le château de Prangins.* Musée suisse avec le soutien de l'Association des Amis du Château de Prangins, 1998.

Larson, Erik. *Peter Paul Rubens with a Complete Catalog of His Works in America.* Antwerp: De Sikkel, 1952.

Laverty, Bruce, Michael J. Lewis, and Michele Taillon Taylor. *Monument to Philanthropy: the Design and Building of Girard College, 1832-1848.* Philadelphia: Girard College, 1998.

Lieber, Francis. *The Life and Letters of Francis Lieber: Letters to a Gentleman in Germany on a Trip to Niagara.* Philadelphia: Carey, Lea & Blanchard, 1834.

Le Prince Lucien Bonaparte et sa famille. Paris: Librairie Plon, 1889.

Logan, Deborah Norris. Manuscript diary. Henry Francis Du Pont Winterthur Library, Joseph Downs Collection of Manuscripts and Printed Ephemera.

McClellan, Andrew. *Inventing the Louvre: Art, Politics, and the Origins of the Modern Museum in Eighteenth-Century Paris.* Berkeley: University of California Press, 1999.

McLynn, Frank. *Napoleon: A Biography.* New York: Arcade, 2002.

Macartney, Clarence Edward, and Gordon Dorrance. *The Bonapartes in America.* Philadelphia: Dorrance and Company, 1939.

MacDonald, Donald. *The Diaries of Donald MacDonald, 1824–1826.* Indianapolis: Indiana Historical Society Publiications, vol.14, no.2., 1942.

Magee, James D. *Bordentown, 1682–1932: An Illustrated Story of a Colonial Town.* Bordentown, N.J.: Bordentown Register, 1932.

Maurois, André. *Victor Hugo.* Trans. Gerard Hopkins. London: Jonathan Cape, 1956.

Meigs, William M. *The Life of Charles Jared Ingersoll.* Philadelphia: J. B. Lippincott, 1897.

Méneval, Claude-François, baron de. *Memoirs Illustrating the History of Napoleon I from 1802 to 1815,* ed. by his grandson, Baron Napoleon Joseph de Méneval. 3 vols. New York: D. Appleton and Company, 1894.

Mérimée, Prosper. *Carmen, Colomba & Selected Stories,* trans. Walter J. Cobb. New York: New American Library of World Literature, a Signet Classic, 1963.

———. *Le vase étrusque.* Paris: Henry Babou, 1930.

Mills, Weymer Jay. *Historic Houses of New Jersey.* Philadelphia: J. B. Lippincott, 1903.

Monneret, Sophie. *David and Neo-Classicism.* Trans. Chris Miller with Peter Snowdon. Paris: Finest SA/Editions Pierre Terrail, 1999.

Murat, Inès. *Napoléon et le rêve américain.* Paris: Librairie Arthème Fayard, 1976.

Napoléon. Catalog of an exhibition at the Grand Palais, June–December 1969.

Nash, Gary B. *First City:, Philadelphia and the Forging of Historical Memory*. Philadelphia: University of Pennsylvania Press, 2002.

Oddie, E. M. *The Bonapartes in the New World*. London: Elkin Mathews & Marrot, 1932.

Olson, Roberta J. M., and Hofer, Margaret K. *Seat of Empire*. Catalog of an exhibit at the New-York Historical Society, 8 October 2002 to 12 January 2003. New York: New-York Historical Society, 2002.

Orieux, Jean. *Talleyrand ou le sphinx incompris*. Paris: Flammarion, 1970.

Physick, Susan Dillwyn. *The Autobiography of S. Dillwyn, Daughter of Dr. Philip S. Physick and Wife to Commander Conner, USN 1826*. Philadelphia: Independence Seaport Museum, 1996.

Raitt, A.W. *Prosper Mérimée*. New York: Charles Scribner's Sons, 1970.

Richman, Irwin. *The Brightest Ornament: A Biography of Nathaniel Chapman, M.D.* Bellefonte, Pa.: Pennsylvania Heritage, 1967.

Ridley, Jasper. *Napoleon III and Eugénie*. New York: Viking Press, 1979.

Robb, Graham. *Victor Hugo: A Biography*. New York: W. W. Norton, 1998.

Roberts, George B. "Dr. Physick and His House." *Pennsylvania Magazine of History and Biography*, 92 (1968): 67-80.

Ross, Michael. *The Reluctant King: Joseph Bonaparte, King of the Two Sicilies and Spain*. New York: Mason/Charter, 1977.

Rostand, Edmond. *L'Aiglon*. Trans. Lewis N. Parker. New York: R. H. Russell, 1900.

Rudé, George. *The French Revolution: Its Causes, Its History, and Its Legacy After 200 Years*. New York: Grove Weidenfeld, 1988.

Savine, Albert. *À la cour du roi Joseph: Souvenirs du Count de Girardin*. Paris: Louis-Michaud, 1911.

Scharf, J. Thomas, and Thompson Westcott. *History of Philadelphia, 1609–1884*, 3 vols. Philadelphia: L. H. Everts, 1884.

St.-Pierre, Bernardin. *Paul and Virginia*. London: George Routledge and Sons, 1879. Translator unknown. Originally published in French in 1788 appended to *Études de la Nature*.

Schom, Alan. *Napoleon Bonaparte*. New York: HarperCollins, 1997.

Schoulepnikoff, Chantal de. *Le château de Prangins*. Zurich: Musée national suisse Zurich, 1991.

Seward, Desmond. *Napoleon's Family: The Notorious Bonapartes and Their Ascent to the Thrones of Europe*. New York: Viking, 1986.

Shackelford, George Green. *Jefferson's Adoptive Son: The Life of William Short, 1759–1848*. Lexington: University Press of Kentucky, 1993.

Sommers, Frank H. "America's First King." *Winterthur Newsletter*, 31 May 1963.

Stacton, David. *The Bonapartes*. New York: Simon and Schuster, 1966.

Staël, Germaine de. *Ten Years of Exile*. Trans. Avriel H. Goldberger. DeKalb: Northern Illinois University Press, 2000.

Stirling, Monica. *Madame Letizia: A Portrait of Napoleon's Mother*. New York: Harper, 1962.

Stroud, Patricia Tyson. *The Emperor of Nature: Charles-Lucien Bonaparte and His World*. Philadelphia: University of Pennsylvania Press, 2000.

———. *Thomas Say: New World Naturalist*. Philadelphia: University of Pennsylvania Press, 1992.

Thompson, J. M. *Napoleon Bonaparte*. New York: Oxford University Press, 1952.

Tinterow, Gary, and Geneviève Lacambre with Deborah L. Roldán and Juliet Wilson-Bareau. *Manet/Velázquez: The French Taste for Spanish Painting*. Catalog of an exhibition 4 March to 8 June 2003 at the Metropolitan Museum of Art. New Haven: Yale University Press, 2003.

Sully, Thomas. "Notes on Pictures and Painting." In William Dunlap, *A History of the Rise and Progress of the Arts of Design in the United States*; Reprint of the original 1834 edition with a new introduction by James Thomas Flexner. New York: Dover [1969].

Titian. Catalog of an exhibition at the National Gallery, London, 19 February to 18 May 2003. London: National Gallery, 2003.

Tower, Charlemagne. "Joseph Bonaparte in Philadelphia and Bordentown." *Pennsylvania Magazine of History and Biography* 42, no. 4 (1918): 289-309.

Valynseele, Joseph. *Le sang des Bonaparte*. Paris: 126 Boulevard de Magenta, 1954.

Watson, John Fanning. *Annals of Philadelphia and Pennsylvania in the Olden Time; being a collection of Memoirs, Anecdotes, and Incidents of the City and its Inhabitants and of the Earliest Settlements of the inland part of Pennsylvania from the Days of the Founders*. Philadelphia: Carey and Hart, 1845.

————. "Trip to Pennsbury & Count Survilliers, 1826." Manuscript diary. Library of the Henry Francis Du Pont Winterthur Museum.

Webster, Constance. "Bonaparte's Park: A French Picturesque Garden in America." *Journal of Garden History*, 6, no. 4 (1986), 330–347.

Weigley, Russell F., ed. *Philadelphia: A 300-Year History*. New York: W. W. Norton, 1982.

Wellington, Evelyn Katrine Gwenfra (Williams) Wellesley, Duchess of. *A Descriptive and Historical Catalogue of the Collections of Pictures and Sculpture at Apsley House, London*. London: Longmans Green, 1901.

Wethey, Harold E. *The Paintings of Titian*, 3 vols. *The Mythological and Historical Paintings*, vol. 3. London: Oxford, 1975.

Wiebenson, Dora. *The Picturesque Garden in France*. Princeton: Princeton University Press, 1978.

Wilson, George. *Stephen Girard: America's First Tycoon*. Conshohocken, Pa.: Combined Books, 1995.

Wilson, James. *The Life and Letters of Fitz Greene Halleck*. New York: D. Appleton, 1869.

Wolf, Edwin. *Portrait of an American City*. Harrisburg, Pa.: Stackpole Books, 1975. Reprint Philadelphia: Camino Books, 1990.

Woodward, E. M. *Bonaparte's Park and the Murats*. Trenton, N.J.: MacCrellish and Quigley, 1879.

[Wright, Frances]. *Views of Society and Manners in America in a Series of Letters From that Country to a Friend in England during the years 1818, 1819, and 1820*. London: Longman, Hurst, Rees, Orme, and Brown, 1821.

ACKNOWLEDGMENTS

Much has been written about Joseph Bonaparte as diplomat and statesman for his brother Napoleon and his reign as King of Naples and then of Spain, but the only full treatment of his life in America is that by Georges Bertin, published in 1893, in French, and difficult to find. I owe much to Bertin for his thorough and scholarly approach to the subject. In my attempt to cover, in English, Joseph Bonaparte's life in America with material unearthed during the more than one hundred years since Bertin published his account, I wish to thank the many individuals and institutions that have given me their time in this endeavor.

First, Francis James Dallett, former Secretary and Librarian of the Athenaeum of Philadelphia and former archivist of the University of Pennsylvania, kindly gave me his large collection of Bonaparte material, gathered over time. There were many treasures and I hope I have made good use of them. I especially thank Jim for reading the manuscript and offering numerous helpful suggestions.

I am deeply grateful to Her Imperial Highness, the Princess Alix Napoleon for her warm hospitality in welcoming me to her homes in Paris and Switzerland in order to read her family collection of Joseph Bonaparte's letters to his wife, Julie, and daughters Zénaïde and Charlotte, and also for introducing me to Bernard Chevalier, director of the château de Malmaison. Louis-Napoleon Bonaparte-Wyse and his wife, Thérèse, graciously entertained my husband and me at their home in Brussels and showed us fascinating Napoleonic *souvenirs.*

The staff at the Bibliothèque Centrale, Muséum National d'Histoire Naturelle, in Paris at the Jardin des Plantes, were most accommodating and I thank them. Also, Peter Hicks at the Fondation Napoléon in Paris for placing my article about Joseph Bonaparte and Point Breeze on the Web.

I wish to thank Monsignore Luigi del Gallo di Roccogiovine, a great-great-great-grandson of both Joseph and Lucien Bonaparte, for allowing me unlimited access to his family's archives in Rome. The staff at the Fondazioni Primoli was most helpful, as was Signora Guilia Gorgone, director of the Museo Napoleonico, especially for allowing the museum's collections to be photographed. Both of these institutions are housed in a grand mansion by the Tiber River in Rome that once belonged to a granddaughter of Lucien Bonaparte and her husband.

In Switzerland, I am grateful to Madame Chantal de Schoulepnikoff for graciously showing my husband and me through Joseph Bonaparte's château de Prangins, now owned by the Swiss National Museum, at an early stage in its development as a museum.

In Philadelphia, the staff at the Historical Society of Pennsylvania and that of the Library Company next door were always kind and helpful, as was Roy Goodman at the American Philosophical Society. Dr. Roger W. Moss, director of the Athenaeum of Philadelphia, is particularly knowledgeable about Joseph Bonaparte as his institution houses a permanent exhibition devoted to the ex-king. I am most appreciative of Dr. Moss's enthusiasm for this project and his perceptive reading of the manuscript. I also wish to thank Ellen Rose, the Atheneum's librarian, and Bruce Laverty, its curator of architectural history.

Also in Philadelphia, I am grateful to Elizabeth Laurent at Girard College for being so generous with her time over many days in providing me with the correspondence of Joseph Bonaparte and Stephen Girard.

For information on Joseph Bonaparte's art collection, Dodge Thompson, director of exhibitions for the National Gallery of Art in Washington, D.C., most kindly allowed me to review his extensive files, which he has been amassing for years. And I thank Wendy A. Cooper, curator at Winterthur, for introducing me to Dodge Thompson. I am grateful to Joseph Rishel, curator of art before 1900 at the Philadelphia Museum of Art, for his interest in the project, and Ann Percy Stroud, assistant curator of prints and drawings, for valuable references: Xavier Bray, curator of European painting at the National Gallery of Art in London, and David Scrase, curator of paintings at the Fitzwilliam Museum at Cambridge. The Philadelphia Museum of Art's library staff was invariably helpful.

Special thanks to the art historian Andrew Cosentino, formerly at the Library of Congress, for organizing a successful symposium at which I was asked to lecture at the very site of Point Breeze, now the Divine Word Missionaries, in the fall of 2003, and for orienting me as to various features of the property. Father Raymond T. Lennon was most gracious in allowing access to the grounds. I also thank the Honorable John W. Collom III, mayor of Bordentown, for imparting his knowledge of the area.

The intense interest of James Turk of the New Jersey State Museum in the world of Joseph Bonaparte and plans for a major exhibit at the museum entitled "A Bonaparte in America," have been stimulating and rewarding. Damon Tvarianos, architectural historian, kindly showed me Pine Grove and its original site in Trenton, and Roman Kuzyk guided me through Bow Hill, now the Ukrainian Cultural Center. Also, many thanks to James Biddle who gave me a fascinating private tour of Andalusia, the home of his ancestors.

The staff of the Sterling Library at Yale where the Louis Mailliard Papers are housed was most helpful. I also wish to thank those at the Jefferson County Historical Society and the Library in Watertown, New York, who assisted my research; also the staff at the Burlington County Historical Society in New Jersey, and the Henry Francis Du Pont Winterthur Library in Delaware.

Individuals with whom I have had great conversations about Joseph Bonaparte over the Internet and who have sent me much pertinent material are Carolyn Mailliard Hacker, in California, a direct descendant of Louis Mailliard; Isadora Rose Viejo, of Madrid, an expert on the former collection of Manuel Godoy in Spain; and Maria Gilbert at the Provenance Index, Getty Research Institute in Los Angeles. Cheryl Liebold, archivist at the Pennsylvania Academy of the Fine Arts, assisted me with information about the academy's early exhibitions.

Fernand Beaucour, director of the Centre d'Études Napoléoniennes in Levallois, France, directed me to his superb thesis on Jean-Mathieu-Alexandre Sari, which contains much helpful information about various persons connected to Joseph Bonaparte.

I thank Alison Ledes, editor of the magazine *Antiques*, for including my article on Joseph Bonaparte and Point Breeze in the October 2002 issue, and the staff at the Bard Graduate Center for Art and Design in Manhattan for inviting me to speak on the same subject that fall.

Institutions and individuals who kindly allowed me to illustrate works from their collections are the Philadelphia Museum of Art; the Athenaeum of Philadelphia; the Barra Foundation; Christopher Forbes; Girard College; Historical Society of Pennsylvania; New Jersey State Museum; New-York Historical Society; J. Paul Getty Museum, Los Angeles; Joslyn Art Museum, Omaha; Indianapolis Museum of Art; New Orleans Museum of Art; Corcoran Gallery of Art, Washington, D.C.; Château de Malmaison; Musée National du Château de Versailles; Musée National du Château de Fontainebleau; Château de Prangins; the National Gallery of Ireland; Museo Napoleonico, Rome; Museo Nacional del Prado, Madrid; Fitzwilliam Museum, Cambridge, England; and the Victoria & Albert Museum for the collection at Apsley House, London.

In closing, I am particularly grateful to the writer Russell Bourne and to Larry E. Tise, former executive director of the Pennsylvania Historical and Museum Commission, for reading the manuscript and offering helpful suggestions, and to Robert McCracken Peck for his constant encouragement and interest in the subject. Quentin Keynes, my late friend, supplied me with important introductions, and I thank Eric G. Schultz, producer of documentaries for New Jersey public television, for his involvement with the story of Joseph Bonaparte. I especially thank Jerome Singerman, Humanities Editor at the University of Pennsylvania Press, for his continued enthusiasm and superb editorial advice on my third book with the Press. Also Noreen O'Connor, for her sensitive copyediting of the manuscript. My husband, Alexander McCurdy III, not only read through many versions but also patiently engaged in endless conversations about my all-absorbing project. My children, Lisa Tyson Ennis, a fine arts photographer, and Peter Tyson, a writer, have been at all times enthusiastic and supportive of my endeavor. Their father, Noel Jon Tyson, who died in 1982, inspired me to write my first book.

INDEX

Bouvier, Michel, 66, 70
Boyer, Christine, 2
Breck, Samuel, 19, 64, 191
Brill, Paul, 94
Bruegel, Jan, 129
Buonaparte, Carlo, 2, 68, Italy, lineage for, 2
Buonaparte, Francesco di, 2
Buonaparte, Guglielmo di, 2
Burr, Aaron, 28

Cadwalader, Thomas, 45, 132, 160, 161, 197
Caesar, Julius, 87
Canova, Antonio, 68, 127, 169–70
Carl XIV Gustav (Bernadotte, king of Sweden), 70
Carman, Alexander, 79
Carnot, Lazare, 13
Carret, Emmanuel Laurent Jacques (James), 1, 22, 23, 172
Castorland, 36–37
Catherine of Württemberg, 68, 97, 197
Catlin, George, 93, 130, 132
Champ d'Asile, 27–29, 111
Chandelier, Monsieur (cook), 214
Chapman, Nathaniel, 19, 43, *20*, 152; Joseph's gifts to, 160, 183, 197, 214
Charles Albert (king of Piedmont), 206
Charles IV, 72, 94
Charles X, 144, 153
Chaumont, M. Le Ray de, 22, 37, 100, 142
Childe Harold's Pilgrimage (Byron), 87
Cisneros, Francisco Jiménez de, 108
Clary, Désirée, 7
Clary, François (nephew-in-law), 202
Clary, Joachim (nephew-in-law), 210
Clary, Julie. *See* Bonaparte, Julie Clary
Clary, Nicholas (brother-in-law), 32
Clauzel, Bertrand, 47
Clay, Henry, 26, 43
Cobenzl, Count Ludwig von, 10
Colins de Ham, Aspasie Saint-Georges, 157
Colins de Ham, Hippolyte, Baron (Colins), 156–57, 160; Vienna mission, 156
Colonna, Maria-Guilia, Duchess d'Atri, 53
Constant, Benjamin, 52
Conwell, Henry, Bishop, 108
Coppet, 51, 148

Cornwallis, Lord, 2, 10, 149
Correggio, Antonio Allegri, 129
Corsican wild boar. *See* Bonaparte, Pierre
Courrier des États-Unis, 123, 160, 185
Coursy, Mathilde de, 123, *125*
Coypel, Noël-Nicolas, 197
Cromwell, Richard, 43

Dallas, Alexander J., 12, 14, 16
Daschkoff, Andrew, 17
David, Jacques Louis, 66, 127, 180; death, 126; Joseph correspondence, 113–14; paints Joseph's daughters, 91, *92*; paints Napoleon, 94–96, *95*; teaches Charlotte, 93, 94
Davillier, Fanny, 108
de la Folie, François Alexis, 142; death, 216
de la Rochefoucauld, Rosalie, 41
de la Rochefoucauld-Liancourt, François-Alexandre-Frédéric, Duke, 15
Degas, Edgar, 166
del Sarto, Andrea, 131, 160, 170
Delafolie, Anna. *See* Savage, Anna
Delessert, Valentine, 209
Denis, Simon, 67
Denham Place, London, 174
Denon, Vivant, 129–30
Denuelle, Eleanora, 174
Dickerson, Mahlon, 23
Du Ponceau, Pierre-Etienne (Peter Stephen), 45, 183
DuBarry, Edmund, 182, 183, 189–90; and Strasbourg affair, 187
Duke of Orléans. *See* Louis-Philippe
Duke of Reichstadt. *See* Bonaparte, Napoleon-François
Dunlop House, *plate 5*, 49–50
Duphot, Léonard, 9
Duranty, Emilie, 166
Duranty, Louis-Edmond Antoine, 166
Duranty, Louis-Emile, 166
Duvall, Edward, 15

Elba, 12, 17, 96, 114
Encyclopedia Americana, 51
England: and Amiens Treaty, 149; Joseph arrives in, 160–62, 200; Napoleon plans inva-